Essentials for Quality and Safety Improvement in Health Care

Standard operating procedure

Evaluation

Audit

Essentials

Quality management

Healthcare research

Safety management

Christopher Ente • Michael Ukpe

Essentials for Quality and Safety Improvement in Health Care

A Resource for Developing Countries

 Springer

Christopher Ente
Patient Safety and Quality Care for Africa
(PASQUA)
Ashford, Kent, UK

Michael Ukpe
Romivic Specialists Hospital
Eket, Nigeria

ISBN 978-3-030-92484-3   ISBN 978-3-030-92482-9   (eBook)
https://doi.org/10.1007/978-3-030-92482-9

This Springer imprint is published by the registered company Springer Nature Switzerland AG
The registered company address is: Gewerbestrasse 11, 6330 Cham, Switzerland

This book is dedicated to our families:

Christopher Ente: To my children, Daniel, David and Esther, for allowing me to spend their valuable weekends working on this book, and my wife, Eno, for her support and for painstakingly editing the first draft.

Michael Ukpe: To my wife, my children and my wonderful grandchildren, Ethan and Jethro. Despite my struggles in life, I find comfort in them all.

About this Book

Safety and quality improvement in health care has since been a global priority. Suboptimal performance is still common in health care in Africa more than a decade after the inauguration of patient safety. This book aims to help in building patient safety and healthcare quality improvement tenets in the region and reinforce actions imperative for Africans to stand up and take charge of their healthcare destiny. It brings together essential components crucial for achieving revolutionary progress in safety and quality improvement in any healthcare system. These include standard operating procedure, audit, research and evaluation. It explains practical steps in designing them with some specific features to aid learning and facilitate their implementation; it provides step-by-step instructions on how to translate, for instance, WHO guidelines into simple and easy to follow procedures for local use. It gives a succinct account of medical errors and adverse events in health care, sources and techniques to contain them. Quality is also explained with improvement approaches and interventions. The book also specifies areas of immediate application of the essentials and highlights topics to explore in order to increase understanding within the local context with the goal of advancing a safety culture and commitment in the subjects.

Foreword

Healthcare safety and quality improvement to ensure patient safety remains a global challenge even 20 years after the release of the Institute of Medicine's publication *To Err Is Human*, which reported startling losses due to medical errors and adverse events. Some researchers believe the report may have underestimated the impact of medical errors by a factor of four. Today most agree that in the United States, medical errors are the third leading cause of death after heart disease and cancer. Even with the devastating impact of the COVID-19 pandemic, medical errors due to suboptimal care and treatment are still likely to outpace preventable patient deaths.

The good news is that most global deaths due to medical errors and adverse events are preventable, and the authors of this important book have laid out a roadmap of evidence-based practices, processes and methods for reducing preventable harm. Many healthcare leaders are either in denial or unaware that deaths are occurring in their clinics and hospitals due to medical errors. Other leaders understand the breadth of the problem but do not know how to solve what has been deemed a 'wicked' problem – a problem that is intractable and difficult to address with simple linear solutions.

The authors bring diverse knowledge and experience in healthcare from global settings and other risk industries such as oil and gas and aviation, two industries which have embraced a systems approach to safety. These industries, known as high reliability organizations (HROs), are able to successfully operate in complex, high-risk activities while minimising risk, injuries and accidents due to their ability to foster a culture of safety that is open, transparent and continuously learning from errors. HROs understand that human error cannot be eliminated but systems can be better engineered to enhance error management at the sharp end (frontline of care) and managed better at the blunt end (through rigorous safety management practices).

The authors provide the reader with practical, well-researched actions they can take to improve patient safety and healthcare quality no matter the level of resources available within their healthcare setting. Simple actions such as hand hygiene dramatically reduces health-care-associated infections yet gaining buy-in from frontline staff to follow hand-washing protocols requires rigorous monitoring, easy access to hand-washing stations and change management over time.

While no intervention described in this book should be construed as a so-called quick-fix, all of the strategies, tools and methods described could easily be adapted and fit to purpose to achieve continuous process improvement, which would lead to better patient outcomes. Every healthcare professional, whether student or experienced practitioner in either developed or developing countries, would benefit from reading this book and applying these healthcare safety and quality improvement essentials in their work settings. Until all healthcare professionals see *improving the safety and quality of health care as part of their work*, the current rates of preventable patient harm are not likely to change. The authors have provided the requisite knowledge and skills for improving patient safety and healthcare quality; your *will* to embrace these principles and diligently apply them will make a positive difference in the lives of your patients, your community, and your nation. There is no time to waste; together we can turn the tide on preventable patient harm now! It is hoped this book will help to encourage healthcare staff in the region overcome all challenges confronting quality care and services and develop and implement strategically driven quality improvement methods with as excellent outcomes and as great effectiveness as their counterparts in developed nations.

Doctor of Health Administration,
MSc Human Factors, Chief Executive Officer, Synensys
Atlanta, GA, USA   Stephen M. Powell

Preface

Complexity is inherent in a healthcare system and has a profound effect on its service and outcomes. The improvement of safety and quality in healthcare systems to ensure patient and staff safety has become a global priority and remains an evolving issue. The science of safety and quality improvement of healthcare systems has remarkably transformed the way healthcare service is delivered and influenced the way patients are treated, especially in the developed world. Over the years, the field has attracted considerable attention from researchers and scholars, whose findings and recommendations have been extended to practices and other related activities to the developing and transitional countries of Africa, the Eastern Mediterranean and the Middle East. Thus, the field has also gained recognition in these countries.

In Africa, the early period of safety and quality improvement in health care dates to 2005, when the World Health Organization (WHO) World Alliance for Patient Safety intensified its call for action in patient safety during meetings held in Nairobi, Kenya, and in Durban, South Africa. Unfortunately, more than 15 years after both meetings, the performance of safety and healthcare quality improvement in the region remains unsatisfactory; vast areas in care and treatment are still operating under what Hale described as "pre-scientific stages of knowledge". The attention to safety and quality in health care in the region is currently much less than deserved, and progress remains sporadic and limited in scope.

Interestingly, the core principle of safety and quality improvement in health care or any safety and quality management systems, which is to assess and identify the root cause when something goes wrong in order to learn from it and do something about it to avoid reoccurrence, is inherently embedded in the African ethos as expressed in the adage "when a child falls he looks forward but when an adult falls he looks back". Adults look back for various reasons, but the one that is probably the most relevant to a healthcare context is for the purpose of assessing why they fell, specifically, to determine what can be done to prevent further falls. Thus, failure in Africa for a very long time represented an opportunity for learning and improvement. However, in the field of health care, particularly in safety and quality improvement, it appears healthcare professionals, policymakers and stakeholders in the region have forgotten this ethical principle and so have not acknowledged failures or honestly considered, with a sense of concern and commitment, why they failed and sought solutions, which, research has shown, is one of the biggest obstacles to safety and quality care improvement.

It is therefore not surprising that in the region, scientific research in health care, which is crucial in improving safety and quality of care, is very scant in the literature and data quality in health care is woefully inadequate and severely limited. This circumstance poses the greatest threat or bottleneck to patient safety research as there is no meaningful traditional patient safety research, which is often largely outcome-driven and retrospective in design, can be conducted without good-quality data.

Moreover, to date, safety and quality improvement in healthcare systems in the region does not rest on a firm scientific foundation; there is no African equivalent to the fundamental reports *To Err Is Human* in the United States or *An Organisation with a Memory* in the UK which would paint a clear picture of the magnitude and nature of the harm experienced in both public and private hospitals in the region. Despite the overwhelming evidence on the benefits of providing information on preventable death due to adverse events as a key patient safety and healthcare quality driver for establishing a foundation for accountability, prioritising problems to address, creating ideas for safer care and determining which interventions work, currently no study has been conducted in Africa on deaths due to adverse events. Thus, at the moment, there is no clear picture of the magnitude and nature of deaths due to adverse events in both public and private hospitals in the region. In this region, a lack of such vital knowledge creates uncertainty among the public, governments and healthcare professionals as to what level of risk patients face each time they are admitted to hospital. It also hampers the development of appropriate solutions to address the problems and associated healthcare safety and quality issues.

It is hoped that the renaissance of the values underpinning this long-standing African philosophy of learning from a fall as expressed in the adage cited earlier will eventually lead to a complete overhaul of the approach to failure in health care in the region and spur authorities to begin taking the steps needed or lay a proper foundation for starting the journey to enhanced safety and quality care practices. To this end, in unpacking the adage in a healthcare context, one can see connections in the use of standards, questioning practices, seeking answers and recognising the need to put a system in place for managing and avoiding the reoccurrence of such failure or falls. In light of these considerations, an inability to acknowledge a fall and why it happens could amount to failure in acknowledging the sub-optimal care and treatment for patients in the region. The reason could be that the basic clinical processes that underpin quality care are still being derived mainly from opinions based on healthcare professionals' experience rather than best-known practices adapted for local use. The commonest solution in this instance would therefore be the use of basic procedures, protocols or standards in practice. Secondly, depending on how a question arising from or relating to practice is framed, it could be addressed using research, audit or service evaluation. Finally, putting in place a system for managing and mitigating the potential risks of further failures constitutes the core idea that undergirding quality and safety management systems.

To this end, the features considered essential for safety and quality improvement in health care in the region covered in this book are standard operating procedures, audit, research, quality management, safety management and evaluation. In the first chapter the concept of safety and quality improvement in health care is presented with a brief explanation of the basic terms from the perspective of health care in Africa and some of the challenges of safety and quality care improvement in Africa. The components necessary for successful implementation of these essential features with superior outcomes are elucidated. These include creating and sustaining a patient safety culture, securing organisational support at all levels, establishing a dedicated operational safety and quality department and effective healthcare management. Chapter 2 discusses standard operating procedures, emphasising the use of evidence-based practice as opposed to anecdotal evidence from healthcare professionals to create basic clinical processes that underpin quality and safe care. Although under certain circumstances, in certain types of patient treatment and care the use of standard operating systems or protocols may not be applicable, a practical method of how to develop, implement and manage a standard operating procedure is presented in this chapter. The benefits and some of the potential areas of application in health care for the provision of daily care and services are also covered. The audit, which is a quality improvement process employed to improve patient care and outcomes, is discussed in Chap. 3. In this chapter methods of designing, conducting and implementing audits with specific outcomes are discussed. The chapter also covers the advantages of a clinical audit with potential areas of immediate application in health care in the region, including barriers and enablers of effective audit.

In Chap. 4, research, which is a core component of safety and quality improvement in health care, is discussed. Healthcare staff of all types and at all levels must be research-informed and research-aware and be able to use research to address specific clinical questions. A core insight of healthcare research in some parts of the continent is presented briefly, along with the principles of research in health care. Planning, designing, undertaking, recording and reporting ethical and scientifically high-quality research is also covered. The preparation of a new application, amendments and annual progress reports for submission to a typical institutional research ethics board is discussed and a template for relevant research documents, such as protocols, participant information sheets and consent forms which can easily be adapted for specific research is provided. Chapter 5 describes quality in health care with its seven core dimensions, including elements of quality and how it can be measured. Different types of interventions and techniques for quality improvement, including their barriers, are presented with evidence of poor-quality care and its socioeconomic implications. Chapter 6 discusses safety management in health care with its core elements explained. The nature of health care, along with its operations and activities, including the human factor, is covered. This chapter also provides insight into setting up a system for incident reporting, monitoring and investigating, including an explanation of feedback obtained from the implementation of incident investigation findings to improve an organisation's safety performance. The chapter ends with a brief concept of Safety II. Finally, Chap. 7 covers evaluation, which may be applied to both the interventions proposed in this book and other healthcare interventions aimed at safety and quality improvement. It gives a succinct explanation of planning, designing, conducting and reporting evaluation and offers insight into the ethical requirements and challenges of carrying out quality evaluation in the healthcare setting of low-resource countries.

The conceptual framework of this book was generated through research, expert advice and feedback from relevant workshops and conferences in the region. It is informed by the experience and expertise of medical practice gained in real life in the region, providing high-quality care within a challenging political, economic and social climate. It is also based on the knowledge and experience gained over a decade of consultancy work in safety and quality improvement in health care within and outside the region. It must be noted that an in-depth understanding of and major advances in safety and quality improvement in health care in the region will only occur, as in other fields of human endeavour, when ordinary people in the region rise to the occasion and take strategic action themselves rather than depending on others to sort out the problems. In other words, the future of the healthcare system in Africa belongs to Africans.

In this regard the primary aim of the book is to help low- and middle-income countries of Africa formulate the tenets of patient safety and healthcare quality improvement to build safer healthcare systems and healthcare facilities. It also aims to encourage and empower healthcare professionals in the region to find ways of overcoming a litany of challenges (e.g. political, economic, cultural, legislative, infrastructural) confronting the healthcare system and develop and implement safety and quality improvement interventions and activities that are appropriate and meaningful within the local context, with outcomes as good and as effective as their counterparts in developed nations. This book is designed for clinical and non-clinical healthcare professionals, both those with some experience in safety and quality care and those coming to the concept for the first time. It can also be used by medical students interested in safety and quality improvement in health care and partners from individuals and organisations outside the region, as it is the responsibility of all stakeholders in the system to support the agenda of improving safety and quality in health care. It is hoped that the book will represent a seminal opportunity to advance safety and quality care in Africa as it provides further materials which, if learned and applied by staff at various levels in health care, can help healthcare professionals and authorities take the strategic action necessary not only to strengthen safety and quality improvement but equally contribute significantly to laying a foundation to handle related issues in the future.

Patient Safety and Quality Care for Africa (PASQUA)   Christopher Ente
Ashford, Kent, UK
Romivic Specialists Hospital   Michael Ukpe
Eket, Akwa Ibom, Nigeria

Acknowledgements

The authors wish to thank Professor Charles Vincent for sponsoring most of the studies used in forming the framework for this book and for his mentorship and guidance, Steven Powell for his unfailing support and encouragement, Dr Ajibike Oyewumi for her pioneering work in healthcare quality and safety improvement, which significantly shaped the framework of this book, and Mr Victor Esenowo, who brought a valuable perspective from a non-healthcare industry. We are indebted to Lagoon Hospital in Lagos, Nigeria, who supported and hosted some of the research studies which informed this publication. We would also like to thank the Society for Quality in Healthcare in Nigeria, whose members furnished the materials and discussions during various conferences and workshops formed the foundation of this publication.

Our gratitude also goes to the management and staff of Romivic Specialist Hospital, Akwa Ibom State, Nigeria, the management and staff of Patient Safety and Quality Care for Africa (PASQUA), Kent, UK, and a host of others, including co-investigators in the region, who contributed to some of the research studies in Africa used to generate the conceptual framework of this book.

Contents

About the Authors

 **Christopher Ente** is Patient Safety and Healthcare Quality Improvement Consultant and a founder of Patient Safety and Quality Care for Africa (PASQUA). He specialises in the use of information technology to drive safety and quality in health care. His background includes information and communications technology (ICT), quality control, quality assurance and quality improvement, healthcare risk management, clinical incident investigation and prevention and the use of research, auditing and monitoring tools. He works as a research regulatory facilitator in the Research Governance and Integrity team, Imperial College London. He was one of the external reviewers of the World Health Organization's *Patient Safety Research – A Guide for Developing Training Programmes* published in 2012. He worked as a consultant for Synensys, a US-based healthcare consulting firm with the Qatar Ministry of Public Health Project in the Middle East. He has years of experience working in various roles in the National Health Service and Higher Education Institution in the UK. He has worked in several ICT-related companies in different roles and as a systems engineer in Shell Petroleum Development Company (SPDC) in various departments, including highly hazardous offshore oil rigs. He earned his Master's in Quality and Safety in Healthcare from Imperial College London and Computer Communications and Networking from Westminster University London. He has a Bachelor of Science degree in Computer Science and Statistics from the University of Uyo in Nigeria and holds a certificate in PRINCE2 project management. He is a member of the Research Quality Association (RQA) in the UK and the Society for Quality in Health Care in Nigeria.

Michael Ukpe is a Consultant Obstetrician and Gynaecologist, a Fellow of the West African College of Surgeons. He has a fellowship in minimal-access surgery and assisted reproductive technology. He is an experienced medical practitioner who has practised medicine in and outside Nigeria. The greater part of his practice has been in the low-resource setting. He has attended several health-related conferences on primary and secondary health care. He is currently Chief Medical Director, Romivic Specialists Hospital Limited, Eket, Akwa Ibom State, Nigeria. The delivery of safe and easily accessible quality health care to the people is what makes his heart beat. In this book, he brings to bear the challenges and next steps to the issues affecting the safety of healthcare workers and patients in the course of delivering quality health care. He obtained his MBBCH (Bachelor of Surgery and Bachelor of Medicine) from the University of Calabar, Calabar in Cross River State, Nigeria. This book is very relevant to all health institutions, healthcare and non-healthcare workers and can be used as a checklist while rendering quality and safe health care to the people.

Chapter 1
Concept of Quality and Safety Improvement in Health Care

Introduction

This chapter begins with a brief discussion on the concept of health care, its complexity and why errors and adverse events cannot be completely eliminated in health care. Errors and adverse events are defined and how they emerged to assume such a top priority in the agenda of the global discussion on health care, specifically patient safety. Their impact on the healthcare system is highlighted with special attention to healthcare systems in Africa. Patient safety is explained with some of the global initiatives championed by the World Health Organization (WHO) for improvement. A brief history of patient safety in African health care is provided, followed by an explanation of the relevance of patient safety. Safety and quality in health care are defined with a brief explanation, and some of the challenges of safety and quality care improvement in Africa are also elucidated. It is worthwhile to implement the essential features of safety and quality improvement in health care as discussed in this book without having a detailed knowledge of various factors that could influence their implementation at different points and the final outcomes in an organisation. However, a better understanding of the prerequisites for making improvements will not only enhance the quality of their outcomes but will also give insight into how to realise their full potential. To this end, this chapter highlights the requirements that could make it possible to design and effectively implement the necessary improvement in the safety and quality of health care in this book in African healthcare systems. This section discusses an attempt to identify in advance what is required to anticipate possible risks and problems and allow for effective planning, organisation and management of other activities related to the essentials to ensure meaningful success regardless of any drawbacks (Lock 2007). In this regard, the success of any organisation or healthcare setting (private or public) in the region will depend to a large extent on meeting the recommended preconditions.

© The Author(s), under exclusive license to Springer Nature Switzerland AG 2022
C. Ente, M. Ukpe, *Essentials for Quality and Safety Improvement in Health Care*, https://doi.org/10.1007/978-3-030-92482-9_1

Health Care and Healthcare Systems in Africa

Health care, sometimes also spelled healthcare according to the Oxford *Advanced Learner's Dictionary*, is simply the service of providing medical care (Hornby 2000). Health care is delivered by a team of multidisciplinary health and allied health professionals to people referred to as patients, consumers or clients. Health care is provided in a platform known as a healthcare service system, healthcare system, health care system or health system, which consists of people, organisations, resources and activities with a common and principal purpose to promote, restore and maintain the health of public and individual well-being (World Health Organization 2007). The complexity and dynamic characteristics of a healthcare system and the impact of these characteristics on its operations are not new and are widely reported in the literature. Other characteristics of a healthcare system that affect its operation include the fact that healthcare activities are often carried out by multidisciplinary teams using new technologies under increasing financial pressure; above all its activities are performed by human beings who are prone to error and other human factors such as stress and exhaustion (Woloshynowych et al. 2005). In addition, medicine itself is complex with inherent risks, and treatments are sometimes complicated, especially when patients present with multiple co-morbidities. Diagnosis is often difficult, and the outcomes of some treatments, such as in surgical and acute medicine patients, are sometimes unpredictable (Kannampallil et al. 2011; Word Health Organisation Regional Office for Europe 2021). The complexity of a healthcare service system can also be a result of socioeconomic and environmental factors, service fragmentation and a lack of adequate supportive funding (State of Queensland 2011).

In Africa, the healthcare system, which is already complex and characterised by factors which make the occurrence of errors and adverse events inevitable, is however also plagued by a lack of vision, commitment and transparency, including misconceived and misplaced priorities on the part of the leadership, causing healthcare facilities to fall apart (Azevedo 2017). In the face of other enormous challenges, including intense political, social and tribal sentiments, there are additional concerns, including a shortage of medicines in public health facilities, inadequate access for the poor and vulnerable members of society including the elderly and very young, poor attitudes among personnel even in emergency situations, where a deposit of money is demanded before treatment begins, and inadequate information technology (WHO Regional Office for Africa 2012). All these factors increase the likelihood of errors and adverse events in health care in the region.

Impact of Medical Errors and Adverse Events in Healthcare Systems in Africa

In health care, the problem of adverse event is not entirely new. As far back as the 1950s and 1960s, studies reported on adverse events, but the subject was treated as insignificant (World Health Organization 2004). The Institute of Medicine's (IOM) landmark report "To Err Is Human: Building a Safer Health System" is one of the reports that brought to light the scale and impact of medical errors or adverse events in the healthcare system and triggered a global debate on the subject. In this report, an error is defined as the failure to complete a planned action as intended (i.e. error associated with execution) or the application of the wrong plan to achieve a particular goal (i.e. error associated with planning), and adverse events are injuries that result from a medical intervention and are responsible for harm to the patient, which can be life-threatening illness, disability at the time of discharge, prolongation of a hospital stay or even death (Kohn et al. 2000). An error may or may not lead to an adverse event. According to this IOM report, errors cause between 44,000 and 98,000 deaths every year in hospitals in the United States and over a million injuries. In a similar report from the United Kingdom, "An Organisation with a Memory," adverse events occur in around 10% of hospital admissions or about 850 adverse events a year (Department of Health 2000a). A body of evidence from hospitals in Australia revealed 16.6% of adverse events occur among patients in hospitals resulting in disability or a longer hospital stay for the patient, 13.7% caused permanent disability and in 4.9% of cases the patient died (Wilson et al. 1995).

In the African healthcare system, although there is no comparable publication on the scale and impact of medical errors and adverse events, as reported by Ente et al. (2010), the situation is very likely to be far more serious compared to what is reported in the United States and United Kingdom on the basis that *"millions of children and adult patients may be suffering from patient safety incidents: unintended or unexpected events that may lead to prolonged ill-health, injury, extended hospital stay, disability, disease or suffering and death caused by unsafe vaccinations, injections and blood transfusion, counterfeit and substandard drugs, unreliable equipment and practices, inadequate infection control, and overall poor health services, facilities and environments"* and several other factors explained in this book. This is echoed by Mekonnen et al. (2018) in a report on the systematic review of adverse drug events and medication errors in nine countries in Africa, which asserted that errors are comparatively common and adverse events are widespread in hospitals in the region.

As mentioned earlier, because there is no comprehensive research on medical errors and adverse events in African health care, there is uncertainty on the picture of the size and nature of deaths due to errors and adverse events in both public and private hospitals in the region, the impact and the scale of the problems is still based on estimates established from the extrapolation of findings from international studies, which are often judged based on the level of development in these countries. For instance, the World Health Organization Regional Office for Africa (2021) reports that if statistics show that as many as 1 in 10 patients in developed countries are harmed while receiving hospital care, then the harm will be higher in Africa and the risk of acquiring health-care-associated infections (HAIs) will be as much as 20 times higher. A study by Jha et al. (2013) estimated approximately two-thirds of all adverse events resulting from unsafe care, including years lost to disability and death (known as disability adjusted life years or DALYs), occur in low-income and middle-income countries. A report from the National Academies of Sciences,

Engineering, and Medicine (2018) also revealed that up to 134 million adverse events occur in hospitals in low- and middle-income countries annually due to unsafe care, resulting in 2.6 million deaths.

Patient Safety

Patient safety is defined in the IOM report as "prevention of harm to patients" (Kohn et al. 2000). As discussed in the previous section, medical errors and adverse events in health care are inescapable as a result of a combination of factors; this is reflected in the definition of patient safety by the World Health Organization (2021), which defined it as "a health care discipline that emerged with the evolving complexity in health care systems and the resulting rise of patient harm in health care facilities". In light of this, patient safety can be defined as a "child" of the global call to improve safety and quality in health care by devising means of preventing and reducing risks, medical errors and associated preventable adverse events which patients suffer when admitted to hospitals, either for a planned visit or for an emergency. The term *preventable adverse events* is important because in health care there are adverse events which are often not caused by errors but rather by other factors which are not preventable, for instance, adverse drug reactions or complications.

In response to the global call for action in patient safety, as reported by Pittet and Donaldson (2005), the 55th World Health Assembly session in 2002 witnessed the adoption of a resolution of WHA55.18 urging countries to pay serious attention to the problem of patient safety. The resolution mandated the World Health Organization to lead in patient safety with the overall objective of developing global norms and standards, encouraging research on patient safety and providing assistance to countries in the development of patient safety policies and practices. According to this report, the 57th Assembly in 2004 supported the creation of the World Alliance for Patient Safety (WAPS), which was launched in the same year (Pittet and Donaldson 2005). The roles of WAPS include coordinating and facilitating the development of patient safety policy and practice across all countries.

As detailed in World Health Organization (2021), WHO contributions to patient safety through WAPS are enormous. These include initiatives such as Global Patient Safety challenges, namely Clean Care is Safer Care, Safe Surgery Saves Lives and Medication Without Harm. The WAPS also produces technical guidance and resources, for instance the Multi-Professional Patient Safety Curriculum Guide, Patient Safety solutions, the Surgical Safety Checklist, Safe Childbirth Checklist and 5 Moments for Medication Safety. WAPS also established the Patients for Patient Safety programme to promote patient and family engagement in the subject, support the creation of networking and collaborative initiatives such as the global Patient Safety Network and the Global Patient Safety Collaborative and organise annual Global Ministerial Summits on Patient Safety. The latest and most outstanding development in patient safety globally is the establishment of the World Patient Safety Day at the 72nd Assembly in 2019 through the adoption of Resolution

WHA72.6 on "Global action on patient safety" and an endorsement for the day to be marked annually on 17 September. The overall objectives of this day are to enhance global understanding of patient safety, increase public awareness and engagement in the safety of healthcare and promote global actions to enhance patient safety and reduce harm (World Health Organization 2020).

Patient Safety in African Healthcare System

In Africa, patient safety was recognised by the World Alliance for Patient Safety in its annual Global Ministerial Summit on Patient Safety in the region on 17 and 19 January 2005 in Nairobi, Kenya, and Durban, South Africa, respectively. In both regional meetings, the urgent need to prioritise medical error and adverse event prevention was the primary focus, and emphasis was placed on the need for health-care organisations in the region to emulate their counterparts in developed countries and redesign their systems to deliver safe and quality care. It was also recommended that the organisations devise a means of capturing and reflecting on patient safety incidents and begin active learning, which is important for preventing further incidents and harm to patients, and finally lay the foundation for building patient safety and making healthcare quality improvements. Three years later, in September 2008, a similar appeal was made at the 58th Session of the WHO Regional Committee for Africa, which took place in Yaoundé, Cameroon. At the end of the session, ministers of health from 39 African countries signed on to the first WHO Global Patient Safety challenge – Clean Care is Safer Care. At another ministerial summit, the WHO African Regional Committee conference held in 2009, about 47 ministers of health in the region demanded urgent action to address the risks patients were facing which at the time was deemed a very serious and imminent threat to the entire healthcare system (WHO Regional Office for Africa 2008). This resulted in the establishment of the African Partnership for Patient Safety (APPS) (World Health Organization 2015), one of the early WHO patient safety collaborative initiatives aimed at strengthening the healthcare system in the region. The APPS was charged with building the capacity for patient safety programmes and facilitating learning from incidents to prevent patient harm. This special partnership started with hospitals in Europe but extended to the United States (World Health Organization 2016).

Importance of Patient Safety

Medical errors and adverse events have been regarded as a leading threat to patient safety globally. As discussed in what follows, they not only cause significant injuries, death, physical, psychological, and economic burdens but also have a considerable impact on families, communities and governments. Medical errors and associated risks within health care cause injuries or death to millions of people, and, as reported by the Department of Health (2000a), errors and adverse events cost the National Health Service (NHS) an estimated £2 billion a year in extra bed days; the cost of HAIs was estimated at £1 billion annually.

The purpose of patient safety is therefore to prevent and reduce risk, medical errors and adverse events that patients experience during provision of care by improving safety and efficiency in the healthcare system. The ultimate goals are to save lives, reduce costs and burdens related to patient harm and assist in reassuring and restoring people's trust in the healthcare system (World Health Organization 2019). Patient safety is a vital driver of safety and quality improvement in health care globally, and its purpose is firmly grounded in the fundamental principles of medicine – First, do no harm. It is therefore essential that the safety of patients during the provision of care be paramount and services provided be safe and of high quality. In this connection, healthcare organisations worldwide are expected to implement good patient safety practices, that is, processes and structures aimed at reducing the probability of medical errors and adverse events resulting from exposure to the healthcare system across a range of diseases, conditions and procedures (Kohn et al. 2000).

Quality and Safety Improvement in Health Care

Quality in health care is defined as "the degree to which health services for individuals and populations increase the likelihood of desired health outcomes and are consistent with current professional knowledge" and the components of quality care are safety, efficacy, patient centredness, timeliness and equitable (Committee on the Quality of Health Care in America 2001). Quality improvement aims to standardise processes and structures to eliminate or reduce variations, achieve predictable results and improve outcomes for patients. In this book, various quality improvement interventions are explained. Safety in health care is defined as freedom or protection from accidental injury or harm in health care (Kohn et al. 2000). The safety management system presented in this book is composed of two major components, risk control and a learning system. Risk control covers organisational support, safety policy, process, procedure and a safety plan, while the learning system covers collecting and analysing errors and other incidents that often lead to adverse events with the aim of reducing or preventing re-occurrence. This can only be achieved in a healthcare setting where a favourable or good safety culture prevails.

Costs of Poor Quality of Care and Services in Africa

Research shows that poor quality or substandard care and services can waste significant resources and cause various kinds of harm to public health. It can destroy human capital because of a reduced work force resulting from in increased incidence of premature deaths. It can also reduce productivity as a result of the number of people suffering from temporary or permanent disabilities. Specific research evidence, such as that obtained by Vincent et al. (2001), shows that poor-quality care can indeed result in adverse events for patients, leading to moderate or severe disability or death and serious consequences. Economically, it is estimated that the cost of harm which causes a loss of life or permanent disability leading to a loss in capacity and productivity of affected patients and families is estimated in the trillions of US dollars annually, and while it is acknowledged to be significant, it is difficult to estimate the psychological cost to patients and their families associated with the loss of a loved one or coping with permanent disability (World Health Organization 2017).

Quality care and services therefore not only prevent human suffering and ensure healthier societies but also ensure better human capital and healthier economies (World Health Organization, Organisation for Economic Co-operation and Development, and World Bank 2018). High-quality care is obtained when appropriate care is provided "to a patient in a technically competent manner, with excellent communication, shared decision making, and cultural sensitivity". Poor-quality care, on the other hand, is providing too much care or using unnecessary services, tests, medications or procedures, with their associated risks and side effects. Poor-quality care is provided as part of essential services, such as indicated diagnostic tests or lifesaving surgical procedures, or the wrong care, such as prescribing medicines that should not be given together and using poor surgical technique (Schuster et al. 2005).

Some of the most common sources of adverse events, according to Leape et al. (1991), include drug complications, wound infections and technical complications, including those associated with surgical procedures such as negligence leading to diagnostic mishaps, non-invasive therapeutic mishaps and error in management. In Kalish et al. (1995), a study of medical complications during and after major surgery in 404 California acute-care hospitals in 1988 across all patients revealed over $647 million of additional costs due to complications. In a study by Baker et al. (2004), about 7.5% of overall incidents suffered by patients in Canada resulted in almost 2.5 million annual hospital admissions. In the UK the rate is estimated at 11.7% resulting in an 8% average increase in the length of stay for patients at a cost of £1 billion. The cost to the Australian health system is $4.7 billion (Vincent et al. 2001), with a 16.6% overall rate at which patients experience adverse events in hospital in Australia (Wilson et al. 1995). Eshani et al.'s (2006) study of adverse events in Australia between 2003 - 04 in victoria hospital revealed that at least 6.9% of admissions had an adverse event with an average extra stay of 10 days and extra costs of $A6,826. Associated with adverse events are the costs of settling litigation claims, which in the UK were estimated at £423 million in 2003–2004. The expected costs for outstanding clinical negligence at the end of the same year were estimated to be in excess of £2 billion (National Audit Office 2005).

In the Institute of Medicine (2000) findings in quality care and services, problems identified were classified as overuse, misuse and underuse of medical procedures or drugs, for instance, underuse of influenza vaccine, overuse of antibiotics and misuse of antidepressant medications. There are also quality care problems associated with variations in the medical procedures leading to over- and undertreatment of patients (Chassin et al. 1986). Research has revealed the high financial costs associated with these problems. In the United States, misdiagnosed and mistreated presumed appendicitis in 1997 was estimated to cost $741.5 million per year (Flum and Koepsell 2002). In the UK patient safety incidents are estimated to cost the NHS about £2 billion a year in extra bed days, and infections acquired in hospital cost an additional £1 billion (Department of Health 2000a). Another study in the UK reported costs of £11,452 incurred when patients fall, resulting in a fracture neck or femur, £234 incurred daily due to for geriatric and rehabilitation care and £584 per day on orthopaedic and operating theatre costs (Walsh and Antony 2009). There are certainly many reports on the impact of poor-quality care and service, and the aforementioned are just a few examples from some developed countries. These examples serve mainly to highlight the impact of poor-quality care and services on patients and their associated costs.

In Africa there is currently no systematic literature review on research evidence for the extent and impact of these problems. However, considering the level of development in the healthcare systems there, the situation is likely to be far more serious with serious economic implications compared to developed countries. There is therefore an urgent need to ensure that integrated solutions to improve quality care and services are built into the foundations of healthcare systems in the region. This could be best achieved through the cooperation of governments, policymakers, healthcare system leaders, healthcare workers and patients.

Challenges of Safety and Quality of Care Improvement in Africa

In developed countries, evidence for the safety and quality of care, investments, strategies and techniques are well documented in the literature, including the impacts of such interventions on care and service outcomes (Schuster et al. 1998; Burstin et al. 2016; Boyle et al. 2009; Øvretveit 2009). But in Africa, only scant research evidence is available on modern techniques used to improve the safety and quality of care (Leatherman et al. 2010; Heiby 2014). Even those interventions which are increasingly applied in developed nations have, up till now, received little attention in Africa. The adoption of these interventions in local healthcare settings in the region remains infrequent. According to research, currently the entire spectrum of safety and quality improvements in health care in the region is still dominated by traditional interventions, which are often poorly designed and have significant limitations, so they have less of an impact in terms of actual change. Some of the traditional quality improvement interventions used in the region include clinical training and supervision (Carlo et al. 2010; Rowe et al. 2010) and audit and feedback (Siddiqi et al. 2005), which remain beset by poor data quality. Health care in Africa is extraordinarily diverse, with differing economies, governments and approaches to public health, infrastructure and services, as is the enormity of the challenges faced when it comes to making improvements. Some of these challenges are explained in "Historical Perspective on the State of Healthcare and Healthcare Systems in Africa" by M. J. Azevedo (2017). The challenges or barriers highlighted in this section are crucial issues which, if resolved, would lead to improvements in the safety and quality of care and service.

Poor Infrastructure

One study involving the direct observation of clinical practice in some countries in the region revealed a lack resources resulting in a poor triage, inadequate initial assessment of patients, diagnosis and treatment and inadequate monitoring (Nolan et al. 2001). There is also a lack of critical infrastructure and weak governance structures (Guest and Namey 2015). In general, especially in the public health sector, healthcare infrastructure in the region is characterised by frequent electricity outages, unreliable cellular networks, fragmented or entirely absent wireless communication networks or inadequate information and communication technologies for supporting an electronic medical record system and an associated clinical and non-clinical information management system (WHO Regional Office for Africa 2012). There is poor access to assistive technology, that is "assistive products and related systems and services developed for people to maintain and improve functioning and thereby promote well-being, such as eyeglasses, hearing aids and wheelchairs", which could benefit people, including elderly, with disabilities and non-communicable diseases (WHO Regional Office for Africa 2021). There is also a lack of adequate funding in health care and geographical accessibility due to the poor transport infrastructure (Azevedo 2017). Healthcare accessibility is greatly hindered in rural or remote areas, although there is better infrastructure in private hospitals and public hospitals in major cities, especially areas frequently visited by tourists.

Workforce Shortage

The shortage of staff, including those with the relevant safety and quality improvement skills and experience, is another factor. Although staff shortages are global in nature, it is evident that the shortage is much worse in developing and transitional countries. The healthcare professionals who are currently struggling with serious clinical workloads are also those expected to drive and lead in safety and quality improvement programmes. According to Kinfu et al. (2009), staff shortages are such that even when there are funds allocated to improve health care in the region, there is simply not enough personnel to make effective and efficient use of them. This confirms Aveling et al.'s (2015) findings that the level of barrier to safety and healthcare improvement in developing nations is such that financial resources on their own will not be enough to achieve the level of change required. In addition, some of the healthcare professionals in the region lack the required knowledge, skills and motivation to embark on continuous personal professional development.

Health Policies, National and Local Guidelines

In developed countries, health policies and national and local guidelines are produced from a range of health research evidence, but in developing continents, such as Africa, health policies and guidelines are rarely informed by research evidence (WHO Regional Office for Africa 2021a). Also, guidelines which are often developed specifically to manage a certain clinical disease or symptom are also usually derived from evidence-based criteria resulting from well-designed clinical investigation or expert opinion (Jamison et al. 2006). As discussed in various chapters in this book, without evidence-based clinical protocols or guidelines, it will be impossible to achieve high-quality care, better health outcomes and cost-effective treatments in Africa. In the countries of Africa there is no equivalent to the UK's National Institute for Clinical Excellence (NICE) or the US Agency for Healthcare Research and Quality with responsibility for producing evidence-based guidelines or protocols aimed at delivering improved, safe and high-quality care. Even where there are similar bodies, they are defunct and non-functioning, thereby compounding the problems of not producing locally relevant health evidence, information and research for the formation of policies and the development of guidelines directed at local needs and priorities and the management of various clinical diseases (WHO Regional Office for Africa 2021a).

Weak Legal Mandates, Accreditation and Administrative Regulations

An effective quality improvement system also depends on legal mandates, accreditations and administrative regulations, which impact quality care by controlling entry into the practice of healthcare. The functions of these policies include the licensing of professionals and facilities, their accreditations or certification to perform certain procedures and the formal delineation of duties that various types of health workers can legally perform (Jamison et al. 2006). There are many accredited healthcare organisations in Africa (Joint Commission International 2018); however, to date there is no published research evidence linking accreditation programmes to improvements in health outcomes in these organisations. There is therefore insufficient regulatory capacity in the region to regulate the healthcare profession to ensure effective maintenance of standards and codes of conduct. There is also no strong regulatory body that can enforce a strict professional development that enables professionalism and enhances excellent judgement through maintenance and enhancement of knowledge, skills, experience, personal qualities and cultivation of professional values and behaviours.

Weak Legal and Judicial System

There is also no strong legal structure in place to support clinical negligence. The healthcare systems in this region do not currently benefit from malpractice litigation, which is known to reduce harm to patients as organisations learn from claims and eventually use the lesson to improve quality (Vincent et al. 2004; Esmail et al. 2004). A study reviewing healthcare sector regulators in Tanzania and Zimbabwe revealed that the regulations mainly controlled entry into the market and ensured a minimum standard of quality are met but fails to address market-level issues of anti-competitive practices and lack of patient rights (Kumaranayake et al. 2000).

Medical-Legal Medical Malpractice Litigation Assocation summit (Pepper and Slabbert 2011). As reported by the country's Department of Health (2016) South Africa has now put in place a national policy for patient safety incident reporting and learning in the public sector. This is one of the recommendations of the Medico-legal Medical Malpractice Litigation Association summit held 9–10 January 2015.

Organisational and Institutional Influencing Factors

The influence of organisational and institutional contexts, professionals and leadership on the quality of care have been extensively researched in developed nations. Other areas with similar studies are the continual design and redesign of systems to ensure quality of care and that services are effective, safe, people-centred, timely, equitable, integrated and efficient. According to Clifford and Clark (2004), in healthcare, organisational support is required for any meaningful quality improvement changes to be successfully implemented.

Quite often a major driver of change in organisational culture to favour any given quality improvement interventions is whether the proposed intervention is linked directly to organisational priorities. As reported by Gilpatrick (1999), a project connected with organisational targets will easily win the support of senior management. This support will impact the backing of the organisation, the resources it will be willing to commit to the intervention and its willingness to persuade staff to accept and implement the new intervention. The challenges of a successful implementation of quality improvement initiatives are also addressed within organisational cultures where innovation and teamwork are valued.

In the developing countries of Africa, it is not clear how these factors could be handled to achieve success in designing and implementing quality improvement interventions. Moreover, in the region there could be factors to be dealt with apart from organisational cultures, capacities and contexts; tribalism and lack of staff engagement; leadership; and staff incentives, as reported in the literature (Dixon-Woods et al. 2012). In the Africa region, improving care and service had previously been a function of procuring new equipment and employing more staff, whereas today the concept of redesign interventions shows that simply adding new resources without improving processes will not result in the desired quality improvements (Jamison et al. 2006). In the region, therefore, a better understanding of organisational change in the African healthcare context will help in assessing the readiness for change, establishing a sense of urgency, forming a steering team, developing an implementation plan, executing a pilot programme and disseminating change (Varkey and Antonio 2010).

Poor-Quality Data in Health Care

Dixon (2011) views quality improvement as "systematic, data-guided activities designed to bring about immediate, positive changes in the delivery of health care in particular settings". As the foregoing discussion explained, the importance of quality data in quality improvement interventions cannot be overemphasised. The prevailing inadequacies of health care in the region, which has been a serious hindrance to quality and safety improvements, as discussed in the previous sections, will pose a similar challenge to successful implementation of quality improvements, largely because all quality improvement interventions depend for the most part on having quality and reliable data to measure structures, processes and outcomes.

Leadership and Governance Problem

Strong leadership and good governance are the leading determinants of a successful healthcare system, and almost all the challenges discussed earlier can be associated less in terms of the impact on the system and more with a lack of vision, commitment, transparency, bribery, corruption, and misconceived and misplaced priorities on the part of African leaders (Azevedo 2017).

In healthcare quality improvement within healthcare organisations, leadership is a major driver because it helps to inculcate the belief that a particular intervention can actually lead to collective action for valuable improvement (World Health Organization, Organisation for Economic Co-operation and Development, and World Bank 2018). Some of the abilities of a good leader or quality improvement initiative advocate include exuding confidence, being able to work well under duress and carefully monitoring performance. Leaders must also be interested in staff well-being and development and be able to recognise and learn from errors and their own inadequacies (Firth-Cozens and Mowbray 2001). In addition, leaders within healthcare organisations must have excellent communication and negotiation skills, as well as a deep understanding of the politics of the particular context, as these are great assets in influencing the implementation climate of any quality improvement initiative.

Prerequisites for Quality and Safety Improvement in Health Care

The essential aspect highlighted in this book of makingmeaningful improvements in the quality and safety of health care in Africa are *standard operating procedures, audits, healthcare research, safety management, quality management system and evaluation.* To successfully design and put in place these essential features and reap their full benefits, strategic actions must be taken. These include but are not limited to creating and sustaining a culture of patient safety, establishing a dedicated safety and quality department, securing organisational support, ensuring effective health-care management and demonstrating excellence in specific skills and abilities.

Creating and Sustaining Patient Safety Culture

The notion of reducing or preventing harm to patients during the provision of care in Africa will require a concerted effort from healthcare and non-healthcare profes-sionals, healthcare organisations and patients themselves. The results of such efforts will lead to the prevention of errors and adverse events and learning from such incidents and building a culture of safety, as explained in the IOM report (Kohn et al. 1999). This idea will require a complete shift from the natural or traditional way of blaming or placing a lot of emphasis on who made a given error and giving little or no consideration to how and why the error or mistake happened. This model of safety culture now used in health care is based on that used by highly reliable organisations (such as aviation, oil and gas and nuclear energy industries), where the occurrence of errors and adverse events is consistently minimized, even though the operations at such organisations are complex and extremely risky in nature (Lee and Harrison 2000; Agency for Healthcare Research and Quality 2019). As stated earlier, the degree of success in safety recorded in these organisations is attributed to the fact that staff at all levels, from frontline staff to managers and executives, recognise their responsibilities with regard to safety and are personally committed to it. The concept of safety culture in this industry has since been successfully inte-grated into the healthcare system. Research shows an encouraging relationship between improved safety culture and better patient outcomes (Singer et al. 2009; Allard et al. 2011), confirming that improving the culture of safety in health care is indeed an essential component of preventing or reducing errors and adverse events and can have a positive and measurable impact on the performance of the healthcare quality of organisations (Department of Health 2000b).

The definition of safety culture is derived from the nuclear energy industry and in a healthcare context, patient safety culture is said to be a product of values, atti-tudes, risk perceptions, competencies and standards of individual and group behav-iour that are committed to and the style and proficiency of the health organisation's safety management (Nieva and Sorra 2003; Sammer et al. 2010). In the reports by

Fig. 1.1 Characteristics of
a successful safety- and
quality-focused healthcare
organisation

these authors, patient safety experts identify the organisational components or properties that can influence the safety culture in any organisation. These include a just culture, which is a culture that considers system failures as a possible source of errors or adverse events and carefully balances such a system malfunction with individual or professional behaviour and accountability. This type of culture is reported to produce an open and honest environment where healthcare staff are confident and feel safe to report patient safety incidents and near misses without fear of blame with the aim of cultivating a quality learning environment, which is one of the major steps in a healthcare safety improvement process (Boysen 2013; Leistikow et al. 2017). On the other hand, an unjust culture is characterised by blame and shame, which hinders people from acknowledging errors and prevents learning (Nieva and Sorra 2003). Other organisational components that can influence safety culture include leadership support, teamwork and communication.

In developed countries, the effect of patient safety culture and various features or components of healthcare organisations mentioned earlier have been extensively investigated and various measurement tools and users' guide developed (Nieva and Sorra 2003; Sorra et al. 2016; Sammer et al. 2010). Unfortunately, in the developing countries of Africa, effective patient safety culture and associated features of healthcare organisations have yet to be adequately explored (Carpenter et al. 2010; Powell et al. 2011; Wami et al. 2016). Much research is required on how to create and sustain a patient safety culture in health care in Africa. It is important that the effects of human factors also be considered as well as the safety culture and the unique environment of Africa. Other notable factors include organisational, social, economic and individual characteristics that are likely to impact individuals' behaviour at work, which could affect patient safety (WHO Patient Safety Methods and Measures for Patient Safety Working Group 2009).

Secure Organisational Supports at all Levels

For any of the essential components to be successfully implemented, the organisation's board and staff at all levels must willingly embrace the evolving paradigm that well-managed and successful healthcare organisations today are those that fully integrate and achieve effective financial control and outstanding service performance, including safe and high-quality clinical care (Scally and Donaldson 1998). As depicted in (Fig. 1.1), this will require a total shift in the hospital management agenda from focusing mainly on finance to service performance as well as safety and quality care issues. This implies devoting full attention and commitment to these three areas in all spheres, including staffing and other resource allocations.

Management must ensure the right infrastructure is in place, which includes but is not limited to information technology, education and training and time for staff to review their care and services. Others will evaluate the evidence applied and plan for either continuing current practices or redesigning the entire system and process of care to achieve improved outcomes.

Create a Safety and Quality Department

More so, any organisation that genuinely wants to witness notable success must urgently set up a department or unit that will be responsible for driving the affairs of patient safety and quality improvement, particularly the essential components proposed in this book, including care and service performance management. Although each organisation will be responsible for working out in detail the role of such a safety and quality department (SQD), it must include influencing the culture of the organisation to prioritise patient safety and quality improvement "through an inspiring vision and positive reinforcement, not through blame and punishment" (Yu et al. 2016). That is, it must create "a working environment which is open and protective, where ideas and good practice are shared, where education and research are valued, and where blame is used exceptionally" (Scally and Donaldson 1998).

Secondly, the SQD must immediately realise the need for cooperation among various disciplines and true partnership with patients as extremely important for success. other words, doctors, nurses, management staff and domestic staff, as well as patients, must all work together towards a common goal of achieving safe and quality care and service. They must devise a means of achieving this by completely eliminating the idea of "god's father", "it won't work without me" and tribal sentiments. They must also treat disrespect and discrimination of any form among staff as unprofessional conduct (Berwick 1998) and adopt a policy of zero tolerance towards it. They must equally work with other staff to identify the skills and competencies required in each area of care and service.

Effective Healthcare Management

One of the suggested responses to the complexity of a healthcare system is forming a collaborative team (communities of practice) equipped with the relevant skills, knowledge and abilities to provide services in various specialties, departments, wards and clinics (State of Queensland 2011). Similarly, to effectively implement the essential components of safety and quality improvement identified in this book, recruiting staff (medical and non-medical) with the requisite skills, knowledge and abilities who are enthusiastic about health care is an essential condition. Therefore, in the African context, with its shortage of healthcare professionals, there is an urgent need to raise the profile of healthcare management and encourage the development of such skills, knowledge and abilities in various fields among non-clinical professionals. Healthcare management is a general term for a career aimed at developing, delivering and coordinating services in various areas of expertise and departments in healthcare organisations (Buchbinder and Thompson 2010).

Healthcare management is a discipline aimed at training both healthcare and non-healthcare professionals to support clinicians at the frontline, patients and service users. Healthcare management is extremely important in healthcare today because it offers relevant degree programmes and courses and produces a range of non-clinical professionals needed to carry out services in health care that are better performed by this group of staff with little or no contribution from clinical counterparts. For instance, the ever-changing landscape of regulations, compliance and policy development and implementation (Lee 2016); healthcare information management, information governance and data protection (Amelung 2019); medical information documentation and coding (Swartz 2021); finance and human resources. Patient safety office and ethusiast capable of creating a safety culture, developing and implementing relevant safety. Healthcare management will also produce patient safety officers and advocates capable of creating a safety culture, developing and implementing relevant safety practices and boosting safety-related management and performance in healthcare organisations (Frankel et al. 2013). However, a detailed consideration of the various knowledge, skills and abilities for integrated solutions to complex problems such as safety and quality improvement is certainly beyond the scope of this book. In addition, in the challenging environment of the healthcare workplace of the developing countries of Africa weighed down with formidable barriers of various forms, one can only imagine the wide array of knowledge, skills and abilities that individuals will require to achieve meaningful and measurable improvements in safety and quality of care and sustain such improvements in both medium- and long-term perspectives. Technology, for instance, particularly the use of computer and mobile technology, which has changed the way healthcare workers live, deliver care and perform other associated tasks, is still not fully integrated into all facets of healthcare settings in the region.

Nevertheless, in health care, success in safety and quality improvement will require "conscientiousness, humility, honesty, self-awareness, confidence, situation awareness, vigilance and open mindedness, anticipation and preparedness, leadership, team working and communication" (Vincent 2010). As discussed by the

Table 1.1 Safety and quality improvement skills. (Reproduced from The Health Foundation 2014)

Technical safety improvement skills	
Identifying where and why improvement is needed; analysing safety risk and measuring/ evaluating data, change and outcomes	*Cause-and-effect diagrams, process mapping/analysis, driver diagrams, swim-lane mapping, understanding clinical variation, understanding clinical risk, proactive risk analysis tools (e.g. failure mode and effects analysis), model for improvement, identifying error and harm, high-reliability systems, human factors, root-cause analysis, safety-critical work (e.g. invasive procedures, infection control, medication safety, emergency), plan-do-study-act (PDSA) rapid improvement cycles, value stream mapping, spaghetti diagrams, fishbone analysis, the five whys, recognising, reporting and managing adverse events and near misses, patient stories*
Measurement skills	
Designing measures and evaluating data, change and outcomes	*Measurement for improvement, setting baselines, Excel, Pareto, Run, SPC, Win charts, balanced scorecards, quality measurement, collecting data/audit, data sampling, analysing data, safety culture measures (e.g. safety culture interaction), measurement of reliability, mortality measures, harm measures, patient experience measures, evaluating improvement*
Engagement and implementation skills	
Influencing and engaging colleagues in patient safety work, involving staff, patients and partners; motivating those involved to change/enhance practice and sustain change over time	*Leading change/improvement, Understanding others' perspectives, creativity and innovation, sustainability, organising for quality, staff engagement, group facilitation skills, creating a culture for improvement/safety, working in partnership, patient and carer engagement, coaching principles and practice, OD cycle and skills (contracting, data collection, data feedback, implementation), effective teams, team diagnostic tools (e.g. Aston organisation development), motivation theory, communication about risk, safety and errors, learning and changing practice from error, Manchester Patient Safety Framework (MPSF), S-BAR handover tool, handling conflict effectively, respectful and non-respectful behaviours*
Research and learning skills	
Extending and deepening knowledge and understanding about safety improvement; sharing learning; applying and transferring research into practice across wider contexts	*Qualitative research methods, quantitative research methods, research findings into practice, peer-reviewed publishing, critical review/appraisal, conducting patient safety research, action research*
System leadership skills	
Creating a culture of values and behaviours which nurture and promote safety improvement across a meso- or macro-system	*Whole system theory, social movement theory, understanding complex systems, leading changes across organisational boundaries, developing shared purpose and values, latent conditions for safety, peer leadership across systems*

Health Foundation 2014, specific skills necessary for effective engagement in safety and quality improvement can be classified into five broad clusters: technical safety improvement, measurement, engagement and implementation, research and learning, and system leadership skills (Table 1.1).

The National Research Council (2001) on twenty-first-century skills, also provided more insight into these aspects. According to the report, there are interpersonal, intrapersonal and cognitive skills which are necessary to *"solve complex problems, to think critically about tasks, to effectively communicate with people from variety of different cultures and using a variety of different techniques, to work in collaboration with others, to adapt to rapidly changing environments and conditions for performing tasks, to effectively manage one's work, and to acquire new skills and information on one's own"*. In the developing countries of Africa, healthcare programmes, initiatives and policies are often stifled by the country's complexity, size, cultural diversity, social and economic conditions and disparity of health resources. Acquisition of these skills by healthcare workers in the region will be a factor in ensuring effective management of these challenges and reducing their influence on a healthcare safety and quality improvement scheme. For instance, interpersonal skills will aid in communicating complex issues within a team and dealing with sociocultural issues with sensitivity and respect for diversity; intrapersonal skills will help in time management, self-development and regulations including adaptability and executive functioning and cognitive skills will assist in non-routine problem solving and support critical and systems thinking (National Research Council 2001).

Conclusion

In addition to the previously mentioned preconditions, the successful design and implementation of these essentials will require sacrifices involving an integrated organisation-wide system approach. Considering various challenges one is likely to face in health care in the region, some of which are explained in the preceding discussion, success will have to be seen and approached as an analogy for the work of digging a well in the region, where one must keep digging until water is found. Practically speaking, it might take a long time to find water in some part of the region or in different communities within the same country for various reasons, especially depending on the hardness of the soil and other geological factors. Digging for a while without finding water is not a sign that no progress has been made; usually perseverance and motivation are needed to maintain focus until water is found, which will benefit the general community. Similarly, various challenges and barriers will be faced in different healthcare organisations within countries or in different countries in the region in the process of putting into place the essential features of a healthcare system discussed here, but everyone – healthcare professionals, policymakers, stakeholders and other parties involved, must make sacrifices in working out the solutions with confidence. That is, people must overcome the challenges to achieving successful outcomes, bearing in mind the price of failure for future healthcare systems and the negative impacts such failure would have on the care and service of future generations of patients and healthcare staff in the region.

References

Agency for Healthcare Research and Quality (2019) Culture of safety. https://psnet.ahrq.gov/primer/culture-safety. Accessed 10 July 2021

Allard J, Bleakley A, Hobbs A et al (2011) Pre-surgery briefings and safety climate in the operating theatre. BMJ Qual Saf 20:711–717

Amelung VE (2019) Healthcare management – managed care organisations and instruments, 2nd edn. Springe, Berlin

Aveling E, Kayonga Y, Nega A et al (2015) Why is patient safety so hard in low-income countries? A qualitative study of healthcare workers' view into African hospitals. Glob Health 11(6):1–8

Azevedo MJ (2017) Historical perspectives on the state of health and health systems in Africa, Volume II: The Modern Era. Palgrave Macmillan, Cham

Baker GR, Norton PG, Flintoft V et al (2004) The Canadian adverse events study: the incidence of adverse events among hospitals in Canada. CMAJ 170(11):1678–1686

Berwick DM (1998) The NHS: feeling well and thriving at 75. BMJ 317:57–61

Boyle BM, Palmer L, Kappelman MD (2009) Quality of health care in the United States: implications for paediatric inflammatory bowel disease. J Paediatr Gastroenterol Nutr 49(3):272–282

Boysen P (2013) Just culture: a foundation for balanced accountability and patient safety. Ochsner J 13(3):400–406

Buchbinder SB, Thompson JM (2010) Career opportunities in healthcare management: perspectives from the field. Jones and Bartlett Publishers, Sudbury

Burstin H, Leatherman S, Goldmann D (2016) The evolution of healthcare quality measurement in the United States. J Intern Med 279(2):154–159

Carlo WA, Goudar SS, Jehan I et al (2010) The first breadth study. Newborn-care training and perinatal mortality in developing countries. N Engl J Med 362(7):614–623

Carpenter K, Duevel M, Lee P et al (2010) Measures of patient safety in developing and emerging countries: a review of the literature. Qual Saf HealthCare 19(1):48–54

Chassin MR, Brook RH, Park RE et al (1986) Variations in the use of medical and surgical services by Medicare population. N Engl J Med 314(5):285–290

Clifford C, Clark J (eds) (2004) Getting research into practice. Elsevier, Amsterdam

Committee on the Quality of Health Care in America (2001) Crossing the quality chasm: a new health system for the 21st century. National Academies Press, Washington DC

Department of Health (2000a) An organisation with a memory. The Department of Health Publication The Stationary Office, London

Department of Health (2000b) An organisation with a memory: a report of an expert group on learning from adverse events in the NHS chaired by the chief medical officer. Department of Health, London

Department of Health (2016) National policy for patient safety incident reporting and learning in public health sector in South Africa, Republic of South Africa

Dixon N (2011) Ethics and clinical audit and Quality Improvement (QI) – a guide for NHS organisations. http://citeseerx.ist.psu.edu/viewdoc/download?doi=10.1.1.457.4981&rep=rep1&type=pdf. Accessed 19 June 2018

Dixon-Woods M, McNicol S, Martin G (2012) Ten challenges in improving quality in healthcare: lessons from the Health Foundation's programme evaluations and relevant literature. BMJ Qual Saf:1–9. https://doi.org/10.1136/bmjqs-2011-000760

Ehsani J, Jackson T, Duckett S (2006) The incidence and cost of adverse events in Victoria hospitals 2003–04. Med J Aust 184(11):551–555

Ente C, Oyewumi A, Mpora OB (2010) Healthcare professional understanding and awareness of patient safety and quality of care in Africa: a survey study. Int J Risk & Saf Med 22:103–110

Esmail A, Neale G, Elstein M et al (2004) Patient safety: lessons from litigation. Case studies in litigation: claims reviews in four specialties. Manchester Centre for Healthcare Management, University of Manchester, Manchester. Report

Firth-Cozens J, Mowbray D (2001) Leadership and the quality of care. Qual Health Care 10(Suppl II):ii3–ii

Flum DR, Koepsell T (2002) The clinical and economic correlates of misdiagnosed appendicitis: nationwide analysis. Arch Surg 137(7):799–804

Frankel A, Leonard M, Federico F et al (eds) (2013) The essential guide for patient safety officer, 2 edn. Joint Commission Resources, Institute for Healthcare Improvement, Oakbrook Terrace Illinois

Gilpatrick E (1999) Quality improvement projects in health care – problem solving in the workplace. Sage, London

Guest G, Namey EE (eds) (2015) Public health research methods. Sage, Los Angeles

Heiby J (2014) The use of modern quality approaches to strengthen African health system: a 5-year agenda. Int J Qual Health Care 26(2):117–123

Hornby AS (2000) Oxford advanced learner's dictionary of current English. Oxford University Press, New York

Institute of Medicine (2000) To err is human: building a safer health system. National Academy of Sciences, Washington DC

Jamison DT, Breman JG, Measham AR (eds) (2006) Disease control priority in developing countries: disease control priorities project, 2 edn. Oxford University Press, Washington DC https://www.ncbi.nlm.nih.gov/books/NBK11728/. Accessed 2 July 2018

Jha AK, Larizgoitia I, Audera-Lopez C et al (2013) The global burden of unsafe medical care: analytic modelling of observational studies. BMJ Qual Saf 22(10):809–815. https://doi.org/10.1136/bmjqs-2012-001748

Joint Commission International (2018) JCI-Accredited Organisations. https://www.jointcommissioninternational.org/about-jci/jci-accredited-organizations/. Accessed 8 July 2018

Kalish RL, Daley J, Duncan DC et al (1995) Costs of potential complications of care for major surgical patients. Am J Med Qual 10(1):48–54

Kannampallil TG, Schauer GF, Cohen F et al (2011) Considering complexity in healthcare systems. J Biomed Inform 44:943–947

Kinfu Y, Dal Poz MR, Mercer H et al (2009) The health worker shortage in Africa: are enough physicians and nurses being trained? Bull World Health Org 87:225–230

Kohn L, Corrigan J, Donaldson M (1999) To err is human: building a safer health system. Institute of Medicine report. National Academies Press, Washington DC

Kohn LT, Corrigan JM, Donaldson MS (eds) (2000) To err is human: building a safer health system. National Academies Press, Washington DC

Kumaranayake L, Mujinja P, Hongoro C et al (2000) How do countries regulate the health sector? Evidence from Tanzania and Zimbabwe. Health Policy Plan 15(4):357–367

Leape LL, Brennan TA, Laird N et al (1991) The nature of adverse events in hospitalised patients. Results of the Harvard medical practice study II. N Engl J Med 324(6):377–384

Leatherman S, Ferris TG, Berwick D et al (2010) The role of quality improvement in strengthening health systems in developing countries. Int J Qual Health Care 22(4):237–243. https://doi.org/10.1093/intqhc/mzq028

Lee V (2016) A profile of health management industry: health administration for non-clinical professionals. Business Expert Press, New York

Lee T, Harrison K (2000) Assessing safety culture in nuclear power stations. Saf Sci 34:61–97

Leistikow I, Mulder S, Vesseur J et al (2017) Learning from incidents in healthcare: the journey, not the arrival, matters. BMJ Qual Saf 26:252–256

Lock D (2007) Project management, 9th edn. Gower Publishing, London

Mekonnen AB, Alhawassi TM, McLachlan AJ et al (2018) Adverse drug events and medication errors in African hospitals: a systematic review. Drugs Real World Outcomes 5(1):1–24

National Academies of Sciences, Engineering, and Medicine (2018) Crossing the global quality chasm: improving health care worldwide. National Academies Press, Washington DC

National Audit Office (2005) A safer place for patients: learning to improve patient safety. National Audit Office, London

National Research Council (2001) Assessing 21 St century skills – summary of a workshop. National Academies Press, Washington DC

Nieva VF, Sorra J (2003) Safety culture assessment: a tool for improving patient safety in health-care organizations. Qual Saf Healthcare 12(Suppl II): ii17–ii23

Nolan T, Angos P, Cunha AJ et al (2001) Quality of hospital care for seriously ill children in less-developed countries. Lancet 357(9250):106–110

Øvretveit J (2009) Does improving quality save money? A review of evidence of which improvements to quality reduce costs to health service providers. Health Foundation, London

Pepper MS, Slabbert MN (2011) Is South Africa on the verge of a medical malpractice litigation storm? SAJBL 4(1):29–35

Pittet D, Donaldson L (2005) Clean care is safer care: the first global challenge of the WHO World Alliance for Patient Safety – special report. Infect Control Hosp Epidemiol 26(11):891–894. https://www.who.int/patientsafety/information_centre/ICHE_Nov_05_CleanCare_1.pdf#:~:text=%E2%80%9CClean%20Care%20is%20Safer%20Care%2C%E2%80%9D%20focusing%20on%20the,countries%20and%20everywhere%20that%20health%20care%20is%-20provided. Accessed 1 July 2021

Powell S, Baily D, Ndili NM et al (2011) Patient safety in Africa: a culture shift? Patient Saf Qual Healthcare:48–51

Rowe AK, Onikpo F, Lama M et al (2010) The rise and fall of supervision in a project designed to strengthen supervision of integrated management of childhood illness in Benin. Health Policy Plan 25:125–134

Sammer CE, Lykens K, Singh KP et al (2010) What is patient safety culture? A review of the literature. J Nurs Scholarsh 42(2):156–165

Scally G, Donaldson LJ (1998) Clinical governance and the drive for quality improvement in the new NHS in England. BMJ 317(7150):61–65

Schuster MA, McGlynn EA, Brook RH (1998) How good is the quality of health care in the United States? Milbank Q 76(4):517–563

Schuster MA, McGlynn EA, Brook RH (2005) How good is the quality of health care in the United States? Milbank Q 83(4):843–895

Siddiqi K, Newell J, Robinson M (2005) Getting evidence into practice: what works in developing countries? Int Qual Health Care 17(5):447–453

Singer S, Lin S, Falwell A et al (2009) Relationship of safety climate and safety performance in hospitals. Health Serv Res 44(2 Pt 1):399–421

Sorra J, Gray L, Streagle S et al (2016) AHRQ hospital survey on patient safety culture: user's guide. (Prepared by Westat, under Contract No. HHSA290201300003C). AHRQ Publication No. 15–0049-EF (Replaces 04–0041). Agency for Healthcare Research and Quality, Rockville. http://www.ahrq.gov/professionals/quality-patientsafety/patientsafetyculture/hospital/index.htm. Accessed 12 July 2021

State of Queensland (2011) Complexity and health care: health practitioner workforce services, roles, skills and training, to respond to patients with complex needs. Queensland Health, Brisbane

Swartz S (2021) Mastering evaluation and Management Services in Healthcare: a resource for professional services. Business Expert Press, New York

The Health Foundation (2014) Building capacity to improve safety, event report. The Health Foundation, London

Varkey P, Antonio K (2010) Change management for effective quality improvement: a primer. Am J Med Qual 25(4):268–273

Vincent C (2010) Patient safety, 2nd edn. Wiley-Blackwell Publishing, London

Vincent C, Neale G, Woloshynowych M (2001) Adverse events in British hospitals: preliminary retrospective record review. BMJ 322(7285):517–519

Vincent C, Davy C, Esmail A et al (2004) Patient safety: lessons from litigation. Learning from litigation: an analysis of claims for clinical negligence. Manchester Centre for Healthcare Management, University of Manchester, Manchester. Report

Walsh K, Antony J (2009) An assessment of quality costs within electronic adverse event and recording systems. Int J Health Care Qual Assur 22(3):203–220

Wami SD, Demssie AF, Wassie MM et al (2016) Patient safety culture and associated factors: a quantitative and qualitative study of healthcare workers' view in Jimma zone Hospitals, Southwest Ethiopia. BMC Health Serv Res 16(495):1–10

WHO Patient Safety Methods and Measures for Patient Safety Working Group (2009) Human factors in patient safety review of topics and tools. World Health Organization. Report number: WHO/IER/PSP/2009.05

WHO Regional Office for Africa (2008) Patient safety in African health services: Issues and solutions, Report of the Regional Director to the 58th Regional Committee. Report No: AFR/RC58/8, Geneva

WHO Regional Office for Africa (2012) Health Systems in Africa Community Perceptions and Perspectives - The Report of a Multi-Country Study. WHO Regional Office for Africa. Report number: ISBN: 978 929 023 2018 (NLM Classification: WA 540 HA1)

WHO Regional Office for Africa (2021) Framework for improving access to assistive technology in the WHO African region – Report of the Secretariat. World Region Office for Africa. Report number: AFR/RC71/11

WHO Regional Office for Africa (2021a) Framework for strengthening the use of evidence, information and research for policy – making in the African region - Report of the Secretariat World Region Office for Africa Report number: AFR/RC71/13

Wilson RM, Runcima WB, Gibberd RW et al (1995) The quality in Australian health care study. Med J Aust 163(9):458–471

Woloshynowych M, Roger S, Taylor-Adams S (2005) The investigation and analysis of critical incidents and adverse events in health care. Health Care Technol Assess 9(19):1–143. iii. https://doi.org/10.3310/hta9190

Word Health Organization (2015) Partnerships for safer health service delivery: Evaluation of WHO African Partnership for Patient Safety 2009–2014. Report No: WHO/HIS/SDS/2015/2015.13

Word Health Organization (2020) World Patient Safety Day. https://www.who.int/campaigns/world-patient-safety-day/2020. Accessed 25 Sept 2020

Word Health Organization Regional Office for Europe (2021) Patient Safety Day. https://www.euro.who.int/en/health-topics/Health-systems/patient-safety/patient-safety. Accessed 23 June 2021

World Health Organization (2004) World Alliance for Patient Safety Forward Programme. https://www.who.int/patientsafety/en/brochure_final.pdf. Accessed 2 July 2021

World Health Organization (2016) Patient Safety APPS Achievements. http://www.who.int/patientsafety/implementation/apps/achievements/en/. Accessed 10 Oct 2016

World Health Organization (2017) Patient safety: making health care safer. World Health Organisation, Geneva. Report number: WHO/HIS/SDS/2017.11

World Health Organization (2019) Patient safety: global action on patient safety. Report by the Director-General. World Health Organization, Geneva https://apps.who.int/gb/ebwha/pdf_files/WHA72/A72_26-en.pdf. Accessed 01 July 2021

World Health Organization (2021) Patient Safety. https://www.who.int/news-room/fact-sheets/detail/patient-safety. Accessed 30 June 2021

World Health Organization Reginal Office for Africa (2021) Patient Safety. https://www.afro.who.int/health-topics/patient-safety. Accessed 29 June 2021

World Health Organization, Organisation for Economic Co-operation and Development, and World Bank (2018) Delivering quality health services: a global imperative for universal health coverage. World Health Organization, Organisation for Economic Co-operation and Development, and World Bank, Geneva Licence: CC BY-NC-SA 3.0 IGO

World Healthcare Organisation (2007) Everybody business: strengthening health systems to improve health outcomes: WHO's framework for action. WHO Press, Switzerland

Yu A, Flott K, Chainani N et al (2016) Patient safety 2030. NIHR Imperial Patient Safety Translational Research Centre, London

Chapter 2
Standard Operating Procedure

Introduction

Delivery of care and service to agreed standards is a fundamental requirement for safe and quality care (Vincent et al. 2014). The agreed standard in this case is based on the current and best evidence obtained through research and development. In essence, this is evidence-based practice (EBP). The most up-to-date best evidence is usually translated into policies, guidelines and procedures for use at the point of care in a healthcare system. Healthcare professionals are often expected to use this evidence as a guide in conjunction with their clinical expertise, experience and patient values while making clinical decisions during care delivery. But according to the World Health Organization (2018a), there is considerable variation between the application of evidence-based recommendations and current practice in many countries in Africa. Even in several health conditions where current best evidence is available, such as cardiovascular diseases, respiratory diseases, neonatal seizures and the treatment of malaria and Ebola patients, the evidence has still not been adopted in practice. For instance, the WHO has developed some standard operating procedures under The High 5s Project aimed at achieving measurable, significant and sustainable solutions to safety and quality improvement in health sector problems (World Health Organization 2018b), but there is still no evidence in the literature on whether any of these SOPs has been adopted and implemented in healthcare facilities in the region.

Nonetheless, there was evidence of SOPs for national initiatives in the regions, for example, SOPs for the management of health information in Uganda (Ministry of Health Uganda 2010), infectious diseases such as tuberculosis in Tanzania (Ministry of Health and Social Welfare 2008), serving as a model for a health sector monitoring framework and strategic plans (Kenya Health Sector 2008), providing operational guidance on social mobilisation and community engagement for Ebola transmission and prevention in Sierra Leone (Burial Pillar 2015) and the management of the Ebola virus in South Africa (Health Department, Republic of South Africa 2014). But again, there is no strong evidence on SOP adoption and use in local hospitals. Moreover, the effective dates on these SOPs showed they had been developed years ago, so it was challenging to establish whether they have been updated or discontinued. However, considering the importance of SOPs as a means of standardisation in clinical practice (Vincent 2010) and their usefulness in improving patient outcomes when followed during treatment (Nachtigall et al. 2008), local adaptation of SOPs will be necessary to achieve meaningful improvements in the safety and quality of care in healthcare organisations in the region.

This chapter discusses a practical method of developing, implementing and managing a SOP in clinical settings. The benefits and some of the potential areas of application of SOPs in health care in the region are also presented. The premise of this chapter is that practical knowledge and skills in the development, implementation and management of SOPs will encourage healthcare professionals in the region to develop and use them in their daily care and service provisions. Above all it is hoped that this endeavour will generate interest and facilitate the process of accessing evidence-based practice resources currently available on the World Health Organization's website, individual country healthcare ministries and other reliable sources. Hopefully, this will lead to the extraction and integration of such resources into one set of procedures useful to frontline staff for informing clinical practice and service planning.

Standard Operating Procedure

A SOP is a set of written instructions for the completion of a routine task, designed to increase performance, improve efficiency and ensure quality through systematic standardisation (Nolen 2009). The SOP enables a routine task or procedure to be carried out in a similar manner (consistency) and correctly (quality) every time it is performed to a specified standard, even if it is executed by different people. SOPs are used in different organisations in various contexts. It is used in both high-risk industries (aviation, construction, nuclear, oil and gas) and other settings (educational institutions and government parastatal organisations and companies). SOPs used in all these organisations share common features. These features include presenting a repetitive task in a systematic format and clearly defined steps to follow in implementing such a task, thereby creating an overall quality system (Nolen 2009). Moreover, these SOPs provide the means of standardising best practices in operations across organisations (WHO African Regional Office 2014).

In health care, SOPs are extensively used in everyday clinical care in different areas of specialty and constitute a long-established practice. SOPs are a cornerstone of consistency and quality in the performance and improvement of care and service delivery. As explained by Sathyanarayana et al. (2011), SOPs used in the healthcare setting are as numerous as the area of care and tasks in healthcare systems. For instance, there are SOPs for physicians to follow in an emergency room for unconscious patients, while other SOPs are for technicians in a laboratory setting for handling, testing and destroying bodily fluids from patients. In an operating theatre, there are SOPs for nurses who need to hand over forceps and swabs to the operating surgeon and effectively manage instruments before, during and after operations.

Development of Standard Operating Procedure

SOP development requires careful consideration as it involves the distillation into precisely defined steps of routine clinical practice processes for treating clinical conditions. Clinical practice processes, which are standards based on the latest evidence-based care, are sometimes complex in nature. Moreover, the processes are made up of series of activities or tasks (such as admission processes or patient care management) that lead to a particular outcome. SOPs are often detailed, but an evidence-based generic plan is applicable to the delivery of care to certain patients afflicted with a given disease (Salleh 2016). Adherence to this evidence-based generic plan by healthcare staff while treating patients with that disease will enable the staff to apply best practices consistently every time for every patient.

A SOP is best presented as a structured and systematic approach (Fig. 2.1). The most important step in SOP development is the identification of the need for one in a clinical or service area of interest. This could mean, for instance, developing a SOP for the diagnosis and treatment of patients with malaria or the diagnosis and treatment of patients with chronic obstructive pulmonary disease. This identification could be initiated by an individual or clinical team, but regardless of the origin, it must be discussed, agreed upon and approved by the management, who will allocate resources for the entire exercise. This is followed by appointing a designated team for detailed review, confirming the need for the SOP and carrying out its actual development. If a safety and quality department (SQD), recommended in Chap. 1 of this book, has been set up in the organisation, a staff from this department must be a member of the team. At this point, the clinical area where the SOP will be applied will have been well established. The purpose and suitable format are also clearly defined. Every member of this team in some sense is an individual author for the SOP being developed. The next essential step is for the team to decide who among them will be the main author. The main author should preferably be a clinician within the specialty with experience and knowledge in the field or the patient's condition. It could also be an advocate of safety and quality care who possesses the relevant skills and abilities and who can work well with the experienced clinicians in the field.

This is followed by agreement regarding the development plan according to a specific timeline and with the specific contents, structure and scope of the SOP. Depending on the team's decision, the SOP may be drafted by the main author and distributed to the other team members for review, contributions and comments. Alternatively, another team member could draft the SOP and forward it to the main

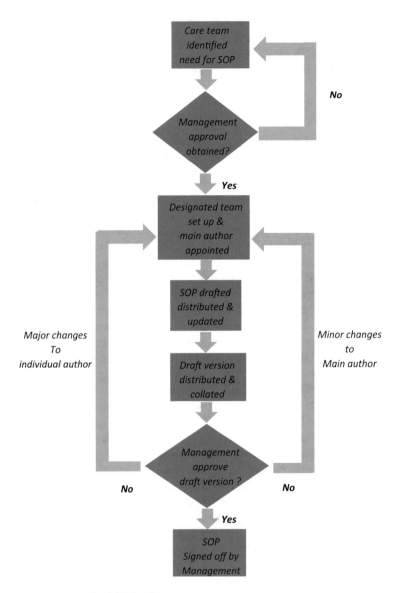

Fig. 2.1 Flow diagram for SOP development

author for compilation. A staff member of SQD in the team can help the main author in the compilation and distribution of the draft to members of the team. The SQD staff can also assist in other administrative duties in the team such as setting up meetings and take notes at the meeting.

In health care it is not always possible to write a single SOP for a single process or service, so alternatives for variations in a disease or patient profile can be incorporated into the same SOP (Salleh 2016). The decision on the structure or format of the SOP should be guided by its purpose, ease of use and efficiency. It is recommended that an existing SOP structure or format in an organisation be adopted. Where none exist, any format selected should provide a description of the processes in sequence and in a form of checklists using short sentences. The sentences should be easy to follow with the main steps using lists with accurate and ordered sub-lists where necessary. The sentences should constitute simple step-by-step and specific instructions on procedures to be followed at the point of care with possible outcomes. It is very important that the SOP agree with relevant evidence-based standards, policies and regulations. It must also provide references and citations of key legislation and regulations.

In developing any SOP, careful attention must be given to the contents. Table 2.1 shows typical SOP contents in health care. The contents of a SOP must be presented in concise, simple, step-by-step and plain-English language that is easy to read, understand and follow for staff at all levels. As a result, staff members' knowledge of terminology and their language ability must be taken into consideration. The SOP must be written in a logical order and in active and present verb tense. A SOP is a control document and so must have version control comprising version number and date. The effective and review date must be clearly stated. Diagrams can be used in the presentation where contents are complex so as to clarify the ideas and make the document easier to read and understand. Where additional information or clarification of elements of the contents is required, relevant personnel on the care or service team who are not on the SOP development team can be interviewed.

Testing and Reviewing Standard Operating Procedure

Testing and reviewing are important aspects of SOP development, implementation and administration. The process to follow depends on whether the SOP was written by a group of individual professionals or one main author. Assuming it was written by separate authors, the individual authors' copies are collated and compiled into a single document by the main author, but if it is written by one main author, a copy is distributed to individual authors within the team for input and comments. In any case, a single copy, referred to as a draft version, is produced at the end of the exercise. The draft version is then distributed to staff in the department where the SOP will be used for testing and comments. It is important that the draft copy be tested by junior staff with limited knowledge and less experience in the care or service area in which the SOP will be applied. This is a crucial step because it will give everyone the opportunity to contribute to the development and take ownership of the SOP. Feedback from these staff members on all aspects of the SOP, including ease of understanding and adequacy of the SOP for satisfying its purpose, is obtained, and relevant revisions are made to the SOP.

Because SOPs go through a review process, it is important that all versions of the document be carefully tracked. This is achieved using version control. It is best practice to ensure that each page of the SOP carries the document version control,

Table 2.1 Contents of standard operating procedure in health care. (Adapted from Salleh 2016)

Contents	Explanation
Title of SOP	Since SOPs are descriptions of steps to perform during care or management of patient group based on identified diagnosis or health condition, SOP title should show clearly specific disease or condition and target population.
Objective	A statement defining the objectives of care the SOP is designed for. The objective can also specify quality features of care and service such as expected outcome with standards and treatment end points. It should also specify the intended degree of restoration or amelioration of patient quality of life, avoidance of side effects or complications. The quality statement covers clarifying targets, and limits and quality standards should be specified.
Workflow	This is a principal component of SOPs. Workflows or clinical pathways of patient-care activities for managing clinical problems are presented as sequential work processes of predicted or planned decision-making steps that may lead to alternative paths or variations. The main work process tasks are as follows: –Establishing patient health problems, severity grading and stages of problems. This is achieved by analysis and interpretation of clinical data documented during initial assessments, investigations and diagnoses, including clinical data from other sources. –Monitoring and charting of clinical parameters through observation, management planning and documentation, implementation of plans including placing orders and performing tasks such as investigation, treatment and administration of drugs. –Documentation of results, procedures, findings and outcomes. These cover reviewing and interpreting results, quality control procedures, progress review, assessment of outcomes, communication (referral notes, replies) and other requests and orders.
Process schedule	The processes or task activities within a SOP are ordered into sets appropriate for scheduled periods. The entire exercise is referred to as a care plan or work schedule. Its contents include a title which clearly states the purpose of the SOP, the phase of care and other indications, objectives and expected outcomes. The list of all tasks is grouped based on the methods or techniques or professional competency.
Work Instruction	Work instructions or protocols provide further details on how certain processes are to be performed. The instructions are usually a description of how to perform a task, e.g. inserting a catheter, taking blood samples or other specimens, and also include information about obtaining consent and documentation using standard forms or charts, use of instruments and operating machines.
Operational policies	These documents are often integrated into work procedures. In any organization, policies define objectives and explain specific constraints within which tasks or processes are performed. Constraints are usually embedded in rules, regulations, targets and standards outlined by the organisation. Policies also provide insight into efficiency, quality, cost, responsibilities, preferences and expectations.
Quality control methods and procedures	This deals with quality control and quality improvement activities detailing how to achieve compliance with process specification and outcome standards. Functions in common use include quality measurements, standards comparisons, compliance monitoring and improvement methods.

including the page number, as a footnote if desired. The updated version is reviewed by the designated team and again forwarded to individual members across the department for rigorous review and comments. The updated SOP, as reviewed by all staff members, is now presented to management for further review and approval. If the SOP is accepted by management (Fig. 2.1), it is signed off as the final copy; otherwise, it is sent back to either the individual authors or main author depending on the level of revision required. When management's recommended revisions are made, the SOP may be sent to team members for further review and comments, if necessary, or the changes are simply communicated to them, especially if the changes were minor.

Implementation of Standard Operating Procedure

The implementation date and next review date are confirmed and documented on the SOP usually on the front page. As pointed out by Salleh (2016), "The SOP/Care plans remain as a reference document until it is converted into an actual plan by customizing it for the individual patient." This makes the implementation stage very crucial in SOP development. Before the SOP is effective, debriefing or training must be conducted. During training, trainers and trainees often sign a training log to show that the training was successfully completed. The main author at this point now makes the SOP available, in either paper or electronic form, at appropriate clinical sites where it will be easily accessible to all the relevant members of the staff or care team. The author must also set up a system for quality assurance and monitoring to ensure compliance and encourage staff members to submit their comments during real-life application. This information is used to evaluate whether the SOP achieved its objectives. It is important for SOPs to remain current and not be allowed to become outdated. All SOPs must be reviewed at agreed intervals, except where an urgent review is required due to sudden changes in care informed by research findings or regulations.

Benefits of Standard Operating Procedures in Healthcare Settings

SOPs are extensively used in health care, especially in developed countries, to improve safety and quality because it promotes uniformity and standardisation in services, care and management of operations. Through conscientious, sincere and disciplined adherence to a SOP, various aspects of health care in the region which are currently not up to standard can be strengthened. A SOP can be developed to routinely check the identity of a patient or equipment. It can also be used to carry out innumerable tasks within a given setting, for example, handing over a patient from one area of care to another, hand washing, prescribing drugs and administering intravenous drugs. SOP is equally used to specify and standardise patient treatment, facilitate a more structured care plan and encourage the proper choice of investigation and treatment based on the latest evidence. Furthermore, it provides management with information, guidance and support for decision-making.

The use of SOPs in the aforementioned areas and others too numerous to mention helps to ensure care is based on evidence and reduce variability in care. It can curb enormous financial losses and serious health consequences associated with such variability in service, care and operations. A classic example is that advanced by Vincent et al. (2013) that some patients who fail to receive standard evidence-based care, such as a failure to provide rapid thrombolytic treatment for stroke and rapid and effective treatment for myocardial infarction, means their disease will progress more rapidly than it might have otherwise (Vincent et al. 2013). The ripple effects of this type of failure can certainly impact service, care and management operations negatively in various ways.

Other benefits of SOPs in health care include facilitation of compliance by setting the standards or specifications for safety and quality measurements and control. SOPs encourage better utilisation of resources by eliminating redundancy, duplication and waste. They also give a clear picture of future actions and provide guidance for staff orientation and training, thereby improving their knowledge, skills and behaviour (Salleh 2016).

As shown in the preceding discussion, there are many potential areas of application of SOPs as an essential component of patient safety and quality care improvement in Africa. However, urgent attention is required in the application of SOPs in the region with respect to optimising healthcare data quality and documentation and improving diagnosis and treatment, facilities and training and development. These are discussed in what follows.

Optimising Healthcare Data Quality and Documentation

High-quality data are the bedrock of any organisation trying to be conscious of the safety and quality of care and service. This is because no meaningful quality improvement activities can be carried out successfully without the use of quality data. According to the World Health Organization (2008), better healthcare information means better decision-making leading to better health. In Africa, there is significant evidence of poor-quality data in health care (Jha et al. 2010; Christian et al. 2006). The effect of this is enormous. As reported by the Global Health Information Network (2009), African countries are among those currently witnessing the deaths of tens of thousands of patients every day simply because healthcare staff lack the quality data and knowledge required to make life-saving decisions. This situation can be improved through the application of a SOP.

A SOP can be used to specify precisely what data should be recorded at the point of care and eliminate excessive healthcare staff data gathering. It can promote best practices in clinical and professional health record keeping. It can also ensure high-quality clinical data on a patient are accessible to the right staff at the right time and that such data are relevant and accurate (Wang and Strong 1996). The SOP can provide a benchmark for continuous monitoring and auditing of patients' health records. Moreover, although medical records have been serving clinical, administrative and legal functions for years (Carpenter et al. 2007), the SOP can help in medico-legal functions, which are attracting increasing attention in Africa due to an increased awareness of clinical negligence. The importance of good health record keeping cannot be overemphasised in the legal system because documentation is regarded as an essential element, and failure to document relevant data accurately is considered a significant breach of and deviation from the standard of care (Gutheil 2004).

SOPs can therefore be referred to as the nexus that binds the wisdom of professionals and scientific evidence to achieve efficiency in care and service. Simple and comprehensive information on good health record keeping is presented in Table 2.2

Table 2.2 Generic medical record-keeping standards. (Adapted from Carpenter et al. 2007)

Standard	Description
1	Patients' complete medical records should always be available during their stay at hospital.
2	Every page in the medical record should include the patient's name, identification number and location in the hospital.
3	The contents of medical records should have a standardised structure and layout.
4	Documentation in medical records should reflect the continuum of patient care and should be viewable in chronological order.
5	Data recorded or communicated on admission, handover and discharge should be recorded using a standardised form.
6	Every entry in medical records should be dated, timestamped, legible and signed by the person making the entry. The name and designation of the person making the entry should be legibly printed near their signature. Deletions and alterations should be countersigned.
7	Entries in medical records should be made as soon as possible after the event to be documented (e.g. change in clinical state, ward round, investigation) and before the relevant staff member goes off duty. If there is a delay, the time of the event and the delay should be recorded.
8	Every entry in the medical record should identify the most senior healthcare professional present (who is responsible for decision making) at the time the entry is made.
9	On each occasion the consultant responsible for the patient's care changes, the name of the new responsible consultant and the date and time of the agreed transfer of care should be recorded.
10	An entry should be made in the medical record whenever a patient is seen by a doctor. When there is no entry in the hospital record for more than 4 days for acute medical care or 7 days for long-stay continuing care, the next entry should explain why.
11	The discharge record/discharge summary should be commenced at the time a patient is admitted to hospital.
12	Advance directives, consent and resuscitation status statements must be clearly recorded in medical records.

below; it shows Carpenter et al.'s (2007) generic medical record-keeping standards, which could be combined with other evidence-based health records standards (WHO Western Pacific Region 2002; Royal College of Physicians 2018) for implementation in different regions.

The use of standards such as above (Table 2.2) could result in excellent medical records keeping in the region adequate to meet both its primary clinical purposes of supporting patient care. It could also support secondary clinical purposes such as Medico-legal, clinical audit and research, service planning, performance monitoring, epidemiology, and resource allocation (Mann and Williams 2003) which are essential activities of patient safety and healthcare quality improvement.

Improving Healthcare Facilities and Environment

Efforts to attain a high degree of patient safety and quality care in Africa are often thwarted by various factors, including inadequate facilities, poor maintenance of existing facilities and poor environmental hygiene. As reported in Government of South Australia (2012), a high level of environmental hygiene, which involves cleaning surfaces with appropriate products, decontaminating medical equipment, safe and appropriate handling of sharp instruments, blood and bodily fluid spills, waste and linen, is essential for the prevention of transmission of infectious diseases in healthcare settings. The use of a SOP can strengthen facility maintenance, improve the hygiene of hospital buildings and equipment, and ensure their use for their intended purposes in a safe way. Specifically, the development and implementation of a SOP can have the following effects:

- effective management of facilities to attain the appropriate level of planned preventive maintenance (PPM) in buildings and facilities, carried out in a timely manner with minimal disruption to care delivery.
- introduction of proactive plan of investment in facilities (utility systems, equipment and site infrastructure), including their upgrade or replacement.
- effective daily cleaning of the environment to agreed standard using associated quality improvement such as a checklist (equipment use and maintenance, daily/weekly/monthly quality assurance, bed space and treatment area checklists) to ensure regular monitoring of compliance and identify non-compliance issues for follow-up action.
- ensuring the buildings, equipment, utility service and site infrastructure do not cause or create hazards to the environment, patients, staff and visitors and creating a safe environment and work practices to achieve high standards of care consistently.

One of the important characteristics of SOPs is that they are usually accompanied by incorporated all relevant standards, policies and regulations, including best practices. In this regard, the use of SOPs in managing hospital facilities and environment can raise awareness of the applicable legislation and regulations at the national and international levels among healthcare professionals and management in the region. The benefits of this knowledge and understanding are enormous. These include enabling better judgement about whether given premises and facilities comply with applicable regulations.

Improving of Procurement Management

The use of SOPs in managing hospital facilities and environment can raise awareness to enhance decision-making during procurement of new equipment and facilities and ensure their regular maintenance. This is very important because, very often, one of the initial responses to questions on how to improve patient safety and healthcare quality in the region is by acquiring new equipment. In most cases, this equipment cannot be used either because there is no one trained to use or maintain the equipment or there is insufficient power supply to run the equipment, which may be left to deteriorate and breakdown. The introduction of a proactive plan of investment in facilities using SOPs will result in the use of the necessary steps in facility planning and conducting adequate feasibility assessment necessary for informed decisions to be taken on equipment acquisition and other capital-intensive projects. It will equally help to resolve what Azevedo (2017) refers to as "a major displacement of health priorities" by the healthcare organisation to take informed decisions to acquire a simple piece of equipment, which will both serve some function and easy to upgrade or maintain, instead of purchasing high-specification equipment, which will be more difficult to maintain.

The diagnostic process, according to Baerheim (2001), is complex and involves the interpretation of symptoms, physical signs and test results. According to Llewelyn et al. (2014), diagnosis requires the use of an intuitive, non-transparent and pattern recognition process. The introduction of SOPs will help healthcare professionals formulate a process to follow to ensure consistent, accurate and reliable diagnosis and treatment. This will lead to effective management and prevention of disease (Republic of Uganda Ministry of Health 2009) and, in turn, improve patient safety and quality of patient care.

Like in other fields, healthcare professionals are trained at various institutions. In the Africa region, it would not be out of place to say that some of these institutions do not conduct regular, rigorous inspections and evaluations of their courses and programmes. These institutions may not have facilities which have been assessed and approved by trusted, external, independent and recognised bodies to ensure expected high standards are always met. Because these staff are educated in different ways using various equipment, the result is variation in practice. The use of SOPs like the one developed based on the latest guidelines from the WHO, for instance, guidelines for the treatment of malaria (World Health Organization 2015) can help to reduce or eliminate the variation. This is because all practitioners involved in treating malaria using this SOP will use the same evidence-based diagnosis and antimalarial drugs recommended in the WHO guideline. In this sense, irrespective of where medical practitioners were trained, they will diagnose and treat in compliance with the clinical guideline recommendation. This will therefore enable them to overcome hindrances to best practice posed by their experience, abilities and skills from various educational settings. SOPs will make it easier to harmonise practice and ensure that no required medical evaluation or test (e.g. blood test, CT scan, electrocardiogram) with specific requirements for a particular treatment is missed because this will be specified in the SOPs.

Similarly, in treatment, there are so many antimicrobial drugs in the region, but the evidence on the effectiveness of these drugs is not common. In medicine it is well established that the drugs commonly used to destroy or stop the growth of microorganisms, including bacteria, to treat malaria tend to become less effective over time as bacteria develop resistance to them (Gillespic 2010; Khudaibergenova 2015). This is a serious threat to patient safety as antimicrobial resistance increases the cost of healthcare by prolonging patient stays in hospital and demanding intensive care (World Health Organization 2018c). It is also known that antimicrobial usage can lead to the development and spread of antimicrobial resistance (Ventola 2015). The use of SOPs can help in carrying out performance evaluation or auditing, providing useful insights into the effectiveness of these drugs and support in connection with the decision on which antimicrobial is best to prescribe to patients.

Enhancing Training and Development

SOPs are an indispensable tool that can facilitate training and development in healthcare organisations. The key characteristics of SOPs which make them suitable for this role are that they contain detailed and step-by-step instruction on how to accomplish a routine or repetitive task. In addition, they also contain references to standards and applicable regulations and policies, which helps in keeping the staff up to date with changes in practice and regulations through continuing medical education, training and development. The use of SOPs can encourage periodic evaluation of care delivery, continuous improvement and information exchange regarding best practices and lessons learned across healthcare organisations.

Barriers and Enablers in SOP Implementation in Health Care in Africa

One major barrier to the use of SOPs in health care is usually a lack of knowledge and skills for developing relevant SOPs. Once this initial barrier has been overcome, other hindrances that will need to be addressed include organisational systems such as leadership style and poor organisational safety culture. Barriers can also include a lack of adequate resources and resistance from staff members who are comfortable with the status quo and are therefore not willing to step out of their comfort zones irrespective of the justification for a change (Katowa-Mukwato et al. 2021).

On the other hand, SOP implementation can be facilitated by the early involvement of the relevant team, such as the department or team that will be affected by the SOP, at every stage of its developed. This is necessary to allow such teams to take ownership of the SOPs. Other enablers include management, whose support will cultivate the environment needed for SOP implementation, as well as the necessary time and resources required by staff. Also essential is an individual who will champion the need for a SOP and who really understands the process and so will serve as mentor to other staff (Katowa-Mukwato et al. 2021). Conducting a trial run of SOPs and providing adequate supervision and training to increase the level of knowledge and skills on the use of SOPs could also facilitate SOP implementation (Alatau et al. 2020).

Conclusion

In general, there is a strong consensus that SOPs developed based on tried and tested practices or evidence are extensively used to improve care and services. However, there is insufficient scientific proof of its valid structure in healthcare systems anywhere in the world. Currently, their design takes various forms, but their purpose remains the same: to specify and standardise diagnosis and treatment for a particular condition and clinical service. Healthcare professionals in Africa can also take full advantage of SOPs by developing, implementing and exploring their usefulness in their local healthcare settings through empirical studies.

Of course, the implementation of SOPs in health care in the region will not be straightforward. Like all changes in health care involving getting evidence into practice, it will require an integrated approach demanding systemic change in both individuals and organisations (Dopson and Fitzgerald 2005; Kitson et al. 2008).

According to Bromiley (2011), monitoring the compliance of SOP use by trained staff in aviation is the major basis for the successful application of SOPs in the sector, which serves as a basis for believing similar success could be achieved by monitoring the application of SOPs in health care. Besides monitoring, it is also recommended that additional support and interdependent actions, such as training, supervision and feedback, are needed for successful SOP implementation (Leatherman and Sutherland 2007).

It is very important to note that in the treatment of patients using SOPs, occasionally it will happen that SOPs cannot be used or will be insufficient. For instance, patients suffering from multiple conditions and ailments cannot easily be treated according to strict guidelines, and in some situations patients themselves might simply decide against a course of treatment. Finally, SOPs in health care will never represent a complete solution to safety, so sometimes it will be necessary to depart from standard procedures in the pursuit of safety (Vincent et al. 2013). In this regard, healthcare staff should be aware of the need to modify SOPs based on their professional judgement and experience and patient preference, where necessary.

References

Alatau M, Aljuhani E, Alsufiany F et al (2020) Barriers of implementing evidence-based practice in nursing profession: a literature review. Am J Nurs Sci 9(1):35–42

Azevedo MJ (2017) Historical perspectives on the state of health and health systems in Africa, Volume II: the modern era. Palgrave Macmillan, Cham

Baerheim A (2001) The diagnostic process in general practice: has it a two-phase structure? Fam Pract 18:243–245

Bromiley M (2011) Can standard operating procedures work in healthcare? https://www.health. org.uk/blog/can-standard-operating-procedures-work-healthcare. Accessed 24 April 2018

Burial Pillar (2015) Sierra Leone emergency management program standard operating procedure for home decontamination after collection of corpses or transfer of suspect/probable Ebola cases, Sierra Leone

Carpenter I, Ram MB, Groft GP et al (2007) Medical records and recording-keeping standards. Clin Med 7(4):328–331

Christian CK, Gustafson ML, Roth EM et al (2006) A prospective study of patent safety in the operating room. J Surg 139:159–173

Dopson S, Fitzgerald L (eds) (2005) Knowledge to action? Evidence-based health care in context. Oxford University Press, Oxford

Gillespic SH (2010) Antibiotic resistance protocol, 2nd edn. Humana Press, Totowa

Global Health Information Network (2009) Information for all by 2015. http://www.ghi-net.org/ campaign/ .Accessed 2 July 2015

Government of South Australia (2012) SA Health environmental hygiene in healthcare. http://www. sahealth.sa.gov.au/wps/wcm/connect/public+content/sa+health+internet/clinical+resources/ clinical+topics/healthcare+associated+infections/prevention+and+management+of+infections +in+healthcare+settings/environmental+hygiene+in+healthcare . Accessed 21 April 2018

Gutheil T (2004) Fundamentals of medical record documentation. Psychiatry Edgmont 1(3):26–28

Health Department Republic of South Africa (2014) PHS/EV-SOP/2014. Standard operating procedure for the management of the EBOLA virus disease in point of entry, Pretoria, South Africa

Jha AK, Prasopa-Plaizier N, Larizgoitia I et al (2010) Patient safety research: an overview of the global evidence. Qual Saf Health Care 19:42–47

Katowa-Mukwato P, Mwiinga-Kalusopa V, Chitundu K et al (2021) Implementing evidence based practice nursing using the PDSA model: process, lessons and implications. Int J Africa Nurs Sci 14:100261. https://doi.org/10.1016/j.ijans.2020.100261

Kenya Health Sector (2008) Indicator and standard operating procedure manual for health workers, Republic of Kenya

Khudaibergenova MS (2015) Antimicrobial use at a multi-disciplinary hospital. Int J Risk Saf Med 27(1):13–14

Kitson AL, Rycroft-Malone J, Harvey G et al (2008) Evaluating the successful implementation of evidence into practice using the PARiHS framework: theoretical and practical challenges. Implement Sci 3(1). https://doi.org/10.1186/1748-5908-3-1

Leatherman S, Sutherland K (2007) Designing national quality reforms: a framework for action. Int J Qual Healthcare 19(6):334–340

Llewelyn H, Ang HA, Lewis K et al (2014) Oxford handbook of clinical diagnosis, 3rd edn. Oxford University Press, Oxford

Mann R, Williams J (2003) Standards in medical record keeping. Clin Med 3(4):329–332

Ministry of Health (2009) Uganda National Health Laboratory Service Policy. The Republic of Uganda, Uganda

Ministry of Health (2010) Standard operating procedures for health information, Uganda

Ministry of Health and Social Welfare (2008) Standard operating procedures for the prevention of tuberculosis in health care facilities. The United Republic of Tanzania, Tanzania

Nachtigall M, Deja S, Tafelski S et al (2008) Adherence to standard operating procedures is crucial for intensive care unit survival of elderly patients. J Int Med Res 36(3):438–459

Nolen JL (2009) Standard operating procedure. Encyclopaedia Britannica. https://www.britannica.com/topic/standard-operating-procedure#accordion-article-history. Accessed 8 April 2018

Royal College of Physicians (2018) Health record standards. https://www.rcplondon.ac.uk/projects/healthcare-record-standards . Accessed 21 April 2018

Salleh A (2016) Development of standard operating procedures and care plans. Health Care Service Delivery. Weblog. https://drdollah.com/care-plans/development-of-care-plans/. Accessed 12 April 2018

Sathyanarayana Rao TS, Radhakrishna R, Andrade C (2011) Standard operating procedures for clinical practice. Indian J Psychiatry 53(1):1–3

Ventola CL (2015) The antibiotic resistance crises: part 1: causes and threats. Pub Med 40(4):277–283

Vincent C (2010) Patient safety, 2nd edn. Wiley, Chichester

Vincent C, Burnett S, Carthey J (2013) The measurement and monitoring of safety – drawing together academic evidence and practical experience to produce a framework for safety measurement and monitoring – report N0: ISBN 978-190646-44-7. Health Foundation, London

Vincent C, Burnett S, Carthey J (2014) Safety measurement and monitoring in healthcare: a framework to guide clinical teams and healthcare organisations in maintaining safety. BMJ Qual Saf 23(8):670–677

Wang R, Strong DM (1996) Beyond accuracy: what data quality means to data consumers? J Manag Inf Syst 12(4):5–34

WHO African Regional Office (2014) SOP Standard Operating Procedures for coordinating public health events preparedness and response in the WHO African region. http://www.who.int/hac/techguidance/tools/standard_operating_procedures_african_region_en_2014.pdf. Accessed 13 April 2018

WHO Western Pacific Region (2002) ISBN 92 9061 005 0. Medical records manual: a guide for developing countries. WHO Regional Office for the Western Pacific, Manila

World Health Organization (2008) WHO/IER/PSP/2008.09. Patient Safety Workshop LEARNING FROM ERROR, Geneva

Word Health Organization (2015) Guidelines for the treatment of malaria, 3rd edn. WHO, Geneva

World Health Organization (2018a) WHO/NMH/NVI/18.2. Hearts Technical Package for Cardiovascular disease management in primary health care: Evidence-based treatment protocol. World Health Organization, Geneva

World Health Organization (2018b) Programmes Patient Safety High 5's Standard operating procedures. http://www.who.int/patientsafety/topics/high-5s/en/. Accessed 11 April 2018

World Health Organization (2018c) Media Centre Antimicrobial resistance. http://www.who.int/mediacentre/factsheets/fs194/en/. Accessed 23 April 2018

Chapter 3
Audit

Introduction

An audit, which is a tool to be used in continuous quality improvement, is essential for improving safety and quality in health care (Paton et al. 2015). It provides the unique ability to review current practices and evaluate the quality of care against agreed-upon predefined standards (Bowling 2009). An audit aims to improve patient outcomes by benchmarking the outcome or process against a well-defined standard established using the latest evidence from scientific research. The use of this tool to compare practice with standards often leads to the formation of strategies to ensure specified standards of care are met consistently. This also results in redesigning a healthcare system to prevent sub-standard quality care. This evaluation of care and services through auditing to determine whether care is delivered to agreed-upon standards or identify changes required to improve and sustain the safety and quality of care is not only important in clinical practice but also useful in financial and health policy planning (Esposito and Canton 2014).

There is ample evidence in the literature on audits as an integral part of healthcare professional practice, with the overarching objectives of ensuring high standards of care and improvement in overall quality in a way that is cost-effective (Ghosh 2009; Sale 2005). These objectives are usually achieved through systematic review and analysis of retrospective data or documented performance and comparing the obtained findings against a predetermined standard. Practically any area of clinical and non-clinical aspects of care and services, including the admission process, procedures used for diagnosis, clinical decisions regarding treatment, resources, patient outcomes and experience, can be audited (Bowling 2014). The main condition in auditing care and service is that there must exist a standard that is expected to be met in the delivery of such care and services.

In healthcare settings in Africa, audits are at best rudimentary and infrequently undertaken, despite their central role in the safety and quality of care and service

C. Ente, M. Ukpe, *Essentials for Quality and Safety Improvement in Health Care*, https://doi.org/10.1007/978-3-030-92482-9_3

improvement. Currently little has changed from the perception of the traditional role of the audit as a tool used by accountants for detecting fraud and monitoring internal control and financial compliance (Omigbodun 2004). In reality, if an audit is carefully planned conducted and the recommended changed suggested by the audit's outcomes are strictly implemented, it can help in confirming the quality of clinical care and services, identifying a gap between the standard and quality of care and services and highlighting the need for improvement. This outcome is equally important as it could provide guidance on care and service re-design tailored to the local setting to address specific issues in the system.

There is therefore an urgent need for healthcare facilities in the region to change their approach to auditing and embrace its inevitability as a quality improvement tool or process, that is, a tool or process required to assess the quality of care and service offered to patients on a daily basis and to identify areas for improvement or good practice that should be sustained. This chapter will present the process of designing, conducting and implementing audit findings. It will also discuss the advantages of an audit with potential areas of immediate application in health care in the region. An insight into the barriers and enablers of an effective audit will also be presented. It is hoped that this chapter will help to revive interest in audits in local healthcare settings by showing exactly how to plan and execute an audit. Furthermore, it is hoped that the chapter will draw the attention of healthcare staff in the region once again to the central role of the audit in fostering the agenda of safety and quality improvement in health care.

Audit

In the National Joint Steering Committee for Maternal Health Kenya (2002), an audit is defined as "*the systematic and critical review of the quality of care where health care providers examine their own practice, attitudes and knowledge against agreed standards with a view to changing their practice to improve or maintain quality services*". An audit may also be defined as a quality improvement process that seeks to improve patient care and outcomes through a systematic review of care against explicit criteria, change implementation and monitoring to confirm improvements in care and service (National Institute for Clinical Excellence 2002). In other words, it is all about measuring the quality of care and services against standards and making improvements where relevant and meaningful (Burgess 2011). The core component of an audit from the preceding definition is a standard; without it no audit can be performed. Standards are an "*agreed level of performance negotiated with available resources*" (Martin et al. 2010). Standards are formulated using the principles of evidence-based medicine and provide a clear statement about the quality of care and service to be provided, including what patients and the public can expect.

In this book, the term audit is used broadly to cover any form of audit in a healthcare system aimed at improving care and services and providing means of assessing risk associated with patient treatment. This includes a clinical audit, which is described by the Secretary of State for Health, Wales, Northern Ireland and Scotland (1989) as a systematic critical analysis of the quality of medical care, review of diagnosis, procedures used for diagnosis, clinical decisions about treatment, use of resources and patient outcome. This book will also cover criterion-based auditing, which is widely based on the analysis of medical records (Shaw 1990). It will include the outcome and process audit, where the outcome is said to measure the effect of care on patients' health, while the process deals with the appropriateness of clinical actions (McIntyre 1995). An audit conducted in specialties will also be covered, for instance, a surgical audit, which is the process of systematically examining surgical procedures against a standard and highlighting and addressing problem areas within the surgical care system (Levy and Rockall 2009).

Remote Audit

During the coronavirus disease of 2019 (COVID-19), pandemic health systems globally have significantly increased the use of digital health technology (DHT) to manage the pandemic itself and to support existing service. This has reduced the risk of infection transmission in healthcare settings while ensuring continuity of care. The pandemic has changed the ways care and service are delivered at an incredible pace, and the landscape of clinical auditing is no exception. Auditing through remote techniques has been sparingly practiced but is gradually being viewed as indispensable as a result of voluntary or mandatory confinement due to the COVID-19 pandemic. It is therefore important that healthcare organisations in low-resource settings of Africa also start planning for remote auditing, which is an innovative and alternative method to the traditional onsite methods where staff usually met face to face during the audit session.

A remote audit is one of the audit methods described in ISO 19011:2018 Annex A1 and Appendix A16. A remote audit, also known as an e-audit or virtual audit, is a method of conducting an audit remotely using information and communication technologies (ICT) to gather information or audit evidence and evaluate the extent of conformity to audit criteria (International Organisation for Standardisation 2020). Its life cycles are typically the same as on site but differ in the sense that planning, preparing, conducting, reporting and following up are all carried out remotely through email, telephone and a range of video conferencing technology platforms such as Skype, Microsoft Teams, ZOOM and others. Typically, a remote audit will require more preparation compared to an onsite audit. It will involve testing of the technology and obtaining system access permission in advance and checking the file sharing platform and the software to be used for meetings and interviews and contingency plans in the event of technology failures (Waddell et al. 2021). Moreover, during the auditing session the presence of both the auditing team (auditor) and a member or members of the team being audited (auditee) must be ensured.

Remote Audit in African Healthcare Settings

The remote audit presents another opportunity or rationale for further investing in electronic medical records and improved ICT as inadequate technology character-ised by poor Internet connection and equipment poses a serious challenge to a suc-cessful remote audit. Access to hard copies of documents during a remote audit is also very problematic. There is a need for further training in ICT skills, which is mandatory in a remote audit because it involves the use of computers, tablets, video cameras and smartphones, and for more scientific research to explore the topic fur-ther in local context.

Audit Design and Conduct, Implementation of Findings

The process of designing, conducting and reporting of an audit, implementing the findings of the audit and re-auditing or following up (Fig. 3.1) can be portrayed as a cyclical or spiral systematic process (Benjamin 2008). The spiral suggests that the process continues, and each cycle seeks to attain an ever higher level of quality. This cyclical and systematic process of audit can be divided into seven distinct steps:

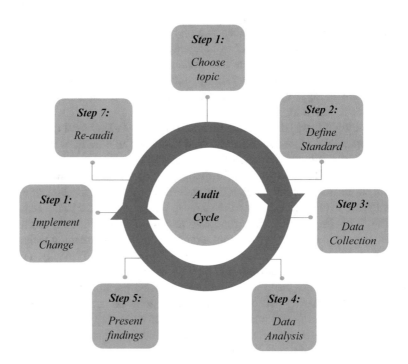

Fig. 3.1 Audit Cycle

choosing a topic, defining standards, data collection, data analysis, presenting the findings, implementing change and re-auditing (Wright and Hill 2003).

Step 1: Choosing a Topic

Choosing a topic is an important step in conducting an audit. This step requires careful thought and planning as an audit project requires a significant investment of resources (National Institute for Clinical Excellence 2002). Once a topic is selected, a thorough literature review and extensive discussion with the specific care management team (i.e. care team in the area selected for audit) should be undertaken prior to the final decision on the topic. The literature review will help members of the team to determine the work that has already been done in the selected topic. The discussion with the specific care management team, on the other hand, will give the team an opportunity to contribute to the topic and eventually take ownership of the project.

As suggested by Shaw (1990), the topic chosen for audit should be of general interest and significance to the team. This could include issues that are common, entail high risk, high costs or conflict or that are of local interest. From Wright and Hill's (2003) perspective, influential factors to be considered in selecting an audit topic should include priority areas with strong potential benefits and the possibility of completing the project within a reasonable time frame with the allocated limited resources. Box 3.1 shows a checklist composed of some questions that could guide the audit team during discussions to select a topic for the audit project.

Once a topic is agreed upon, a brief background of the project and its aims and objectives should be given. The aims of the audit project consist of the overall purpose of the audit, that is, the ultimate desired goal of the audit process. This can be presented as statements about what is expected to take place as a result of the audit, for instance, to improve care of patients with malaria. The aims can also be framed as a question that the audit intends to answer, for example: Are we meeting standards for best practice in the management of malaria?

Specific steps required to assess whether the goals of the audit have been met are known as the objectives. Objectives should be based on clear evidence and definition of what constitute good and quality care or service. They could be presented in the form of series of tasks to be undertaken to achieve the aims.

An Example of a Typical Audit Project Background, Aims and Objectives for Medical Record is Shown in What Follows:

Audit topic: Medical Record Keeping Audit.

Background: Clinical record keeping is an integral part of healthcare professional practice designed to inform all aspects of multidisciplinary care. Accurate and effective record keeping is fundamental to improving safety and quality in health care. It allows effective communication with other professionals involved in patient care and expresses individual professional accountability and responsibility. It is therefore important that medical records be accurate, complete, consistent,

1. Is the topic an important public health problem in terms of size (prevalence or incidence) cost to the health service or clinical risk to patients?

2. Is there evidence that current quality of patient care should be improved?

3. Is data source adequate to provide sufficient information for analysis and drawing a valid conclusion?

4. Is this change in patient achievable?

5. Are there measurable clinical outcomes which can be used to monitor change?

6. Is there good research evidence available about the most clinically effective and cost-effective management of patients?

7. Does the audit have a clear patient focus?

8. Is there multidisciplinary involvement?

9. Are the training needs for implementation of the recommended change taken into consideration?

10. Is the implementation feasible in terms of resources?

Box 3.1 Checklist for choosing an audit topic. (Adapted from Wright and Hill 2003)

easily accessible and comply with relevant regulations to reduce risk to patient and liability in the event of complaint or litigation.

The main reason for conducting the audit is to comply with the requirements of medical record keeping policies and procedures in relation to the auditing of patient records. It is also recognised that an audit helps to identify both good practice and compliance, which are useful in designing remedial actions. Conducting this audit will provide insight on whether all medical and non-medical staff involved in medical record documentation and maintenance are aware of the relevant requirements. This audit will ensure efficiency, professionalism and cost effectiveness in medical record keeping.

Aims of the Audit: The aims of the audit are to:

- ensure medical records are kept to the highest standards and follow the relevant national, professional and local medical record keeping requirements to reduce risks associated with poor record keeping;
- raise awareness of the importance of medical records, good record keeping and the need for responsibility and accountability at all levels.

Objectives: The objectives of the audit are to:

- give evidence-based assurance that medical record keeping standards and best practice are being carried out during care;

- ensure a consistent approach to medical record keeping practices;
- identify, encourage and share areas of good practice within a team;
- identify areas of concerns in medical record keeping practices;
- develop prevention and corrective action plans to address concerns identified; and
- identify areas for further training.

Step 2: Defining Standards

In general, standards or criteria in an audit are a set of requirements used as a reference against which objective evidence is compared. These may include policies, procedures, work instructions, legal requirements and contractual obligations (International Organisation for Standardisation 2020). So once the topic has been agreed upon, the next step is to decide on the standards with which the current clinical practice or services will be compared. At this stage it is important to agree on indicators, criteria and intervention strategies (Esposito and Canton 2014). Indicators describe the performance that should occur for a patient or the related outcome and allow the quality of care and services to be measured against a defined criterion. These indicators must be evidence-based and provide a quantitative basis (expressed in number, percentage, rate or average) for healthcare staff aiming to achieve improvements in care or sustain improvement to base their decisions (Mainz 2003). A criterion, on the other hand, is an item or variable which enables the achievement of a standard and the evaluation of whether or not it has been achieved (Royal College of Nursing 1990). It is a definable and measurable element of health care which describes quality and can also be used to assess it (Irvine and Irvine 1991). It is a systematically developed explicit statement that can be used to assess the appropriateness of specific healthcare decisions, services and outcomes (Institute of Medicine 1992). Audit criteria declare what should happen based on good practice (Burgess 2011). A standard, therefore, consists of quantifiable statements detailing the specific level of care that should be achieved for each specific criterion. It is usually expressed as a percentage of events that should comply with the criterion and define the range of value at which quality care is considered to be appropriate (Baker and Fraser 1995). The choice of criteria and standards is the most critical point in clinical audit design. It is important that there be agreement locally on the criteria and standards chosen before they are used, especially as the final audit result, which will show the quality of care provided, will be evaluated on the basis of comparison with these parameters (Esposito and Canton 2014).

Clearly identified criteria will help in defining standards for comparison (Ghosh 2009). Standards selected for a clinical audit must be valid and should be able to lead to improvements in care. For this, they must be based on evidence, related to important aspects of care and measurable (National Institute for Clinical Excellence 2002). The sources of standards may be international guidelines such as WHO guidelines; scientific literature such as systematic review of randomised controlled trials (RCTs); expert consensus, for instance, clinical experience of respected authorities like the Academy of Medical Royal Colleges. Other sources are data obtained by other healthcare organisations, local standard operating procedures, personal case study experience and opinion (Hearnshaw et al. 2001; Esposito and Canton 2014). Strength of evidence is essential, and evidence from RCTs or developed directly from a literature search of specific journal articles will certainly be stronger and more reliable than that of personal experience because RCTs can eliminate or reduce bias. Where standards are based on strong evidence, the outcome of the comparison with clinical practice will be more reliable as well.

It is also important that the standards to be used be shared and agreed upon by the clinical team prior to the review of the data collection process. Where there is disagreement as to what constitutes good practice during the design of criteria and standards, this should be resolved because it could make it difficult to implement changes in practice recommended in the findings. It is equally vital for the audit team to define and agree on the intervention strategies to be implemented should there be a critical finding such as important discrepancies between standards and actual clinical practice (Espositi and Canton 2014). The principle of specific, measurable, agreed, relevant and theoretically sound (SMART) evidence (University Hospitals Bristol NHS Foundation Trust 2021) could be adopted during the design of an effective audit to evaluate its proposal (Paton et al. 2015) and ensure that valid criteria and standards that will lead to improvements in safety and quality are chosen. SMART standards are shown in Table 3.1.

In the National Institute for Clinical Excellence (2002) recommendation, the means of vigorously assessing the strength of evidence should be established and a checklist used to ensure that an explicit process is used to identify, select and combine the evidence for standards. For medical records selected as an example of audit topic in this chapter, generic medical record keeping standards (Table 2.2) will be used.

Step 3: Data Collection

This is another essential step in an audit which must be carefully planned. In an effective audit, data collected either retrospectively or prospectively must be robust enough that, when analysed, they make a clear case for improvement that can

Table 3.1 SMART standards for audit

Keyword	Interpretation
Specific	It must be precise and mean the same thing to everyone involved in the auditing exercise
Measurable	It must be easy to measure the outcome after analysing available data, identifying, for instance, whether the findings relate to training or inadequate supervision
Agreed	It must be accepted by all responsible for the delivery of the aspect of care or service to be audited
Relevant	It must be relevant to the care or service area being audited
Theoretically Sound	It must be derived from updates and current evidence on the care and service area audited

withstand challenges (Paton et al. 2015). Retrospective data collection provides a picture of care provided during some earlier period. Such data, which provide a baseline of care provision, are collected from medical records and other clinical documentation. Prospective data collection, on the other hand, provides an instant snapshot of current performance because these data are collected in real time as events occur. Prospective data give a team immediate feedback on its current performance and help to identify where improvement is required or good practice needs to be maintained (National Institute for Clinical Excellence 2002).

In Africa, where the poor quality of healthcare data is a major problem, before proceeding with data collection, initial sampling and auditing of the data source could be conducted. This would help to establish whether there are sufficient data to complete the audit and draw valid conclusions. The main benefit of such an initial data source auditing is to avoid the pitfall of abandoning an audit project halfway through owing to data constraints.

The audit data can be quantitative or qualitative. The potential sources include but are not limited to medical records, patient complaint, incident reports, questionnaires, interviews, diagnoses, tests results and direct observations. To ensure that the data collected are precise and that only essential data are collected, important details of the audit must be established at the early stage before data collection. These include identifying the study population, defining the data to be collected, designing the data collection form and specifying the sample size. These are covered in the next section.

The patient population or user group to be audited must be identified. Take as an example patients treated for malaria. Specific inclusion and exclusion criteria will have to be defined, for example, patients who are 60 years and above and were treated for malaria over the 6-month period from January to June 2018. If records obtained for this period are not enough to provide sufficient data, then the criteria can be reviewed and the duration extended.

Define what information will be required from each patient record. Early involvement of the care team of the defined population will help in gaining insight into the range of information available. Who will collect the data, what data will be collected and how the data will be collected are identified at this point. A data collection form (Table 3.2), also known as a data extraction sheet, is designed and tried out at this stage too. The use of a data extraction sheet helps in clarifying the data items to be collected and how the data should be recorded, for instance by specifying the format, like the number of decimal places required and the units of measurement, if applicable. Other factors worth considering at this point are how much data should be collected, how long it will take and resources, in terms of time, staff and management support, that will be required. It is best practice to test out a trial data extraction sheet to ensure only relevant data and all the required data are collected within the allotted time frame. The feedback from the pilot can be used to improve the form and ultimately the quality of data collected.

The next thing to consider is the sample size that will provide sufficient information that, when analysed, can provide generalisable and valid results. In selecting the sample, care must be taken to avoid introducing bias, which could invalidate the results. The sample size could be drawn from records of every patient that meets the inclusion criteria, or random sampling from the list of patients that meet the criteria could be used.

Table 3.2 Sample of medical record audit data collection form

Patient identification and hospital location on every page

RESPONSE – please mark the correct box		YES	NO	Comments
Q1	Hospital number			
Q2	First name			
Q3	LAST name			
Q4	Date of birth			
Q5	Location of hospital			
Q6	Other personal details (optional)			

Step 4: Data Analysis

Data analysis is another significant step in an audit, and it influences both the type and amount of data collected. Both data variables to be recorded and analysis to be performed on the data generated during the audit are often decided at an early stage of audit planning (Esposito and Canton 2014). Data analysis can vary from a simple calculation of percentage to complex statistical techniques (National Institute for Clinical Excellence 2002). Data analysed by the team are then compared with the pre-set standards. In settling on the analysis techniques, a simple technique that everyone in the care process can understand should be chosen to aid a better understanding of the results, which will stimulate change (Plsex 1999).

Table 3.3 presents an analysis of medical audit data using a percentage where 30 patient records were reviewed. The variables, patient name, hospital and hospital number, all contain non-identifiable information. This information is anonymised to comply with data protection regulation, confidentiality and security of patient information, as a good audit must do.

Step 5: Presentation of Findings

This is a very important step in the audit cycle since the essence of auditing is to generate findings which can be shared to improve care and service. Just like the analysis, the findings should be presented in a simple format which is clear and easy to understand. Figure 3.2 give a graphical representation of the data analysis of the medical record audit used as an example in this book. The bar chart is the most common format used in audit findings, though control charts, pie charts, histograms and time trends can also be used. However, where sophisticated statistical procedure is involved, it is important to seek expert advice (National Institute for Clinical Excellence 2002).

Table 3.3 A simple data analysis of medical records audit

	Response in %	Yes	No	Comment
Q1	Hospital number	100%	0.00%	
		N = 30	N = 0	
Q2	First name	50%	50%	
		N = 15	N = 15	
Q3	Last name	100%	0.00%	
		N = 30	N = 0	
Q4	Date of birth	90%	11.10%	In 2 records dates are missing, and entry in 1 is illegible
		N = 27	N = 3	
Q5	Location of hospital	100%	0.00%	
		N = 30	N = 0	
Q6	Other personal details	0.00%	0%	
		N = 0	N = 0	

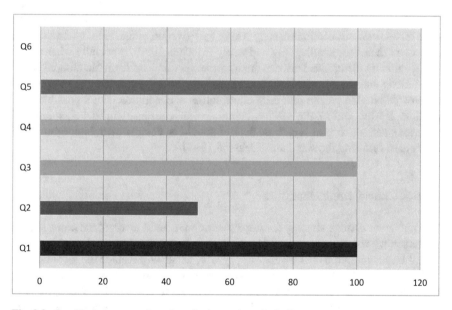

Fig. 3.2 Graphical representation of medical records audit findings

As pointed out by Esposito and Canton (2014), the team of professionals involved in the audit should be cautious in reviewing the findings for both compliance and non-compliance with standards. This is because interpreting an audit as an inspection of their clinical activity could unconsciously influence their analysis of the data. To this end, Robertson et al. (1996) suggested that the meeting at which the findings of a clinical audit are to be discussed must be carefully planned and involve the use of strategic communication and interpersonal skills. Moreover, it would be beneficial to start the presentation with areas where the findings demonstrate compliance and good practice to encourage the team to think of further improvements.

Figure 3.2 shows the findings of the audited 30 medical records. It shows full compliance in the completion of patient hospital number, last name and hospital location but non-compliance in the completion of first name and date of birth. In 15 patient records, the first name was not given, the date of birth was not given in 3 records and other personal details were missing in 20 records. This kind of incomplete data could lead to a failure to identify the right patient, which could eventually result in a wrong diagnosis and, hence, medication, transfusion and testing errors. It could also result in procedures for the wrong patients and even improperly discharging of patients.

Another important point was raised by Esposito and Canton (2014) regarding a determination of compliance or non-compliance with standards following comparison of the actual data with the theoretical standards. If standards are not met, the authors suggest assessing whether real improvements are possible. However, where the findings are not in line with standards but there is no significant difference, it might be useful to invest resources in the assessment of other problems as further improvements might be difficult to attain. It is essential that meetings be conducted in an atmosphere without fear and blame. Effective leadership is needed to establish an effective communication strategy which will give individual team members time to present their views collegially and freely (McCrea 1999), especially where there is a significant difference between the information obtained from the clinical documentations and the standards. The sessions must also be carefully led to prevent endless debate but ensure that each contribution is concluded with a possible suggestion. By the end of the session, some sort of consensus must be established regarding actions to take, and those actions should be documented, highlighting the barriers to fulfilling the standards (Oakland 1993).

Step 6: Change Implementation

The choice of change strategy for implementing the audit recommendations should fit the setting and circumstances of health care in the region. The most effective strategy of implementation is a systematic approach, which will include the identification of local barriers to change and team and management support (National Institute for Clinical Excellence 2002). Identification of barriers to change in advance, through interviews with key staff, observation of patterns of work and discussions at team meetings, can help in the development of practical implementation plans necessary to overcome obstacles that may be encountered (Robertson et al. 1996).

Effective management of sub-groups within the team is essential because of the potential for such groups to hinder change implementation. As explained by Robertson et al. (1996), a powerful sub-group in the team may resist change, and the less powerful majority may be obligated to go along with the sub-group unless the less powerful team members form alliances with experts to reduce the influence of the powerful minority view. There is also another circumstance where a group could exert pressure on its members to conform, and there is a possibility that an individual will not only comply with the group's view but come to believe that the group's view is valid and so adopt it (Reberton 1999; Hayes 1994). One of the ways a minority can influence the larger group is if it has a powerful role and makes its case consistently. The minority may also increase its power by forming alliances within the team or outside the group. The management of this undue influence on change implementation in the team will require a strategic and integrated approach taking into consideration the local context in which the audit takes place because there is no single approach or theory that fully explains the process of change in healthcare setting anywhere in the world (National Institute for Clinical Excellence 2002).

Moreover, any intervention strategy for implementation must identify organisational factors required in terms of time, resources and dedicated staff. It must also accommodate recommendations involving modification of care activities, such as documentation and reviews of standards and guidelines. The choice of educational method of implementation must be appropriate and specific, for instance, a training seminar or workshop or discussion among peers. Finally, monitoring and feedback on the implementation is indispensable, and the methods for achieving both must be detailed in strategies to implement change.

Step 7: Re-audit

An audit process is an ongoing exercise, and re-auditing is an important part of the audit cycle. After changes have been introduced based on the audit findings, data should be collected on performance and review on a regular basis. A period within 6 months to a year following implementation of the corrective and preventive actions is recommended. This is referred to as a re-audit or follow-up audit. In re-auditing, the same method, process and strategy as was used in the first audit are adopted to ensure the data are valid and comparable with each other (Benjamin 2008). This exercise allows for verification on whether the changes were implemented and improvements made or whether an agreed-upon standard is met; if it is not met, then the re-auditing is continued until the results meet the standard.

The development and implementing structures, including systems that integrate scheduled regular monitoring as part of the audit process, are essential for sustaining improvements. However, if performance deteriorates, a full audit will have to be reactivated (Benjamin 2008).

Benefits of Audit in Health Care in Africa

The views on whether audit works and its benefits vary widely in literature. Benjamin (2008) acknowledges a lack of strong scientific evidence in support of this quality improvement tool but stressed the importance of audits in assessing whether patients are receiving the best quality of care by measuring current practice against standards. This author added that an audit is crucial in deciding when to advocate for change. One success story cited by the author is that of the national stroke audit, which made it possible to achieve improved quality of care for stroke patients across the UK.

Paton and colleagues reiterated a similar opinion of scant evidence on auditing as a healthcare practice improvement strategy. In their view, an audit and the feedback it generates are widely promoted as a strategy to improve professional practice as healthcare professionals can improve their practice in response to data on their performance which fall below predefined standards. They also acknowledged the importance of reliable data on current performance, generated during an audit, as a major driver for evaluating the performance and outcomes of a healthcare system to aid improvement. In their conclusion, the role of an audit includes a means of obtaining essential data to enable quality improvement. According to these authors, audits are not only technique for improvement but also a tool to obtain data to support-quality of care (Paton et al. 2015).

Auditing also allows assets and resources to be used appropriately. The work of Jones and Woodhead (2015) provides another insight into the use of audits during decision-making in building capacity. According to the authors, there is no one approach to building capacity; each organisation is expected to devise an integrated strategy to appraise the assets and resources they already have so that they can make full use of healthcare professionals and teams with existing quality improvements and patient experience, and this is best achieved through audit.

Another benefit is that, because audits tend to focus on specific point-of-care processes, they help in measuring reliability, which is the probability that a system will function properly over time (The Health Foundation 2016). As a quality assurance tool, an audit helps in understanding variation in care and services. Data generated through an audit could be used to identify areas of concern in care and service or where there is potential for improvement.

In view of the benefits of the audit, Benjamin (2008) recommended that audits be included in medical education foundation programmes. Some reasons for the recommendation include that fact that audits enable junior doctors to gain skills on how to maintain and improve their immediate and future services. In addition, conducting an audit may help in their own learning and understanding of the healthcare process in a particular field and may also enable them to contribute to the formation or refining of a clinical protocol (Benjamin 2008).

In African health care, auditing could be beneficial in various ways. Some of these ways, covered in the next section, include encouraging the use of modem medicine, evaluating health policy and guidelines, developing and implementing educational programmes and improving the quality of clinical documentation.

Encouraging the Use of Modern Medicine in the Region

In Africa, to this day, many natives still prefer alternative medicine to modern or orthodox medicine, which whose methods fall outside mainstream health care. As explained by Abdullahi (2011), alternative medicine, also known as native healing, traditional or folk medicine, ethno-medicine and complementary medicine, is well established in Africa, and care including services in this domain is provided through the combination of spiritual beliefs and herbalism. In Chan's (2015) report, alternative medicine in the region is accepted and in high demand by locals, and alternative medicine practitioners are well respected and trusted in the community. A study by Mhame et al. (2010) showed that at present in the region many antenatal and post-natal cases are still handled by alternative medicine practitioners. They also use locally produced medicine to treat coughs, mental health, hypertension and liver disorder. In a report issued by the World Health Organization Office for Africa (2010), traditional medicine is the main source of health care for about 80% of the population in the region, but the real concern is on the safety of the products.

In traditional medicine, information on the quality, efficacy and safety of medicinal products is not sought out before the products are marketed in comparison to products of modern medicine. Furthermore, traditional medicines or treatments are based on principles and evidence that are not recognised by the majority of independent scientists, and, unlike modern medicine, their practitioners are not regulated like healthcare professionals, making patient safety and treatment quality management more challenging. In Omigbodun's (2004) view, as result, an audit which demonstrates significant improvement through the use of modern medicine in maternity care, for instance, if widely disseminated among opinion leaders in the community and other influential members of society, could encourage and persuade a greater proportion of the population to use modern healthcare facilities instead of alternative medicine, though this is a hypothesis those validity requires verification.

Evaluating Health Policies and Guidelines

Auditing can be used extensively in the evaluation of existing policies and guidelines. It can help in understanding whether agreed-upon standards of care issuing from them are relevant and lead to quality improvement. This is very important because it will help in decision-making before a new guideline is created, in addition to numerous ones already in place (Black and Gruen 2005). For instance, Ibrahim et al. (2012) found that in the management of care of patients with asthma, the problem was not the guideline but adherence to it because there was a significant gap in discharge planning and documentation as recommended in the guidelines.

Designing Educational and Training Programmes

Professional education is an ongoing life-long endeavour designed based on the learning needs of an individual professional (Grol et al. 2013). An audit can help to identify training needs and a strategic educational programme designed to address those needs. A classic example is the work of Weeks and colleagues in curbing maternal mortality in Uganda. This programme, apart from leading to significant improvements in maternity care, also motivates healthcare workers to take responsibility for analysing situations encountered during care and providing creative solutions to address such problems (Weeks et al. 2004). Feedback is an essential component in professional development and performance improvement (Lockyer 2003). Feedback and audit findings can provoke social interaction among healthcare workers, and this interaction could motivate staff and facilitate the development of valuable relationship with peers and senior team members (Grol et al. 2013).

Improving the Quality of Medical Records

Complete, accurate and high-quality medical records are indispensable for effective auditing (Omigbodun 2004). An audit can help to identify inadequacies in clinical documentation with recommendations on how to improve the system. It can also be used in developing countries to monitor data quality, identify areas of concern such as completeness, accuracy and consistency and ensure that health records are kept to the highest standard. The availability of high-quality data in the region will ensure that healthcare practitioners will be more able to make evidenced-based informed and accurate decisions (Osungbade et al. 2010) during patient care, including healthcare policy and strategy.

Barriers and Enablers for Effective Audits in Health Care in Africa

An audit, which is used in developed countries' healthcare systems with adequate basic infrastructure to improve the quality of care, can also be used in the developing countries of Africa with very limited resources for the same purpose. It could also be used to empower local healthcare workers in health care in the region to find their own solutions to common problems (Weeks et al. 2004). Mgaya et al.'s (2016) study in the region showed that auditing helps in detecting substandard diagnosis and management of foetal distress. But the benefits associated with audits can only be obtained when hurdles that can hinder effective and efficient auditing are overcome.

In a review of 93 studies on a wide variety of audits across different professions by Jonnston et al. (2000), some of the barriers to a successful audit include a lack of resources, expertise in project design and analysis, supportive relationship between clinicians and managers and poor relationships between professional groups. Moreover, a lack of commitment from senior doctors and managers and a lack of protected time and practical support are reported by Cheater and Keane (1998). Designing, conducting and applying the findings can pose a barrier as well. Some of the associated problems at levels explained by Sealey (1999) include losing sight of the audit cycle due to the complexities of the audit process, complacency with reasonable findings and underestimating the time needed to complete the audit.

Specifically, in African health care, some of the constraints on an effective audit include healthcare workers' level of competence and motivation, low morale of staff probably due to delays in monthly salary payment, continual strike action by the healthcare staff and availability of equipment (Hunyinbo et al. 2008). The difficulties in finding medical records, inadequate documentation, fear of blame and the lack of a dedicated team that could grant approval for conducting an audit are other barriers (Kediegile and Madzimbamuto 2014) including work pressure.

The enablers of an effective audit, on the other hand, will demand addressing the aforementioned barriers adequately. As summarised by the National Institute for Clinical Excellence (2002), conducting a successful audit that will result in significant improvements in care requires a strategic approach using a combination of various types of support from healthcare organisations. This will require the allocation of adequate facilities, time and management support. A culture of openness where staff can freely identify and document failures in care without fear of blame is essential. It is only in this atmosphere that failures can be identified, thoroughly investigated and the outcomes used to put in place corrective and preventive measures. In addition, in Africa, health care will require involving and training all staff members, beginning with the clinical staff on clinical audit processes, including how to translate audit results into action plans (Weeks and Ononge 2001; Kellett et al. 2001) and seeking expert advice where relevant. Adeleke et al. (2012) and his colleagues pointed out a lack of motivation among healthcare practitioners as a contributory factor in poor medical record keeping. The introduction of auditing with an annual reward for the best audit team can encourage participation.

Conclusion

The essence of an audit is to develop healthcare practice (Morrell and Harvey 2001). Hunyinbo and colleagues are working on improving the quality of obstetric care in a healthcare setting in the region is one of many success stories on using audits to advance healthcare practice. This study identifies non-clinical causes of poor performance that, when promptly and adequately addressed, can result in an instant impact on improving the quality of care (Hunyinbo et al. 2008). Another study is that by Weeks et al. (2004), in which an audit enabled some participants to develop a very important skill and ability in medicine, which encouraged them to continue thinking about a problem until an idea or solution was found. What these stories demonstrate is that it is possible to change practice in African healthcare systems, but it is not a simple and straightforward process. What is therefore required for the widespread use of clinical audits across the entire healthcare practice in Africa is a real commitment from everyone involved in healthcare practice. In Swage's (2003) view, this will require active participation from multidisciplinary teams of clinicians and non-clinicians, including service support departments such as catering and cleaning. Though strengthening clinical auditing in the region will involve multidisciplinary teams from various departments, it is important that such audits comply with the fundamental principles discussed by Sealey (1999). These include ensuring audits are professionally conducted, seen as an educational process and form part of routine practice.

Moreover, a lack of objective scientific evidence on the evaluation of audit measurement properties and sampling methods in the region, as highlighted by Pirkle et al. (2011), must be addressed. Rigorous and empirical studes, in other words, rigorous and empirical studies are required to validate and test auditing methodologies and implementation strategies to determine which ones suitable taking into consideration cultural, social and organisational factors in the African context. Similar research will be required to identify the best and most effective means of integrating audit findings into practice in the region.

Lastly, an audit offers an opportunity to low-income countries for whom securing funding for improving healthcare practice is challenging. For instance, Weeks et al. (2004), through auditing, achieved a simple, cost-free or low-cost but significant improvement in maternity care, which the healthcare staff who participated in the audit initially thought would be achievable on with financial assistance and the intervention of powerful politicians. In their words, "Often an apparently insurmountable problem can be improved by surprisingly simple acts—a guideline posted on the labour suite wall, the repair of a broken machine, allowing women to keep their placentas after delivery as an incentive for institutional delivery, making accessible the equipment from the ward sister's cupboard, and regularly checking stocks. Because these small improvements can be made cheaply and by many members of staff, the combined effect can be impressive." Audits are therefore feasible, valid and reliable measurement tools for assessing and improving patient safety and quality care in the region.

References

Abdullahi AA (2011) Trends and challenges of traditional medicine in Africa. Afr J Tradit Complement Altern Med 8(s):115–123

Adeleke IT, Adekanye AO, Onawola KA et al (2012) Data quality assessment in healthcare: a 365-day chart review of inpatients' health records at a Nigerian tertiary hospital. J Am Med Inform Assoc 12:1039–1042

Baker R, Fraser RC (1995) Development of review criteria: linking guidelines and assessment of quality. BMJ 311(7001):370–373

Benjamin A (2008) Audit: how to do it in practice. BMJ 336(7655):1241–1245

Black N, Gruen R (2005) Understanding health services. Open University Press, Berkshire

Bowling A (2009) Research methods in health investigating health and health services, 3rd edn. Open University Press, Maidenhead

Bowling A (2014) Research methods in health – investigating health and health services, 4th edn. Open University Press, London

Burgess R (ed) (2011) New principles of best practice in clinical audit. Radcliffe Publishing, Oxford

Chan M (2015) Opening remarks at the internal forum on traditional medicine in China, Macao SAR. World Health Organisation. https//www.who.int/dg/speeches/2015/traditional-medicine/en/. Accessed 17 Sept 2015

Cheater FM, Keane M (1998) Nurses' participation in audit: a regional study. Qual Health Care 7:27–36

Esposito P, Canton AD (2014) Clinical audit, a valuable tool to improve quality of care: general methodology and applications in nephrology. World J Nephrol 3(4):249–255

Ghosh R (2009) Clinical audit for doctors. Developmedica, Nottingham

Grol R, Wensing M, Eccles M et al (eds) (2013) Improving patient care – the implementation of change of change in health care, 2nd edn. Wiley, West Sussex

Hayes N (1994) Foundation of psychology. Routledge, London

Hearnshaw HM, Harker RM, Cheater FM et al (2001) Expert consensus on the desirable characteristics of review criteria for improvement of health care quality. Qual Health Care 10(3):173–178

Hunyinbo KI, Fawole AO, Sotiloye OS et al (2008) Evaluation of criteria-based clinical audit in improving quality of obstetric care in a developing country hospital. Afr J Reprod Health 12(3):59–70

Ibrahim SMH, Haroun HM, Ali HM et al (2012) Audit of acute asthma management at the paediatric emergency Department at Ward Madani Children's Hospital Sudan. Sudan J Paediatr 12(1):104–114

Institute of Medicine (1992) Guidelines for clinical practice: from development to use. National Academic Press, Washington DC

International Organisation for Standardisation (2020) ISO 9001 Auditing Practices group guidance on: REMOTE AUDits. International Organisation for Standardisation (ISO) & International Accreditation Forum (IAF)

Irvine D, Irvine S (1991) Making sense of audit. Radcliffe Medical Press, Oxford

Johnston G, Crombie IK, Davies HTO (2000) Reviewing audit: barriers and facilitating factors for effective clinical audit. Qual Health Care 9:23–36

Jones B, Woodhead T (2015) Building the foundation for improvement how five UK trusts build quality improvement capacity at scale within their organisation. The Health Foundation, London

Kediegile G, Madzimbamuto FD (2014) Obstacles faced when conducting a clinical audit in Botswana. South Afr J Anaesth Analg 20(2):127–131

Kellett S, Newman DW, Hawes A (2001) The elusive final stages of the audit cycle: do we put results into action? J Clin Gov 9(4):187–191

Levy B, Rockall T (2009) The role of clinical audit in clinical governance. Surgical 27(9):367–370

Lockyer J (2003) Multisource feedback in the assessment of physician competencies. J Contin Educ Heal Prof 23(1):4–12

Mainz J (2003) Defining and classifying clinical indicators for quality improvement. Int J Qual Health Care 15(6):523–530

Martin V, Charlesworth J, Henderson E (2010) Managing in health and social care, 2nd edn. Routledge, New York

McCrea C (1999) Good clinical audit requires teamwork. In: Barker R, Hearnshaw H, Robertson N (eds) Implementing changes with clinical audit. Wiley, Chichester, pp 119–132

McIntyre N (1995) Evaluation in clinical practice: problems, precedents and principles. https://onlinelibrary.wiley.com/doi/pdf/10.1111/j.1365-2753.1995.tb00003.x. Accessed 15 Sept 2018

Mgaya AH, Litorp H, Kidanto HL et al (2016) Criteria-based audit to improve quality of care of foetal distress: standardising obstetric care at a national referral hospital in a low resource setting Tanzania. BMC Pregnancy Childbirth 16(343):1–10

Mhame PP, Busia K, Kasilo OMJ (2010) Clinical practices of African traditional medicine. Afr Health Monitor 13:32–39

Morrell C, Harvey G (2001) The clinical audit handbook – improving the quality of health care. Harcourt Publishers, Edinburgh

National Institute for Clinical Excellence (2002) Principles for best practice in clinical audit. Radcliffe Medical Press, Oxon

National Joint Steering Committee for Maternal Health Kenya (2002) Standards for maternal care in Kenya. The Professional Societies of Kenya and the United Kingdom. ISBN 9966-9755-1-9

Oakland JS (1993) Total quality management. The route to improving performance, 2nd edn. Butterworth-Heinemann, Oxford

Omigbodun AO (2004) Improving standards in practice through medical audit. Ann Ibadan Postgrad Med 1(2):23–26

Osungbade KO, Oginni SA, Olumide EAA et al (2010) Clinical audit of intra-partum care at secondary health facilities in Nigeria. Niger J Clin Pract 13(2):210–214

Paton JY, Ranmal R, Dudley J (2015) Clinical audit: still an important tool for improving healthcare. Arch Dis Child Educ Pract Ed 100(2):83–88

Pirkle CM, Dumont A, Zunzunegui M (2011) Criterion-based clinical audit to assess quality of obstetrical care in low-and middle-income countries: a systematic review. Int J Qual Health Care 23(4):456–463

Plsex PE (1999) Quality improvement methods in clinical medicine. Paediatrics 103(1):203–214

Reberton N (1999) A systematic approach to managing change. In: Barker R, Hearnshaw H, Robertson N (eds) Implementing changes with clinical audit. Wiley, Chichester, pp 37–56

Robertson N, Bker R, Hearnshaw H (1996) Changing the clinical behaviour of doctors: a psychological framework. Qual Health Care 5(1):51–54

Royal College of Nursing (1990) Quality patient care – the dynamic standard setting system. Scutari, Harrow

Sale D (2005) Understanding clinical governance and quality assurance – making it happen. Palgrave McMillian, New York

Sealey C (1999) Two common pitfalls in clinical audit: failing to complete the audit cycle and confusing audit with research. Br J Occup Ther 62(6):238–243

Secretary of State for Health, Wales, Northern Ireland and Scotland (1989) Working for patients. HMSO, London

Shaw CD (1990) Criterion based audit. BMJ 300(6725):649–651

Swage T (2003) Clinical governance in health care practice. Elsevier, Edinburgh

The Health Foundation (2016) A framework for measuring and monitoring safety: a practical guide to using a new framework for measuring and monitoring safety in the NHS. The Health Foundation, London. ISBN 978-1-906461-53-9

University Hospitals Bristol NHS Foundation Trust (2021) How to: set an audit aim, objectives & standards. http://www.uhbristol.nhs.uk/media/2978983/4_how_to_aim_objectives___standards_v4.pdf. Accessed 28 Aug 2021

Waddell A, Brummitt B, Ovington C (2021) Remote auditing course. Paper presentation at Remote Auditing Course, Research Quality Association (RQA), Zoom online, 2–3 Feb 2021

Weeks A, Ononge S (2001) Audit in maternity care: a better practice 1. Qual Forum 2(2):1–9

Weeks AD, Alia G, Ononge S et al (2004) Introducing criteria based audit into Ugandan maternity units. Qual Saf Health Care 13:52–55

World Health Organisation Regional Office for Africa (2010). Regulation of traditional medicine in the WHO African Regions. https://www.aho.afro.who.int/en/ahm/issue/13/reports/regulation-traditional-medicine-who-african-region. Accessed 30 Nov 2016

Wright J, Hill P (2003) Clinical governance. Elsevier

Chapter 4
Research

Introduction

Research is fundamental to improving healthcare as its discoveries can be used to provide the best patient outcomes and improve the quality of life in society. The scientific body of knowledge generated from research is incredibly important in preventing ill health and improving health outcomes and services in the healthcare environment (Bowling 2014). Research is also essential in determining which treatments work best for patients. Besides patients, other beneficiaries of research in health care include care providers, healthcare organisations, professional societies, the government and regulatory agencies. There is a strong consensus that research can be used by these beneficiaries to inform the choice of care, provision of care, care coverage, financial planning and policy development (Reynolds 2015). Research can lead to innovations that could be used to improve the health and quality of life of participants and others with similar conditions. Research is therefore a core component of safety and quality improvement in health care.

Embracing and incorporating research into daily clinical practice is therefore indispensable as a starting point in effecting meaningful improvements in patient safety and healthcare quality in all countries. However, in the developing countries of Africa, research in the health sector has received far less attention than it deserves. In the region there are ongoing discussions about the urgency of improving safety and quality, but it is unclear how this will be achieved given the current rate of participation in healthcare research. The Royal Tropical Institute (2011) advocates promoting research to ensure evidence-based and cost-effective interventions as the highest priority in the region. According to the report, this is to meet the health needs of the public, which currently represents a serious challenge. Moreover, the institute is of the opinion that focusing on and prioritising healthcare research in the African context will help identify solutions to health problems in the region. The idea is that this could provide relevant evidence which could be systematically reviewed to produce more guidelines and policies which could enhance clinical and non-clinical decisions in the healthcare system. However, even when healthcare practice is based on the best scientific evidence, the efficiency and effectiveness of this practice still must be questioned. This is to determine whether the practice leads to the best patient outcomes, delivers safer and higher-quality care and whether there is any need for further improvement. Research is therefore the fundamental tool available to raise such questions in practice to seek new insights and solutions (Parahoo 2014).

This chapter is therefore aimed at renewing interest in research among healthcare staff in the region. It is designed to simplify planning, designing, conducting and reporting healthcare research specifically for healthcare professionals in the developing countries of Africa who face enormous challenges in a very difficult environment. The environment is characterised by poor infrastructure, limited resources and competing demands on time to deal with an increasing workload due to acute shortages in the workforce. The real motivation is evidence that engagement of healthcare staff in research can in reality improve healthcare performance (Boaz et al. 2015). The main purpose, therefore, is to encourage all healthcare staff in the region, particularly the young generation of clinical and non-clinical professionals, to embrace and develop passion for healthcare research.

To achieve this purpose, the chapter provides a brief discussion of healthcare research in Africa and covers in general ethical, scientific and best practice in research. To minimise the effort required in the preparation of various aspects of research, a decision tool is provided to aid in identifying whether a project is research or an audit. Some templates of various documents are provided which can be easily adapted for specific research needs, and guidelines for different functions are included. These resources will be useful for both healthcare staff with some research experience and those who plan to conduct research for the first time. Precise information on how to prepare a research application and make a submission to an ethics committee or review body is provided. It also includes what ethics committees expect of a researcher during a study. It is hoped that this information and resource will help healthcare staff in the region to plan and carry out more research studies. This will also enable them to evaluate their practice and work with patients to develop research focused on actual live clinical and non-clinical issues. It is hoped that findings produced from the research will help them to develop and implement strategically driven local patient safety and quality improvement interventions with outcomes as good and as effective as their counterparts in developed nations.

Healthcare Research

Healthcare research as presented in this book refers to the entire spectrum of research studies used in generating knowledge for improving or enhancing activities in healthcare settings. This is described in various terms by different publications.

They include but are not limited to clinical trials, clinical research, experimental medicine, translational research, and epidemiological and behavioural research. These also include public health studies, basic scientific laboratory research, patient-oriented research, such as the study of disease pathology and mechanisms, and the development and testing of therapeutic interventions or technologies (British Medical Association 2014 and Institute of Medicine 2013). Clinical research also includes health service research, which covers the effects of a wide range of parameters on healthcare outcomes, for instance the financial system. In the class of this research are studies on the effects of the costs of healthcare services; accessibility to healthcare; planning, delivery distribution and quality of healthcare services; workforce, organisational structure and processes of healthcare systems; and innovation and health technologies and research on economic and social factors affecting health (Institute of Medicine 1995). In Bowling (2014) suggestions for health service research also deals with increasing knowledge and understanding of the healthcare needs of local populations, designing and providing care to meet their needs, taking into consideration the impact of social factors. According to the author, studying the effectiveness of care delivery and employing health services in meeting the needs falls under this section. In addition to the study of health systems which aim at improving the efficiency and effectiveness of the healthcare system to solve health-related problems.

Healthcare research as presented here also covers biomedical research, which deals with the processes of life and the prevention and treatment of diseases including genetic and environmental factors related to health and diseases. Translational research is included, which is a field of study in which basic science and preclinical discoveries are translated into human subject research and then incorporates clinical trial results and other research breakthroughs into practice in clinical and community settings (Institute of Medicine 2013). Translational research emphasises making new research discoveries and translating them into medical advances, new therapies, new interventions, techniques, treatments, practices and health policies for direct clinical benefits for patients and the public. Healthcare research as just described and other types of research not covered in this book must be planned, designed, conducted, recorded and reported according to approved good clinical practice (GCP) compliance protocol. This is covered in the next section.

Research Ethics, Governance and Integrity Training

To comply with GCP principles, including regulations and guidance covering healthcare research, training is required. This training will enable healthcare staff in the region to gain a better understanding of ethical principles and related regulatory requirements applicable to their specific research. Ethics deals with the protection of the interests and well-being of all trial participants; governance, on the other hand, refers to managing the roles and responsibilities of key stakeholders and continuous quality improvements in all aspects of research. Integrity emphasises the need for honesty in designing and conducting research, which instils trust and confidence in the methods and findings of the study. This training is therefore referred to in this book as research ethics, governance and integrity training because the courses aim to provide knowledge and skills needed to ensure all aspects of research processes are carried out to the highest scientific and ethical management and professional standards.

The training course is often designed based on International Council for Harmonisation - Good Clinical Practice (ICH GCP). ICH GCP sets standards for all aspects of the conduct of clinical research. The goals of these standards are two-fold: ensure the protection of human participants and the maintenance of the highest standards of scientific practice (Karlberg 2009). Compliance with the GCP principles also ensures the integrity of research data generated and the validity of the results. Table 4.1 shows a summary of GCP principles relating to designing, conducting, reporting and managing healthcare research. All principles are highly interrelated, but they may not necessarily occur in the order presented below.

Training is also usually based on the local policy and procedures of potential research sites. Another aspect of the training is known as research ethics. During ethics training, the review of previous abuses in clinical research are often discussed for a better understanding of what prompted the publication of guidelines and regulations in the conduct of research and why the publication must be followed (Friedman et al. 2015). Some of the abuses that changed the landscape of clinical research include an experiment in the Tuskegee study of 1972. This study was aimed at observing the natural progression of untreated syphilis in African Americans in Alabama under the pretence of giving free health care (Shavers et al. 2000). Another study is known as the Nazi or Doctor's trial, which took place at a concentration camp in Nuremberg in 1947 (Ghooi 2011). Others include Salgo and the Stanford University Board of Trustees in 1957 and Moore and Regents of the University of California in 1990. Courses often cover various aspects of research, such as study design and methods, data collection and management, data monitoring and safety reporting. Research ethics and integrity training is an ongoing exercise owing to the constant changes in the regulation and conduct of research. It is best practice to maintain a training record, documenting all training attended by members of a research team.

Planning, Designing, Conducting, Recording and Reporting Healthcare Research

Every step in planning, designing, conducting, recording and reporting healthcare research, especially clinical trials that involve people, must incorporate GCP, which is a set of internationally recognised ethical and scientific quality requirements covering research activities (World Healthcare Organization 2005). Compliance with the GCP ensure that the rights, safety and well-being of research participants are

Table 4.1 Healthcare research GCP principles

Principles	Interpretation
Safety and quality	The safety and well-being of participants must be considered the most important factor compared to the benefits of such a research study for science and society. There must be a system and procedure in place for quality assurance of every aspect of the research.
Research proposal	Project plan or research protocol or proposal should provide a clear, complete and detailed picture of the study design, methodology and what is expected of the study participants, including a description of how the relevant laws and regulations will be met.
Competence of research team	The team of researchers for the design, conduct and reporting of the study should be qualified by education, training and experience to carry out their roles or should be supervised by a suitable qualified person.
Patient and public involvement	Patient, service users and members of the public should be encouraged and permitted to help researchers in the design, set-up, conduct, management and dissemination of research reports.
Scientific and ethical justification	There must be scientific justification for a research study and all aspects of the research including the design, conduct and reporting should follow ethical principles.
Integrity, quality and transparency	Research should be designed, reviewed, undertaken, managed, recorded and reported in a way which enables those in the scientific community and society to have confidence and trust in how the research study was carried out and in the findings.
Legal and regulatory requirements	The main ethical and regulatory issues covering research design, conduct and reporting must be identified and respected in all aspects of the research study.
Potential risks and burdens	The potential benefits for science, society and participants must be balanced against the identified potential risks and burdens – distress, discomfort or inconveniencies of the research study. The benefits must outweigh the risks.
Ethical and management approvals	Research should receive approval from an independent ethics committee, institution or other relevant body or organisation prior to initiation of the study.
Insurance and indemnity	Adequate insurance and indemnity must be in place to cover liabilities which may arise from the design, conduct and management of the research.
Data protection and confidentiality	Measures should be taken to ensure data collected for research are recorded, processed and stored securely, accurately and in accordance with applicable data protection principles or regulations, respecting the privacy and confidentiality of the data.
Participant consent	Informed consent should be obtained from all participants before any research activities involving that participant commence. The consent should be voluntarily given, and when a participant is not willing to take part in the research, it must not affect the participant's relations with the study team or organization.
Research findings	Data collected for the research should be handled in a way that allows their accurate reporting, interpretation and verification. The findings of the study (both negative and positive results) should be made publicly available to research participants, interested groups and communities.

(continued)

Table 4.1 (continued)

Principles	Interpretation
Compliance and serious breaches	Compliance with the foregoing principles is essential. Therefore, non-compliance, serious breaches or violations must be appropriately sanctioned by the sponsor, funders, employer, relevant professional body or statutory regulators.

Adapted from Health Research Authority (2017b) and World Health Organization (2005)

protected and respected in conformity with the principles of the Declaration of Helsinki developed by the World Medical Association and other internationally recognised ethical guidelines (World Health Organization 2001).

Planning and Designing Healthcare Research

Other projects are aimed at improving patient safety and healthcare quality that are not necessarily research. These projects include auditing, service evaluations and even surveillance systems. One of the initial steps in planning, designing, conducting and reporting a research project, therefore, is to make sure the project constitutes research and not a non-research project such as an audit or a service evaluation. This distinction between these three essential components for improving patient safety and the quality of healthcare can prove difficult for inexperience researchers (Twycross and Shorten 2014). The difficulties stem from the similarities between researching and auditing. For instance, both start with important questions, involve collecting formal data on patients (or process) and analysing quality data to answer questions and in the expectation that the answers will change or influence clinical practice. In addition, both use a rigorous and systematic design methodology to reach a sound conclusion (Wade 2005). The same is applicable to service evaluation. These components also have some distinctions which relate to the scope and overall objectives of a project. It is therefore essential that the decision on whether a project is a research study, an audit or a service evaluation must be accurate. Any wrong decision, whereby a research project is mistaken for an audit or service evaluation, could have serious implications.

One important requirement applicable to research but not an audit or service evaluation is the requirement for ethical review (Health Research Authority 2017a). All research studies require ethics review but ethics is not required in audit and some service evaluation. However, in service evaluation involving patients, ethics review may be required. There is also the need for informed consent because research by nature involves some degree of risk, burden or intrusiveness for participants (Department of Health 2011). Non-research projects, such as a clinical audit or service evaluation, on the other hand, pose minimal risks, burdens or intrusions and so do not require ethics approvals but do require clinical governance approval or approval from an equivalent local review body in the organisation (Rix and Cutting 1996 and Car 1999). Early identification of whether a project is a research

Table 4.2 Difference between research, service evaluation and audit

Criterion	Research	Service evaluation	Clinical audit
Definition	A quality improvement process that uses scientific, rigorous and multiple strategies to address clearly defined questions, aims and objectives resulting in the most effective and efficient form of care and services.	A quality improvement process that uses the scientific method and the rigorous and systematic collection of data to assess the effectiveness of current services or completed without reference to standards	a quality improvement process that seeks to improve patient care and outcome through systematic review of care against a standard and the implementation of change (NICE 2002).
Aims	To derive generalisable new knowledge or generate hypotheses and test hypotheses.	Solely to define or judge current or completed care and service.	To produce information to inform delivery of best care and service.
Design	To investigate hypotheses or identify and explore themes following established methodology to determine what should be done.	To investigate what standard the service has achieved.	To investigate whether we are doing what should be done and meeting a predetermined standard.
Intervention	May involve evaluating or comparing interventions, particularly new ones, including how interventions and relationships are experienced.	Involves intervention in use only. The choice of treatment is that of the clinician and patient according to guidance, professional standards and/or patient preference.	Involves an intervention in use only. The choice of treatment is that of the clinician and patient according to guidance, professional standards and/or patient preference.
Sample and source	Involve collecting data that complement those for routine care but may include data collected routinely. May involve treatments, samples or investigations in addition to routine care.	Involves analysis of existing data but may include interviews or questionnaires.	Involves analysis of existing data but may include simple interviews or questionnaires.
Allocation to treatment groups	Involves allocating patients to intervention group and uses clearly defined sampling framework underpinned by conceptual or theoretical justifications.	No allocation to interventions: the health professional and patient have chosen intervention before service evaluation.	No allocation to intervention: the health professional and patient have chosen intervention before audit.
Randomisation	May involve randomisation	No randomisation	No randomisation

(continued)

Table 4.2 (continued)

Criterion	Research	Service evaluation	Clinical audit
Ethical review	Ethics review required.	Ethics review require only when patients are interviewed and data are used that could identify patients.	Does not require ethics review.

Adapted from Health Research Authority (2017) and Twycross and Shorten (2014)

study, an audit or a service evaluation is very important because it will prevent waste of resources. It will also enable researchers to identify the GCP principles, regulations and standards applicable to the proposed research and ensure the study protocol is designed to conform to them (Page et al. 2012). Table 4.2 provides key criteria which can help to guide this decision-making.

Identification Research and Framing a Question

According to Creswell (2009), the choice of topic is crucial, and it is better that the decision be made by the investigator rather than by an adviser or a committee. The reasons advanced by the author include the fact that the topic or research question has the potential to give an insight into the entire research project and to help reflect on whether the study is practical and useful to undertake. Finally a research question can help in understanding how the study will address the area of concern. In DePoy and Gitlin's (2016) view, the identified topic should be taken from a problem area that holds strong personal interest and meaning to the investigator. The authors also assert that the question or topic should be fascinating enough to keep the researcher motivated throughout the process irrespective of the challenges that may be encountered or the time and commitment required. In line with the theme of this book, the research question or the topic could aim at changing policy, exploring the effect of current standard treatment and investigating whether new treatments offer any benefits. It could also focus on the opinions of patients, staff and service users about the treatment and how best to organise and provide services.

Of importance at this stage also is a research title. Creswell (2009) recommends a brief title that indicates what the study is about. It should also convey the central idea of the research to readers. The author suggested that posing the topic as a brief question would be an effective strategy in the topic's development. In addition, a brief title is better in the sense that it will eventually become the actual idea that researchers can continue focusing on and modifying, if necessary, as the project progresses (Glesnce and Peshkin 1992). Wilkinson (1991) suggests keeping titles as brief as possible by eliminating articles, prepositions and phrases, for example "an approach to …, a study of …," and keeping it to no more than 12 words. It is common these days to find a short and a long title, with the short one presented in the form of acronyms. For instance, a long title would be "Adverse events in health care in Africa: a retrospective study" and the short title "AVERICA". It is important that the study title be used on all study documents (e.g. protocol, participant information sheet (PIS), consent form, participant invitation letter)

At the end of this section, the investigator should be able to address why the research is considered worth undertaking, the benefits, the main research question that will be addressed and whether the study will expand our understanding of the topic or areas of concern. The investigator should be able to establish whether a similar study has been carried out previously and what difference the proposed study will make. One of the ways of addressing these issues is through identifying and evaluating the literature discussed in the next section.

Literature review and Evaluate Literature

A literature review, which is the art of "interpretation and synthesis of published work" (Merriam 1988), is essential in all aspects of research. It includes a review of existing theory and background, leading to establishing the contribution of the proposed research to the existing literature. A systematic literature review is a requirement for all types of research because it helps researchers to have clarification about their proposed study, to build confidence in their work and show the rigour of their methods (Booth et al. 2016). In embarking on this process there is a need to critically appraise all identified relevant publications. This is to eliminate poorly designed publications and ensure the proposed study is based on sound and valid literature relevant for addressing specific research issues (Rogers 2010). Depending on the type of study, the review may take the form of a thorough systematic review or a less in-depth review. However, the importance of a critical review of the existing literature is enormous because it will lead researchers, for instance, to uncover the results of other studies closely related to their own and become familiar with the contribution and ongoing dialogue in the literature. All this information enables the investigator to identify and specify the direction of the study, make meaningful contributions to the knowledge base in the area of concern by filling gaps and extending previous studies (Marshall and Rossman 2006; Cooper 1984).

In summary, a critical review of the literature provides an investigator with an up-to-date overview of the current knowledge and studies in the field of interest. It enables the investigator to scientifically justify the need for the research because it will allow the researcher to assess the originality of the research proposal based on the existing body of evidence. It eliminates the likelihood of trying to address a research question that has already been answered. It also helps to place the study in context to demonstrate that the researcher is knowledgeable about previous studies, informs the design and methodology of the research, and shows how the research will contribute to the current body of knowledge.

Research Team and Responsibility

It takes an effective team to successfully conduct high-quality research. In planning and designing a research study, it is important to consider the roles and responsibilities of the team, which is often composed of a group of individuals (e.g. doctors, nurses, pharmacists, statisticians, laboratory technicians) working on a research project, department (e.g. human resources, imaging, pathology, pharmacist, finance) and other organisations supporting the project. Everyone involved in the research must have the appropriate clearance and contract required for their roles (National Institute for Health Research 2018). The chief investigator (CI), who is responsible for the overall conduct of research and a lead researcher for research projects, will have to form the research team and delegate responsibility to individual members within the team based on qualifications, training and experience in research. The CI must have full understanding of research procedures and requirements. This is documented using a delegation of duties log (Fig. 4.1). The CI has overall responsibility for ensuring that the ethics committee requirements and applicable regulatory requirements are met and that the study personnel have knowledge of ICH GCP (Karlberg 2009a).

Research Sponsor and Responsibility

The sponsor is another important role. All clinical research must have a sponsor, which is the person, organisation or partnership that takes on overall responsibility for initiating, conducting, reporting and financing (or arranging the financing for) a research project. It is also the responsibility of the sponsor to demonstrate that the research serves the interest of the public and is conducted to the highest scientific and ethical standards. The sponsor can delegate some of the responsibilities to the investigator. In non-commercial research, the sponsor is normally expected to be the employer of the chief investigator and the funder, The funder of the study can be a different organisation while in commercial research the sponsor is usually the same as the funder (Health Research Authority 2017b). The CI or principal investigator (PI) will have to identify, discuss and agree to the potential research sites and the corresponding local PIs, especially if it is a multi-centre research study. In some studies, especially in clinical trials, this might require undertaking a site selection visit. This is one of the responsibilities of the sponsor often delegated to the CI or PI, particularly in non-commercial research study.

The sponsor must also ensure that appropriate insurance and indemnity are in place before the study commences. The insurance and indemnity to meet the potential legal liability of the sponsor concerning harm to participants arising from the design, conduct and management of the research are specified in the protocol and also stated in study PISs. Indemnity is a written assurance inserted in a sponsorship letter or study contract confirming liability (financial compensation) that will be

Study Title:								
Study Site:					Study R&D Reference:			
Principal Investigator (PI):								
No	Name	Signature	Initials	Study Role	Study procedures	Study Duration From	To	PI Signature
1.								
2.								
3.								
4.								
5.								
6.								
7.								
8.								
9.								
10.								

Study Procedures:

4. Obtaining informed consent 2. Taking samples (blood, Urine, etc.) 3. Reviewing Health Record 4. Completing CRF 5. Examining Participant (physical examination) 6. Dispensing drugs 7. Obtaining medical history 8. Others.

Fig. 4.1 Study staff delegation log

provided in the event of an accident during the study, while insurance is a premium that has been or must be paid into a fund from which payment for compensation will be made in the event of a claim.

Feasibility Assessment and evaluation of a study site

This is another critical stage in research planning and design. The focus on the assessing the capacity and capability of the study site is to ensure clarity on the resources (personnel, finance, facility/equipment) implication and their requirements for the success of the study (Ahmed et al. 2018). The cost of the project should be evaluated at this stage. The involvement of a support department (such as pharmacy, human resources, imaging, pathology, medical records) is also assessed and the cost of their procedures and services estimated. The main contact in each department should be identified and the contact details documented. The required contractual arrangement put in place for the research is appraised. This includes but is not limited to a clinical research study contract agreement, material transfer agreement, confidentiality or non-disclosure agreement and memorandum of understanding.

Ethical Review of Healthcare Research

Healthcare research, as discussed earlier, is vital for protecting and improving the health and well-being of patients and the public. However, research in any context involves trying something new, so it can sometimes involve an element of risk whose impact is often unpredictable. In addition, healthcare research may also involve additional burdens or intrusions beyond those experienced in usual care. In light of this, it is important that in planning, designing, conducting and reporting research risks be minimised, methods be put in place to ensure the dignity, rights, safety and well-being of participants are not compromised and the potential benefits

Table 4.3 Some of the basic responsibilities of research ethics committees or institutional review boards

Establish a scientific justification for the proposed research by considering whether the research question is worth asking and can be adequately addressed by the proposal. Verify the potential benefits for science, society or research participants against the potential risks and burdens and verify the existence of peer review of the study by other competent experts.
Ensure that all ethical and design issues arising in the research are satisfactorily addressed. Consider the research question, how it will be addressed and the methodology that will be used, and justify how the study will build on or contribute to the existing body of knowledge. Issues of recruitment, consent, confidentiality, conflict of interest, risks, burdens and benefits, and possible use of sample in future research are all addressed.
Consider the qualifications of the researchers, including education and experience in the principles of research practice, and whether there are adequate resources at the proposed research site to carry out all aspects of the research effectively ensuring the safety of the participants.
Determine that all proposed research, particularly studies involving the administration of gene therapy, radioactive substances, drugs and vaccines or the use of medical devices or procedures under development are acceptably safe in humans and ensure a review was conducted by a relevant competent expert advisory committee.
Ensure that data/samples generated from the research will be properly stored and analysed in compliance with data protection principles and information security standards, respecting privacy and confidentiality.
Maintain records of decisions and take appropriate measures to monitor ongoing research projects and ensure various reports are obtained in a timely manner.

to participants and society be justifiable (Department of Health 2011). To achieve all this, all research studies must be reviewed by a research ethics committee (REC) or institutional review board (IRB) to assess whether the research conforms to recognised ethical and scientific standards. In addition, to assess the systems put in place to comply with standards regarding respect for the dignity of the participants and protecting their well-being, safety and rights during the research (World Medical Association Declaration of Helsinki 2013). Some of the basic responsibilities of RECs or IRBs are summarised as follows in Table 4.3.

Composition of Research Ethics Committee

Members of the committee could range from someone with specific knowledge and skills (expert members in the relevant fields of care), who would be useful in better understanding of the research proposal, to lay members, who are people independent of care service whose main professional interest is not care-related research. This includes, for example, someone with no knowledge of the research area, patients, lawyers, administrators and someone from the local community. While the expert members during the review will deliberate to ascertain whether the research is based on sound scientific and ethical standards, the lay members will help to provide different perspectives, such as a societal perspective which could give investigators insight into how members of the public might view the research. The lay members could also raise issues that researchers deeply involved in the study might not identify and help to ensure the integrity of the committee. However, although members of the committee often come from various backgrounds that allow them to scrutinise the ethical aspects of a study proposal (Page et al. 2012), it is important that these members be individuals with no vested interest in the research under review. They must be independent of the researchers, the organisations funding the research and organisation where the research will take place, that is, the research site (Department of Health 2011).

In some countries in Africa where there is no formal national REC or IRB, an ad hoc ethics committee may be required. In forming such a committee, members should be carefully selected with a process put in place to prevent undue influence on the decisions of the committee by any of the members. For transparency and openness, any conflicts of interest (COIs) should be effectively resolved. One of the ways of achieving transparency is by written COI policies and procedures that are made publicly available to all members of the research team. To ensure the COI does not compromise the rights, safety and well-being of the research participants or the integrity of the review process, every member selected should sign a COI agreement before the ethical review of the research commences (Bhatt 2018). The selected members must be willing to volunteer freely and should undertake special training in conducting an ethical review appropriate to their role. The committee as a whole must be independent and impartial in its operation. They must be free from undue pressures of *"political influence; institutional affiliations; trades union or profession-related interest; direct or indirect financial inducement or any impression thereof; coercion; market forces; and agency-, discipline- or topic-related bias"* (Department of Health 2011) and tribal sentiments. Moreover, there must be established operating procedures stating the principles, requirements and standards that the committee should meet in its review. The decision of the committee must be respected in the sense that the research must not commence until approval is granted.

Ethical Considerations in Healthcare Research

There are key ethical principles in healthcare research that a research proposal must conform to. The detailed information on these principles in relation to the research must be provided with clear demonstration of how these ethical issues will be addressed in the project. It is this information that will help the REC or IRB understand the project so that an informed decision can be made about whether or not to approve the research project. These principles are as follows.

Science and Society

In the proposal it is important to demonstrate conformity of the research to scientific and ethical standards. There must be a clear demonstration that the potential risks and burdens associated with the research have been identified and weighed in relation to the benefits. This is referred to as the beneficence principle. The implication of this is that the potential benefits to science, society or research participants at present or in future should be balanced against the potential risks and burdens which might be experienced by study participants. In Levine (1988) the risks and burdens are classified as follows:

- Physical, such as pains, injury and bruises
- Psychological, or risk associated with emotions such as anxiety, distress, discomfort, embarrassment over divulging sensitive information, breaches of confidentiality, stigma and discrimination.
- Social risks, which are associated with low morale affecting social interactions with others; and
- Economic risks, where participants incur financial costs or are influenced to take part as a result of financial benefits.

Sample size is another element to consider. For a research study to be scientifically valid and ethically sound, it should have the appropriate sample size, meaning it should be large enough to produce statistically significant scientific results (Page et al. 2012). It is therefore important that the sample size be decided with the help of a statistician (Nayak 2010).

The criteria for recruiting participants in a study constitute another important factor for ethical consideration. Researchers must demonstrate that the selection criteria do not unjustifiably and discriminatingly exclude potential participants due to age, culture, disability or gender. This is to ensure that the benefits of the research evidence for improved health will be fairly distributed throughout society (Department of Health 2011). In effect it is ethical that research should only be conducted in a population that will benefit from the outcome, for instance, it is unethical to conduct research on polio with participants in Europe instead of African countries, where this disease is prevalent.

Protection of Research Participants

In healthcare research, the principle of respecting and protecting the interests of the participants is paramount to the interest of researchers and research for science and society. It is vital that the research proposal contain details on the manner in which research participants will be given necessary knowledge about the purpose of the research and the nature and scope of their involvement including study procedures, risks and benefits. The proposal should also show how the participants' anonymity, privacy and confidentiality will be respected. The protocol should also demonstrate that participants' decision on taking part in the study is voluntary, informed by their full knowledge of the research purpose and the nature and the scope of their involvement. In addition, investigators should ensure that the treatment and procedures involved in the study are safe and all the necessary precautions are taken to minimise the potential risks, in other words, that the chance of serious injury or death is very remote (Royal College of Physicians 1990).

The process of ensuring adequate protection for healthcare research participants could be summed up in three primary ethical principles: consent, confidentiality and voluntary participation (DePoy and Gitlin 2016). A detailed explanation of these principles is provided in the next section.

Consent

Informed consent as defined by the Council for International Organisations of Medical Sciences (2002) is a "*decision to participate in research, taken by a competent individual who has received the necessary information; who has adequately understood the information; and who, after considering the information, has arrived at a decision without having been subject to coercion, undue influence or inducement, or intimidation*". Consent can be obtained by the investigator or some designated person. Consent is a continuous process and not a single event. Once a participant gives consent, the process of consent continues throughout the duration of the study. Every time a participant interacts with research staff, consent and other new information on the trial can be updated.

COVID-19, an infectious disease caused by the coronavirus – SARS-COV-2, has completely changed research recruitment and consent processes (World Health Organization 2020). With the advent of this pandemic, the use of electronic methods for providing information to research participants without direct contact is now preferred over traditional text-based information on paper. The use of these electronic methods to disseminate information and to seek, confirm and document informed consent (eConsent) will not only help in reducing the risk of infection but also in

- Improving understanding
- Testing and reinforcing participant comprehension
- Providing feedback on how consent materials could be improved
- Improving patient recruitment process and reducing drop-out rates
- Enabling process efficiencies (Health Research Authority 2020).

Electronic methods of communicating include the use of electronic devices such as a tablet, smartphone or digital multimedia, which makes it possible to record or document informed consent using electronic signatures. One way of using implied consent is as an online questionnaire survey where consent clauses precede the survey questions. The participant will first access and grant consent before moving to the survey questions, and, depending on how it is designed, participants may not be able to proceed to the survey questions until all the applicable clauses are selected. Other methods include using a pre-recorded text which is played to participants or information is read out via a video link, eliminating contact between researchers and participants. In a situation where contact cannot be completely eliminated, a laminated information sheet could be used since the surface can be readily cleaned and appropriate COVID-19 measures, such as the use of masks and maintaining social distancing during the consent process, are taken.

A PIS is given to participants by researchers to explain the purpose, procedures, risks, participant involvement in and duration of their participation in the study. Information on the PIS must be presented in a simple, non-technical language or in a language that participants will understand. A patient/participant information sheet (Table 4.4) must be provided to participants in advance and participants must be given time to consider their participation before commencement of research activity. Participants are often encouraged to discuss the study with their relatives or personal clinicians.

The investigator or designated member of the research team obtaining consent must be qualified by training and experience to take the informed consent. The researcher taking consent must have excellent knowledge of the research purpose and its procedures and risks. The researcher must explain the study clearly to the participants, answer any questions they may have and ensure each participant understands each procedure (CIOMS 2002).

If the participants willingly participate, a consent form (Table 4.5) is signed by the investigator and signed or thumb-printed by the participants. A copy of the signed form is made available to the participant, and a copy is stored in the research file.

Table 4.4   Patient/participant information sheet template

Participant Information Sheet (PIS)

Study Title:

Study R&D reference:

Principal Investigator/Co-investigators:

Purpose and background of the study: *This section gives a brief explanation of the study background and why the study is being conducted.*

Invitation to the participant: *In this section explain to the participants why they are invited and how their taking part will be useful in the study. It should made know to the participants at this point that their taking in the study is voluntary.*

What is required from participant: *At this point information on informed consent is provided. The research procedures/activities (questionnaire, interview, focus group, clinical assessment) that the participant will be involved is explained including the duration, where such activities will take place and other expectations from the participants. Depending on the study, if the study involves site visitation, the number of visitations is specified and where tests, for instance, blood tests and other clinical assessment are involved these are included. Lifestyle restriction, for instance, fasting due to a test is also mentioned.*

The benefits of the study to participants and the risk including the burdens for participating: *The benefits and the risks of involvement in the study are explained to the participants. If there are no benefits, it should be specified.*

If there is a problem during the study: *This is where an insurance statement of the organisation is provided and must correspond to the nature of the study, that is, whether the research activities will involve invasive (taking blood sample) and non-invasive interventions (interview or questionnaire). Contact details for queries and complaint are also provided in this section.*

Participant confidentiality and data protection: *In this section explanation on what information will be obtained from the participants is provided including how such information will be stored, shared and how data regulations and confidentiality will be maintained.*

Study sponsor and funder: *The sponsor and funder are mentioned in this section. There may not be any funder, but it is mandatory that a sponsor name is provided*

Study ethics or institutional review body: *The name of the ethics committee or institutional review board that reviewed and provided favourable ethical opinion or approval is mentioned in this section*

Study contacts for further information: *Contact details of a member of study team with an excellent knowledge of the study is provided*

Participant Information Sheet Version number: Date:

Table 4.5 Consent form

			Study R& D	
Study Consent Form				
Study Title:			**Reference:**	
Study Principal investigator/Co-investigators:				
No	**Clauses**			**Initials**
1.	I confirm that I have read the information sheet version .... dated.............. for the above study and had the opportunity to consider the information, ask questions which had been satisfactorily answered			
2.	I understand that my participation is voluntary, and I am free to withdraw at any time, without giving any reason and without affecting my relationship with the research team or their organisation			
3.	I give permission for the sponsor, the study team and regulatory authorities to access my research records that are relevant to this research			
4.	I consent to take part in the above study.			

_____   _____   _____

Name of participant   Signature   Date

_____   _____   _____

Name of person taking consent   Signature   Date

(if different from Principal Investigator)

_____   _____   _____

Principal Investigator   Signature   Date

1 copy for participant and 1 copy for Principal Investigator

Consent form version: Date:

The consent form clauses vary depending on the research data collected or the method of data collection, for instance, where a study involves interviewing and recording, clauses such as "I give permission for the interview to be recorded. I understand that this recording will be deleted once it has been transcribed" must be included. A clause such as "I give consent to being contacted about the possibility to take part in other research studies" could be inserted in the consent form to seek permission from potential participants to be invited to take part in future research studies. Best practice is to store the PIS and consent used during the process together.

Vulnerable Groups

In healthcare research vulnerable participants are those who are relatively or completely incapable of protecting their own interest because they have insufficient power, intelligence, resources, education and strength to do so (CIOMS 2002). Vulnerable population include elderly people, children, people with learning difficulties and those suffering from serious illness, dementia, brain injury, stroke or mental health illness. Other health conditions include stigma sickness, such as AIDS or HIV, and unconsciousness caused by sudden accidents. They also include other forms of disabilities that may impair their communication, reasoning and decision-making. As a result of their conditions, they may find it difficult to fully understand what the research is about, their involvement and expectations of them, even when they are provided with the relevant information about the study.

Informed consent is obtained on the conditions that participants can read PIS, comprehend and retain information long enough and believe information to be true. The participants must be able to consider such information appropriate and make an informed decision based on this and at a specific time. Because vulnerable participants do not have the capacity to meet these conditions, there is no ethical justification to exclude them from research versus having a third party represent them. The representative could be a family member, carer, authorised professional or legal representative. Such a representative is enlisted is to ensure this group of participants is not manipulated or misled in deciding to participate in a given study, a decision they might regret later (Page et al. 2012).

Moreover, researchers are often required by ethics committees or guidelines to justify their research on the basis that it could not be conducted with a similar outcome by involving those who are not vulnerable participants. Secondly, researchers are expected to demonstrate that the main purpose of the research is to obtain knowledge relevant to the health needs of the vulnerable and their clinical conditions.

There are specific and standardised tools designed to aid capacity assessment of vulnerable participants to consent (Appelbaum and Grisso 2001; Kim et al. 2001). Ethics committees often want to know whether such a tool was used before the decision to recruit them was made. Ethics expects researchers to also clarify that there are adequate safeguards (psychological and medical support) in place for a vulnerable population recruited for a study.

In a research study involving children, the decision of parents or guardians on behalf of a child regarding the child's participation in a study must reflect the wishes of the child in line with local laws. If a child is over the age of 12 or 13 years and capable of understanding what is essential to give adequately informed consent, it is recommended that the child's consent, which is known as assent, must be obtained and respected. However, this assent must be complemented by the permission of a parent or guardian. In a situation where a parent or guardian gives permission for a child to participate in research, the parent or guardian is expected to be given the opportunity to observe how the research is conducted to a reasonable extent that will enable the parent or guardian to decide whether it is in the overall interest of the child to withdraw from or continue in the study. However, RECs may waive parental permission in a situation where parental knowledge of the subject matter may place the child at some risk. In some countries, when it comes to social research, adolescents below the general age of consent, referred to as *emancipated* or *mature*, can give consent, and such consent can be authorised without the agreement or awareness of parents or guardians. This is usually the case in social research involving the investigation of adolescents' beliefs and behaviour relating to sexuality, use of recreational drugs, child abuse or addressing domestic violence (CIOMS 2002).

Consent in Emergency Research

Emergency research arises when there is an urgent need for treatment and demand for urgent action to be taken for the purposes of the study but prospective patients or participants are not able to comprehend and retain information about the study or treatment and make an informed decision or consent based on the information available at the time, and it is not possible to obtain consent from a relative or legal representative (Health Authority Research 2021). In such circumstances, informed consent in emergency research or situations can be waived where the researcher anticipates that the participant will be unable to grant consent before any research activity is done. However, these participants are expected to give their consent as soon as they are able, or consent should be obtained from their relatives or legal representative as soon as possible.

A typical example is stroke and cardiopulmonary arrest conditions, which occur suddenly and render the patient incapable of giving informed consent. In this situation, due to the time constraints of this critical condition, there may be no time to contact relatives or legal representatives to give consent on the patient's behalf; it is often necessary for research interventions to commence as quickly as possible immediately after the event so as to evaluate an interventional treatment or develop relevant knowledge. The sudden outbreak of the coronavirus (COVID-19) global pandemic is another example. During this period research was undertaken as part of a public health emergency, much like the Ebola outbreak in Africa. Studies in this category were facilitated by an ethics committee through an expedited review process. In both cases, the stroke patients and COVID-19 and Ebola patients are expected be contacted and invited to give informed consent to their involvement as research subjects as soon as they regain consciousness and are fully capable of doing so; otherwise, informed consent should be sought from their relatives or legal representatives (CIOMS 2002).

Confidentiality

Researchers must ensure there are adequate safeguards in place to protect the confidentiality of information shared in the course of and after a research project. In addition, research findings are expected to be published in a way that is respectful of the interests of all concerned, and no information that would identify participants should be disclosed; where such information is absolutely necessary, its disclosure must be done with consent (CIOMS 2002). To ensure confidentiality, a hard copy of identifying information and other research data or records, such as consent forms, completed case report forms, lab results and X-ray results, must be stored in a locked filing cabinet in a secure location. All electronic data or records, for example video and audio records, must be stored in a password-protected file and held in a computer system that can only be accessed using a password. Identifying information includes clinical information on diagnosis and treatment, photographs, video, audiotapes, addresses, date of birth, names and other data that may directly or indirectly identify participants either as a unit data or in combination. In addition, researchers must ensure that information provided by participants cannot be linked to their identity. This is particularly relevant in research related to sensitive and potentially stigmatising subjects, such as AIDS and social care research on teenage pregnancy, mental health and drug abuse. Confidentiality can be protected by limiting access to participants' data and denying access to those who do not need it. This could also be achieved by the use of anonymisation and pseudonymisation. In anonymization, participants identifying data, such as name, address and date of birth, are separated from details that could make it possible to identify research participants. Under pseudonymisation, on the other hand, identifiable data are substituted with a code or unique reference number (British Medical Association 2007).

In conducting telephone or face-to-face interviews, confidentiality must be maintained by ensuring the interview or phone communication is carried out in a secure room where privacy can be guaranteed. During the discussion, the voice should be kept as low as possible to keep others nearby from hearing (DePoy and Gitlin 2016). In general, researchers are expected to obtain, process, store, encrypt and transmit research data or records safely and securely in compliance with the UK Data Protection Act and applicable local regulations and policies. The Data Protection Act also requires that details of how participant data will be collected and how those data will be used must be explained to the participants.

As highlighted by DePoy and Gitlin (2016), in research involving patients, only a certain member of the research team is granted access to identifying information or make initial contact with patients for research without obtaining consent. This often occurs at the patient-identification stage of research. Access to this information or patients at this stage is limited to a member of the research team who is also a member of the patient's direct care team. With consent from patients, both researchers who are members of the direct care team and those outside the direct care team can approach patients to initiate research activities or review and obtain their relevant data for research.

Voluntary Participation

Voluntary participation in a research study is very important in various ways because any form of influence on people to take part in a research study could have negative impacts on the findings. Participants must therefore always be made aware that their participation is voluntary. They must be made aware that they can refuse to take part in the study without this decision impacting their clinical care in a negative way or affecting their relationship with their clinician or member of the research team. In addition, even if they had confirmed their participation by giving consent and starting the study, they can still withdraw their consent at any stage of the research or refuse to participate in a particular procedure without a reason for doing so if they so desire. As summarised by DePoy and Gitlin (2016), participants must be made aware of their voluntary participation at the stages of their initial enrolment in the study and over the entire course of the study. They must be made aware of their right to refuse to answer specific questions or participate in a study procedure.

During the enrolment process, researchers must explain to participants the risks involved in the study and the measures in place to protect them. Researchers must ensure that no form of coercion will be used. With regard to payment, only fair remuneration for expenses, such as fare reimbursement and other expenses, should be offered. Large sums of money or payments in kind to participants should be avoided because they could encourage or persuade people to take part in the study mainly out of financial incentives. However, those who receive no direct benefit from the research may receive token amounts of money for the inconvenience of participating in the research, but all financial rewards must be documented in the protocol, including the PIS, and approval of payment must be obtained from the REC or IRB (CIOMS 2002). Researchers must also ensure that participants are not intimidated or under undue influence or unjustified deception in making decisions. In a situation where researchers are clinicians and the participants are their patients, the researchers must be aware of their influence on their patients and be careful that the participants are not intimidated and feel no pressure to participate as this could damage the doctor–patient relationship (Page et al. 2012).

As the study progresses and new information becomes available or significant changes are made in the conditions or procedures of the research, this must be communicated to participants and new informed consent must be sought. This information or change should be made known to participants, even if it might affect their willingness to continue taking part in the study (CIOMS 2002).

In circumstances where participants refuse to participate or withdraw their participation, according to DePoy and Gitlin (2016), it is essential that the researcher understand the reason for their decision, for example whether it is due to the nature of the procedures, sensitivity of questions, demands placed on them or behaviour of the research team. If a participant refuses to provide a reason for their willingness to participate in the study, this decision must be respected. However, as explained by the authors, knowledge of the reason for their refusal may have implications for the ethical conduct of the study, interpretation of results and generalisation of the findings. It may also help to inform the planning and design of similar studies in the future.

Participants' decision not to answer a question may lead to missing information that could impact data analysis and the study outcome. Participants' decision not to participate, withdraw participation and refuse to answer a particular question can lead to an extension of the study recruitment period in order to achieve a better sample size or obtaining missing information, and this extension may require additional resources in terms of time and finance. It is therefore important that participants not only be encouraged to take part in the study but also continue to participate.

Dissemination of Findings and Publication

The publication of research findings also carries ethical concerns. Researchers are responsible for not only performing their study but also reporting their findings, whether negative or positive, by publishing them in journals or other venue. It is also best practice to share the findings of the research with participants and others since the results may influence clinical care and inform further research in the field (Page et al. 2012). The idea of making research findings available to clinical and public health practitioners is an evidence-based strategy aimed at improving health care and preventing disease. This is a very crucial aspect of healthcare development which the strategy of dissemination and implementation seeks to address (Brownson et al. 2018). In the design of the study protocol and PIS it is necessary that information about the publication arrangement be included.

Preparation and Submission for Ethical Review

The final steps in planning and design in healthcare research is submitting a study proposal to a REC or IRB. Depending on the country and REC or IRB, it may be necessary to submit an additional application form with the study protocol and associated documents. It is therefore advisable to contact the REC or IRB of choice in advance for clarification on their specific requirements. In addition, it is also important at this stage to contact and check with the local research site(s) the requirements and site approval processes in parallel with that of the ethics committee. This method will help to reduce the waiting time for commencing the study at a site once the REC issues a favourable opinion.

The research documents that need to be submitted to the ethics committee could be referred to as study essential documents. These are documents which individually and collectively allow evaluation of the conduct of a study and the quality of the data generated (International Conference on Harmonisation 1996). The essential documents vary depending on the type of research, and some ethics committees do provide a checklist of the required documents. The essential documents include but are not limited to the study protocol, PIS, consent form, study questionnaire, participant invitation letter and personal clinician letter. Table 4.6 shows information that should be covered in the study protocol or proposal or plan, which is the most important of all the essential documents. A protocol or proposal must be designed

Table 4.6 Some relevant sections in a research study protocol

Study Protocol			
Study Details			
Study Title:		*Study R&D reference:*	
Sponsor/Funder			
Study Team			
Study Principal Investigator/Co-investigators			
Others (study manager, co-ordinator, etc.)			
Lists of Contents			
Protocol Summary	*Title, Population, Site, Duration, Objectives, Hypothesis, Design, sample size and Statistical analysis.*		
Introduction/background and literature review			
Rationale/justification			
Study questions			
Study aim(s) and objectives			
Methodology	*Study Design, Data collection and tools, Data storage and management, Data and Statistical analysis*		
Recruitment	*Recruitment process - study site, population and recruitment materials (letters, email, advertisement), Inclusion criteria, Exclusion criteria, Withdrawal criteria, Participation duration, Sample size and justification, Consent process*		
Study safety	*Definition of study related adverse event, Reporting*		
Ethical considerations	*Ethics/review board/site approval, Study risks, burdens and benefits, Consent, Data protection and confidentiality, Quality assurance, Dissemination of finding and publication*		
Protocol version: Date:			

for every research study; it describes the objective(s), design, methodology, statistical considerations, organisation and management of the research.

Moreover, a protocol usually details the background and justification of the study. Study protocol for researchers could be referred to as a manual that guides and governs all aspects of the research to ensure compliance with applicable governance guidelines, standards, policies and regulations. The protocol provides a means of oversight monitoring and evaluation of a study outcome. Specifically, a GCP-compliance protocol provides a plan of action and detailed accounts of how the proposed research will be conducted to achieve its specific aims and objectives (Robert and Priest 2010) in compliance with all applicable regulations.

Submission of Research Application for Ethical Review

Prior to submitting essential documents to a REC for review, it is good practice to have these documents subjected to peer review by experts in the relevant research topic. These experts must be completely independent of the research team. Peer review is important as it can help to identify flaws or errors in the study design that may have been missed by researchers (Page et al. 2012). Peer review also provides insight into the quality and suitability of the protocol and the associated documents. The essential documents are what the REC will review to judge whether the dignity, rights, safety and well-being of research participants will be protected in a research study. In preparing these documents, it is imperative that sufficient evidence be given in the protocol with associated documents to demonstrate how related ethical issues in the study will be addressed. It is important to note that providing false or misleading information to a recognised REC in the research application is an offence (Health Research Authority 2017c). Lastly, to ensure the validity of the application submitted to the committee, it is advisable that the REC be contacted for specific requirements or a checklist for application submission.

Conducting and Recording Healthcare Research

Once the REC has reviewed an application and issued a favourable opinion, which is not the same thing as an approval, the study is ready to commence. It is therefore necessary that written approval or management permission be obtained from the involved research site, that is, the organisation responsible for carrying out any of the research procedures at a given locality. This site approval must be obtained before the study begins. A research study is deemed to have started when any of the procedures set out in the protocol are initiated. However, some RECs recommend that research projects should start within 12 months of the date on which ethics committee or review board approval was given (Health Research Authority 2017c). Essential documents are also used to demonstrate the compliance of the study conduct with GCP standards and applicable regulatory requirements. These documents are usually kept in a file known as the trial master file (TMF). If this file is properly

Table 4.7 Sample of trial master file index

Study Master File (Trial Master File –(TMF)			
Study title:		Study R&D Reference:	
Lists of Contents			
Study management	Study progress reports, contact details and other related documents and correspondence		
Sponsor/funder	Sponsor approval, funding information, insurance and indemnity information, contracts and agreements, budget and other related documents and correspondence		
Study staff information	Staff CVs with training certificates, study delegation log,		
Study protocol	Final approved protocol, protocol amendments and related correspondence		
Participant information	Final approved participant information sheet and amendments, final approved consent form and amendments, recruitment letters, advertisements and related correspondence		
Study Safety	Incident reporting guidelines, incident forms and related correspondence		
Ethics or Institutional review board	Applications submitted, the main approvals and subsequent approvals from amendments, other related documents and correspondence		
Local site	Application submitted, local site approvals, Investigator Site File, site investigators and contact details, other related documents and correspondence		
Study Data Management	Final CRF forms and amendments, instructions for completing CRF, study sample questions, interview and focus group protocol, other documents and related correspondence		
Quality Assurance	Risk assessment report, monitoring plan, audit and monitoring reports, study oversight management reports, other related documents and correspondence		
Publication	Statistical information, publication policy, study manuscripts and other related documents and correspondence		
Study Master File version number: Date:			

maintained, with documents filed in a timely manner using an index (Table 4.7), it can greatly help in the successful management of research and aid in the reconstruction of the conduct of the research in the event of auditing, monitoring or regulatory inspection.

The TMF is usually kept at the site where the CI is based along with copies of relevant documents. In a situation where a research study is taking place in more than one site, site-specific documents and approvals from each participating site are kept in another file known as an investigator site file (ISF). The content of the TMF/ISF varies depending on the type of study, for example in clinical trials of investigational medicinal products (CTIMPs), a pharmacy section will be included in the index (Table 4.6). However, a sponsor will usually provide detailed contents of the TMF and ISF in the local SOPs and policies. There is a useful guideline from the European Medicines Agency on setting up a TMF and its contents (European Medicines Agency 2017).

Data Collection, Analysis and Management

The validity and usefulness of the results of healthcare research depend on the quality of the data and their robustness in addressing the research questions. It is therefore important that data be collected in accordance with the study protocol and in compliance with GCP. A concerted effort must be made to ensure that the data collected are of high quality, accurate, complete, reliable and consistent. In research, data could be collected directly from participants through interviews, questionnaires and patient diaries. Other sources of data include medical records, physical examination of participants, observations, laboratory tests and public databases such as death registers. One of the ways to optimise the collection of high-quality data is through identifying and addressing problems that could lead to poor data quality. Some of the major problems in data collection that could result in unreliable results, as explained by Friedman et al. (2015), include

- Missing data and incomplete data that could be due to an inability of participants to provide the necessary information, for instance, due to withdrawal of consent or loss of follow-up, or to carelessness in completing data entry forms and inadequate assessment of participant during a physical examination;
- Error which could be due to unintentional actions such as mislabelling of the test sample and error in reading due to poorly calibrated equipment or intentional actions, such as falsification and fabrication of data;
- Variability may be a result of different researchers performing the same tasks using different methods or making entries of dates using different formats or weights with different units; and
- Delayed submission of participant data from the research site in a multi-centre study where a paper-based system is still in use.

Some of the approaches put forward by Friedman and colleagues for addressing this problem include the use of well-designed and tested CRFs. A CRF must relate to the study protocol and truly represent the collection of specified data in the protocol. There is also the need for standardisation in terms of putting in place procedures for performing specific tasks, data format standards such as time and date formats and units of measurement. Other possible solutions suggested are pretesting of data entry and procedures, monitoring and data quality auditing, and defining corrective actions to be taken to address the problems.

It is essential that the sample size agreed on at the planning and design stage of a study be met. As discussed earlier, there is an option of extending the research end date if the sample size is not reached, provided there are enough resources to cover the extended period. Statistical analysis of data based on appropriate sample size will produce sufficient power to draw accurate conclusions from the research findings (Nayak 2010).

In terms of data management, besides ensuring that data generated from the study are of high quality, best practice is to ensure that data generated during the course of research are maintained in safe and secure conditions. The records should be prepared and archived in line with the local procedure as soon as the study is fully completed and made accessible if required for the purposes of auditing and regulatory inspection. The documents stored in archives are important in reconstructing steps if the need arises following study completion.

Study Amendment

An amendment to a research study is a change made to the terms of the research application, the research protocol or any other supporting documents after the study begins. The study is normally considered to start with the commencement of any protocol procedures (Health Research Authority 2017d).

Study amendments can be requested for various reasons, some of which are presented in Table 4.8. An amendment can be classified as substantial or non-substantial depending on the nature of the study and the impact of the intended changes on the

Table 4.8 Some reasons for amending a research tudy

Area of change	Amendment
Design	Changes to design, background, methodologies, inclusion and exclusion criteria, data and sample collection, data transfer, processing and storage, number of participants, extension of study end date beyond period specified in application, change or addition of study arm
Researchers	Changes to CI, PI, other members of research team at research site
Participants	Changes to participant identity, recruitment approach, consent procedure, procedure undertaken by participants, changes to procedure due to safety information to protect participants
Sites	Changes to sites, addition of new site, early withdrawal or termination or closure of study site
Documentation	Changes to study protocol, PIS, consent form, questionnaire, invitation letters and other study documents
Management	Changes to sponsor, funders, legal representative, site management, study equipment and facility arrangements, insurance arrangement, contract and agreement arrangements

safety and integrity of participants, the scientific value of the study and the conduct and management of the study.

It is the responsibility of the research sponsor to determine whether the required amendment is a substantial or non-substantial amendment. Researchers must report intended amendments to the sponsors as soon as the need is identified and forward the relevant documents to the sponsor for review and amendment classification. Once a study sponsor has reviewed and classified an amendment, the researcher can send the amended documents to the REC that granted initial study approval. The researcher can only implement the amendment after receiving a favourable amendment opinion from the ethics committee or IRB.

Research Oversight Management

Oversight management is a process aimed at ensuring a research study is conducted to the highest scientific and ethical standards. It involves setting up a specific management group to guarantee that a research study is managed and delivered to the agreed-upon scientific and ethical values defined in the study protocol. The nature of the oversight used in a study depends on the type of study, the number of research sites and associated risks. For instance, oversight set up for a multi-centre clinical trial that will run for many years will be different that for a non-drug study. The most common oversight management groups or committees include trial management committees (TMGs), trial steering committees (TSCs) and independent data monitoring committees (IDMCs). However, it is essential that appropriate oversight management be established based on the need for the particular research study. In the Institute of Medicine (2002) recommendations, the best systems approach to research oversight is one that involves researchers, an ethical review board and funders. In any research where oversight is needed, it is best practice to define it in the protocol, and a detailed study monitoring plan must be agreed by the researchers with the sponsor before approval is given to commence the study.

Research Reports

These are reports that researchers are expected to send to the REC or IRB that reviewed and approved the study. These include the following items.

Annual Progress Report

In a non-clinical trial of an investigational medicinal product study, that is, a non-drug study, the researchers are expected to send an annual progress report to the ethical review body that approved the study. This report should be submitted annually until the ethics committee is informed of the end of the study. The due date for the report is usually 30 days following the anniversary of the date on which the study was given a favourable opinion. Some ethical review bodies have a form detailing the information requirements for this report. This information includes the commencement date of the study; if the study has not started, then the reason for the delay should be provided. Other information is whether the study has been completed, the number of sites in the study, the number of participants recruited, the participants who withdrew, safety information, amendments and other developments in the study that the researchers wish to report to the committee (Health Research Authority 2017c).

Annual Safety Report

In a CTIMP, researchers are expected to send annual safety reports to the ethical review body that issued a favourable opinion on the study and the regulatory authority that issued clinical trial authority (CTA). The due date for this report is usually the anniversary of the first CTA approval. The reports must cover safety information, information on adverse events and adverse reactions, suspected serious adverse reactions (SSARs), suspected unexpected serious adverse reactions (SUSARs) and serious adverse events (SARs). The format and details of this report are available in the ICH E2F guideline (ICH Harmonisation for Better Health 2005).

Final Report

The definition of the end of study is usually defined in the study protocol. Depending on the type of research, in most cases the end of a study is often defined as the date of the last visit of the last participant or completion of any follow-up monitoring and data collection. The end of study notification and a summary of the final report of a research outcome in both CTIMPs and other research studies are expected to be submitted to the ethical review body that approved the study. It is the responsibility of researchers to prepare and submit the final report of their study, whether it is positive, neutral or negative, in a timely manner to appropriate body (Friedman et al. 2015). Some ethics committees recommend that the report be submitted within a year of the conclusion of the research (Health Research Authority 2017c). In a situation where a research study was terminated early, probably due to non-compliance with the GCP, inaccurate or incomplete data collection, falsification of records and failure to adhere to the study protocol, provision of a final report is at the discretion of the sponsor.

The research community has provided some guidelines to assist researchers in reporting study findings (Norris et al. 2015; European Medicine Agency 2006). The aim of the guideline is to ensure that sufficient information about the rationale, design, sample population and conduct be captured to enable the intended audience to understand the results, assess the adequacy of the methods used in the study and learn from the results. To fulfil this aim, researchers are expected to view their findings critically and avoid publication bias. These include overinterpretation and playing down adverse findings. The reports should contain an introduction, literature review, discussion, limitations, conclusion and references.

Benefits of Research in Health Care in Africa

The benefits of healthcare research in Africa are enormous and beyond the scope of this book. The following discussion aims at providing insight into how research could change patient safety and healthcare quality and impact the quality of life in general in the region. Research will help healthcare professionals in the region to systematically build knowledge and test treatment efficacy, participate in research activities, have an impact on health policy and service delivery, enhance understanding of daily practice, become a critical consumer of the research literature, understand the methods of various research studies including clinical trials and apply this knowledge and precision of research to all their professional practice, thinking and actions (DePoy and Gitlin 2016). Specifically, it will improve healthcare outcomes, promote economic growth and strengthen partnerships for healthcare service development and improvement.

Improving Healthcare Outcomes

Some evidence suggests safer and higher-quality health care is provided by organisations that actively participate in research, embrace a learning culture and implement research findings (Boaz et al. 2015; Krzyzanowska et al. 2011; Ozdemir et al. 2015). Conversely, it is very challenging to improve patient safety and quality of care in healthcare organisations with low or no participation in research. Active participation in research can result in acquiring relevant knowledge, developing essential infrastructure and bringing in required resources that can be used to improve clinical care and services (Rochon and du Bois 2011; Christmas et al. 2010). Downing et al. (2016) demonstrated the positive relationship between patients treated in hospitals active in research and treatment outcomes.

Research is essential in determining which treatments work best for patients. Besides patients, other beneficiaries from research in health care include care providers, healthcare organisations, professional societies, the government and regulatory agencies. There is a strong consensus that research can be used by these beneficiaries to inform the choice of care, provision of care, care coverage, financial planning and policy development (Reynolds 2015). Research can lead to innovations that could be used to improve the health and quality of life of participants and others with similar conditions. It is time for healthcare and non-healthcare professionals in the region to increase their participation in high-quality research studies. This will allow them to test cutting-edge therapies aimed at early detection, prevention and treatment of diseases. This is one of the ways of obtaining radical solutions to the looming challenges and burdens posed by numerous diseases on the quality of life and economy in the region. Thus, healthcare professionals in the region must find a better way of engaging their patients and the public in research, particularly because it is not ethical to carry out research on diseases specifically suffered by the African population on any other continent without any compelling need (Friedman et al. 2015). Secondly, as asserted by Downing et al. (2016), patients who participate in research are likely to achieve better outcomes irrespective of allocated treatment. Research is therefore a core component of safety and quality improvement in health care. Patient safety and healthcare quality improvement in African health care will represent impossible goals unless healthcare staff in the region take centre stage in designing, conducting and reporting cutting-edge research and applying the study outcomes in their daily practice.

Improving the Economy

In addition to a better quality of life, high-quality research can also provide great economic benefits. For instance, it can lead to further development and transformation in the pharmaceutical sector. The value of the African pharmaceutical industry was projected to reach $30 billion by 2016 (Dong and Mirza 2016). This growth is continuing at a very rapid pace, and a McKinsey report predicted the market will be worth $40 billion to $65 billion by 2020 (Iweka 2019). At the moment, according to a Goldstein Research forecast, the African pharmaceutical market size is set to reach $160.7 billion by 2024 (Lucchini 2018). Africa is now the world's second fastest growing pharmaceutical market, and engaging in high-quality research will be a good and effective return on investment. This will support the expansion of the pharmaceutical industry to other countries in Africa and strengthen the existing pharmaceutical industries in the region, such as in South Africa, Kenya, Morocco and Egypt. This action will also address the huge demand for safe, effective and affordable medicines in the region and reduce the percentage of imported pharmaceutical and medical consumables, which currently stands at over 80% (Byaruhanga 2020). This will help promote the mission of the Federation of African Pharmaceutical Manufacturers Association (FAPMA), inaugurated in 2013, which is to strengthen the pharmaceutical manufacturing capacity required to produce quality, affordable and efficacious medicines for cures and treatment options to fight countless illnesses and diseases affecting Africans today (Dong and Mirza 2016). It will help those suffering from such diseases and illnesses to recover, allowing them to live longer and more productive lives (Durrant 2001).

Effective engagement in high-quality research will also contribute in no small measure to solve the problem of unemployment in the region. The pharmaceutical sector can independently create millions of opportunities in project management, quality assurance management, manufacturing, packaging and sales, laboratory, domestic production, logistics, information communication technology and research roles such as investigators, project management, research administrators, statisticians, research nurse, data managers, clinical trial pharmacists, monitors, regulatory specialists and others, resulting in huge financial returns (Song et al. 2013).

Strengthening Partnership for Healthcare Service Development and Improvement

Active participation in research will encourage partnerships with researchers in other healthcare organisations and higher education institutions within and outside African countries. There are various benefits associated with such partnerships or collaboration. However, building sustainable partnerships requires careful consideration of the diverse issues surrounding relationships and trust between people, the influence of organisational and cultural values and political processes (Hunter and Perkins 2012). A detailed discussion of these issues is beyond the scope of this book as further research will be required for an extensive investigation of them in an African healthcare context.

Nevertheless, forming active collaborative and interdisciplinary research teams can increase the chance of securing research funding. Research shows that a more collaborative approach to applying for funding or research grants is more likely to yield success as most of the funding bodies prefer an interdisciplinary and collaborative research team (Nyström et al. 2018). This application also includes application for research fellowships and scholarships.

Secondly, working in partnership with public or private organisations or universities brings together different skills, expertise, knowledge and experiences which complement one another in the service delivery process. As a result, the decision-making and the entire service delivery process improves significantly (Alison et al. 2013). In light of this, research collaboration will allow sharing of experience with experts outside the region and can contribute to the redesign and development of all aspects of healthcare systems, including infrastructure development. Partnerships with healthcare professionals in developed countries will offer the opportunity to participate in world-class research training and staff development programmes. It will enhance and empower the ability of healthcare staff in the region to design and carry out high-quality and innovative research, improve their approach to leading, managing and developing practices in African health and social services.

Moreover, collaboration between healthcare organisations and academic institutions will enhance the working relationship between healthcare organisations and associated medical schools with affiliated teaching hospitals. This relationship has the potential to align the research, education and clinical care mission of academic institutions and healthcare organisations and ensure that medical research breakthroughs are immediately translated into patient care and treatment (Dzau et al. 2010). The combination of in-depth knowledge of healthcare sectors and academia within and outside Africa can lead to the design and implementation of innovative and high-quality medical education and training systems.

Barriers and Enablers to Effective Research in Health Care in Africa

According to the literature, research started in some countries in Africa as early as the mid-1990s. According to the Rockefeller Archive Center (2018), the International Health Division (IHD) of the United States government established a West African research laboratory in Lagos, Nigeria, in 1929 for research projects aimed at the eradication of yellow fever and malaria. In another development, the British government established the West African Council for Medical Research in Sierra Leone, Gambia, Nigeria and Ghana in 1954 (Nwabueze 2003). Certainly, there are similar stories in other countries of Africa, and their involvement in research could very well have started earlier, but a thorny question remains: What is the level of development in healthcare research infrastructure in the region today? The Rockefeller Foundation report shows that medical research facilities in some African countries predate two landmark publications which immensely shaped healthcare research globally: the Nuremberg Code of 1949 and the Declaration of Helsinki of 1964. To date, however, the region remains inept in public health emergency research, as witnessed during disease outbreaks such as the 2015 Ebola virus outbreak in West Africa. As expressed by the World Health Organization (2018), the outbreak exposed a significant gap in research capacity. Considering how far back research started in the region as mentioned earlier, the inability to effectively contain Ebola demonstrated a state of deterioration or stagnation in scientific research instead of advancement. Even though the Ebola virus was first identified in 1976 with sporadic outbreaks reported in the region, little was done until the 2013–2016 outbreak in West Africa, which resulted in more than 11,300 deaths (World Health Organization 2017). Now it seems little was learned from the outbreak, and there is no resilience system in place to address a repeat or similar occurrence. The current policy and structure that is in place for emergency, public health and health service research which Rhodes and Pollock (2006) described as being essential in monitoring healthcare access and surveillance of diseases remain extremely weak. The COVID-19 pandemic has confirmed these deficiencies, and according to Byaruhanga (2020), the pandemic has really "exposed Africa's inadequate capabilities and capacity to manufacture and supply essential drugs and personal protective equipment (PPE) needed to curb the disease".

Thus, the major problem in healthcare research in Africa is that the research infrastructure, that is, facilities, resources and related services, which are the prerequisite for conducting research and promoting innovation, is grossly underdeveloped.

In the African healthcare research landscape, growth is impeded by inadequate human resource capacity, weak regulatory systems, poor technology infrastructure and quality assurance systems, policy incoherence, lack of research funding and financial incapacity. According to Byaruhanga (2020), the lack of financial capacity accounts for the fact that companies make little to no investment in research and development and in intellectual property protection.

The enablers, as reported by Dong and Mirza (2016), include incentives such as preferred public procurement, soft loans and non-fiscal arrangements, support for capacity building and creation of an investment-friendly environment, in addition to human capital development, innovation, development of cohesive policy frame-works, infrastructure development, strengthening national regulatory authorities and establishing an independent medicine regulatory authority. If the continent wants to see leading global pharmaceutical companies build plants in Africa or part-ner with African pharmaceutical companies to manufacture safe, affordable, essen-tial and patented medicines for diseases and sickness in Africa, then putting these enablers in place must be seen as a priority. The report also suggested countries in Africa interested in strengthening their pharmaceutical sector should encourage their pharmaceutical manufacturers to apply for WHO prequalification.

Increased research funding is a major enabler, and this could be achieved by ensuring that the necessary facilities, resources, management and leadership are in place to demonstrate effective stewardship of the existing research funding pro-grammes and grants. Convincing accountability and transparency could illustrate that funding and grants secured for healthcare research were being used solely to support relevant research; in addition, credible evidence of the outcomes from the research findings would very likely boost the confidence of funders and increase the potential for new investments. The topic of barriers and enablers is a very broad one, but it is hoped that the brief reflection on the topic presented here will provoke extensive discussion and lead to taking remedial actions, such as further research, to investigate the common barriers and enablers in the specific culture and environ-ment within countries in Africa.

Conclusion

There remains a profound difference between care that could be delivered if health care in the region were informed by scientific research evidence and the care that is currently delivered in practice. The primary objective of this chapter was to present practical steps for designing, conducting and reporting research with findings rele-vant to improving care outcomes, thereby reducing the difference in healthcare practice. It is anticipated that this chapter will increase the desire to participate in healthcare research among healthcare staff in the region, especially in the younger generation. It will inspire them to develop interest in the field of healthcare research and take concrete steps to increase their research efforts, in the face of all the numer-ous challenges, some of which were mentioned in the preceding sections. This will enable healthcare professionals to embark on studies that will generate outcomes that will lead to safe and quality care and provide research evidence in specific areas where resources could be immediately committed. This will encourage critical thinking about healthcare problems and spur attempts to resolve these problems using solutions generated through research evidence. Further, it will also lead to increases in the publication of research findings, thereby reducing the current knowledge gap in the literature in the region. Ultimately, it is anticipated that researchers and professionals will gain proficiency in applying healthcare research vocabularies in their daily clinical and non-clinical practice and services, thereby strengthening healthcare research capacity and in the long run reshape the history of healthcare research in the region.

References

Ahmed N, Durkina M, Jones H (2018) Standard operating procedure for feasibility assessment and set-up of clinical research at Imperial College Healthcare NHS Trust (ICHT). Imperial College Healthcare NHS Trust, London

Alison P, Cook A, Miller E (2013) Partnership working and outcomes: do health and social care partnership deliver for users and careers? Health Social Care Commun 26(6):623–633

Appelbaum PS, Grisso T (2001) MacCAT-CR:MacArthur Competence assessment tool for clinical research. Professional Resources Press, Sarasota Florida

Bhatt A (2018) Managing conflict of interest in ethics committee. Perspect Clin Res 9(1):37–39

Boaz A, Hanney S, Jones T et al (2015) Does the engagement of clinicians and organisation in research improve healthcare performance: a three-stage review. BMJ Open; 5: ee009415. https://doi.org/10.1136/bmjopen-2015-009415

Booth A, Sutton A, Papaioannou D (2016) Systematic approaches to a successful literature review, 2nd edn. SAGE, London

Bowling A (2014) Research methods in health – investigating health and health services, 4th edn. Open University Press, England

British Medical Association (2007) Confidentiality and disclosure of health information tool kit. BMA Medical Ethics Department, London

British Medical Association (2014) The role of the clinical academic. https://www.bma.org.uk/advice/career/studying-medicine/clinical-academic-careers. Accessed 14 Feb 2017

Brownson RC, Colditz GA, Proctor EK (eds) (2018) Dissemination and implementation research in health translating science to practice, 2nd edn. Oxford University Press, New York

Byaruhanga, J. (2020) How Africa can manufacture to meet its own pharmaceutical needs. https://www.un.org/africarenewal/magazine/september-2020/how-africa-can-manufacture-meet-its-own-pharmaceutical-needs. Accessed 16 March 2021

Car ECJ (1999) Talking on the telephone with people who have experienced pain in hospital: clinical audit or research? Journal of Midwifery Women's Health 29(1):194–200

Christmas C, Durso SC, Kravet SJ et al (2010) Advantages and challenges of working as a clinician in an academic department of medicine: academic clinicians' perspectives. J Grad Med Educ 2:478–484. https://doi.org/10.4300/JGME-D-10-00100.1PMID:2197

Cooper JH (1984) The integrative research review: a systematic approach. SAGE, Beverly Hills

Council for International Organisations of Medical Sciences (CIOMS) (2002) ISBN 92 9036 075 5. International ethical guidelines for biomedical research involving human subjects. CIOMS, Geneva

Creswell JW (2009) Research design qualitative, quantitative, and mixed methods approaches, 3rd edn. SAGE, Thousand Oaks

Department of Health (2011) Governance arrangements for research ethics committees. A harmonised edition. https://assets.publishing.service.gov.uk/government/uploads/system/uploads/attachment_data/file/213753/dh_133993.pdf. Accessed 24 May 2018

DePoy E, Gitlin LN (2016) Introduction to research understanding and applying multiple strategies, 5th edn. Elsevier Inc, St Louis Missouri

Dong J, Mirza Z (2016) Supporting the production of pharmaceuticals in Africa. Bull World Health Organ 94(1):71–72

Downing A, Morris EJA, Corrigan N et al (2016) High hospital research participation and improved colorectal cancer survival outcomes: a population-based study. Gut 16 (0): 1–8.doi:https://doi.org/10.1136/gutjnl-2015-311308

Durrant C (2001) The responsibility of the pharmaceutical industry. Clin Microbiol Infect 7(6):2–4

Dzau VJ, Ackerly DC, Sutton-Wallace P et al (2010) The role of academic health science systems in the transformation of medicine. The Lancet 375(9718):949–953

European Medicine Agency (EMEA) (2006) CPMP/ICH/137/95. ICH topic E3 structure and content of clinical study reports. EMEA, London

European Medicines Agency (2017) Guideline on GCP compliance in relation to trial master file (paper and/or electronic) for content, management, archiving, audit and inspection of clinical trials. http://www.ema.europa.eu/docs/en_GB/document_library/Scientific_guideline/2017/04/WC500225871.pdf. Accessed 2 June 2018

Friedman LM, Furberg CD, DeMets DL et al (2015) Fundamentals of clinical trials, 5th edn. Springer, Cham

Ghooi RB (2011) The nuremberg code – a critique. Perspect Clin Res 2(2):72–76

Glesnce C, Peshkin A (1992) Becoming qualitative researchers: an introduction. Longman, White Plains/New York

Health Authority Research (2021) Research in emergency settings. https://www.hra.nhs.uk/planning-and-improving-research/policies-standards-legislation/research-emergency-settings/. 30 September 2021

Health Research Authority (2017a) Determine whether your study is research. http://www.hra.nhs.uk/research-community/before-you-apply/determine-whether-your-study-is-research/. Accessed 14 May 2017

Health Research Authority (2017b) UK policy framework for health and social care research. https://www.hra.nhs.uk/planning-and-improving-research/policies-standards-legislation/uk-policy-framework-health-social-care-research/. Accessed 14 May 2018

Health Research Authority (2017c) Standard operating procedures for research ethics committees. HRA, London

Health Research Authority (2017d) Approvals and amendments. https://www.hra.nhs.uk/approvals-amendments/amending-approval/examples-of-substantial-and-non-substantial-amendments/. Accessed 31 May 2018

Health Research Authority (2020) HRA and MHRA joint statement on seeking consent by electronic methods. https://www.hra.nhs.uk/media/documents/hra-mhra-econsent-statement-sept-18.pdf. Accessed 17 Oct 2020

Hunter D, Perkins N (2012) Partnership working in public health: the implications for governance of a systems approach. J Health Serv Res Policy 17(2):45–52. https://doi.org/10.1258/jhsrp.2012.011127

ICH Harmonisation for Better Health (2005) ICH E2F guideline. http://www.ich.org/products/guidelines/efficacy/article/efficacy-guidelines.html. Accessed 4 June 2018

Institute of Medicine (1995) Training and work force issues. Health services research: workforce and education issues. National Academy Press, Washington, DC

Institute of Medicine (2002) Responsible research: a systems approach to protecting research participants. Committee on Assessing the System for Protecting Human Research Participants. Federman DD, Hanna KE, Rodriguez L L (eds). The National Academies Press, Washington, DC

Institute of Medicine (2013) The CTSA Program at NIH: Opportunities for advancing clinical and translational research. The National Academies Press, Washington DC

International Conference on Harmonisation (1996) ICH harmonised tripartite guideline for good clinical practice E6(R1). https://www.ich.org/fileadmin/Public_Web_Site/ICH_Products/ Guidelines/Efficacy/E6/E6_R1_Guideline.pdf . Accessed 31 May 2018

Iweka K (2019) Africa's pharmaceutical industry and its potential to create jobs. https://www. africa-ontherise.com/2019/02/africas-pharmaceutical-industry-and-its-potential-to-create-jobs/. Accessed Mar 2021

Karlberg JPE (2009) Study Site Standard Operating Procedure SOP No: P11 Investigators' Meeting and good clinical practice training. Clinical Trials Centre, The University of Hong Kong

Karlberg JPE (2009a) study site standard operating procedure SOP No: P7 study team; Definition of responsibilities. Clinical Trials Centre, The University of Hong Kong

Kim SY, Caine ED, Currier GW et al (2001) Assessing the competence of person with Alzheimer's disease in providing informed consent for participation in research. Am J Psychiatry 158(5):712–717

Krzyzanowska MK, Kaplan R, Sullivan R (2011) How may clinical research improve healthcare outcomes? Annals of Oncol 22 (7):vii10–vii15

Levine RJ (1988) Ethics and regulations of clinical research, 2nd edn. Yale University Press, New Haven

Lucchini C (2018) African pharmaceutical market. https://www.pharmaworldmagazine.com/ african-pharmaceutical-market/. Accessed 16 March 2021

Marshall C, Rossman GB (2006) Designing qualitative research, 4th edn. SAGE, Thousand Oaks

Merriam SB (1988) Case study research in education: a qualitative approach. Jossey-Bass, San Francisco

National Institute for Health Research (2018) Research and impact of research passport and streamlined human resources arrangements. Available from: https://www.nihr.ac.uk/about-us/ CCF/policy-and-standards/research-passports.htm. Accessed 6 June 2018

Nayak BK (2010) Understanding the relevance of sample size calculation. Indian J Ophthalmol 58(6):469–470

Norris JM, Plonsky L, Ross SJ et al (2015) Guidelines for reporting quantitative methods and results in primary research. A Journal of Research in Language Studies 65(2):470–476

Nwabueze RN (2003) Ethical review of research involving human subjects in Nigeria: Legal and policy issues. Ind Intl Comp Law Rev 14(1):87–116

Nyström ME, Karltun J, Keller C et al (2018) Collaborative and partnership research for improvement of health and social services: researcher's experiences from 20 projects. Health Res Policy Sys 16(46). https://doi.org/10.1186/s12961-018-0322-0

Ozdemir BA, Karthikesalingam A, Sinha S et al (2015) Research activity and the association with mortality. PLoS ONE 10(2):1–15

Page P, Carr J, Eardley W et al (2012) An introduction to clinical research. Oxford University Press, Oxford

Parahoo K (2014) Nursing research principles, process and issues, 3rd edn. Palgrave Macmillan, Basingstoke

Reynolds HW (2015) Health services research. In: Guest G, Namely EE (eds) Public health research methods. SAGE, London, p 313

Rhodes KV, Pollock DA (2006). The future of emergency medicine public health research. http:// repository.upenn.edu/spp_papers/106. Accessed 7 May 2018

Rix G, Cutting K (1996) Clinical audit, the case for ethical scrutiny? Int J Health Care Qual Assur 9(6):18–20

Rochon J, du Bois A (2011) Clinical research in epithelial ovarian cancer and patients' outcome. Ann Oncol 22(Suppl 7):vii16–vii19. https://doi.org/10.1093/annonc/mdr421PMID:22039139

Rogers D (2010) Can we trust the evidence? Critical reviewing a research paper. In: Roberts P, Priest H (eds) Healthcare research – a textbook for students and practitioners. Wiley, West Sussex

Royal College of Physicians (1990) Guidelines on the practice of ethics committees in medical research involving human subjects, 2nd edn. RCP, London

Royal Tropical Institute (2011) Collaboration for Evidence Based Healthcare in Africa (CEBHA). http://www.cebha.org/. Accessed 7 May 2018

Shavers VL, Lynch CF, Burmeister LF (2000) Knowledge of the Tuskegee study and its impact on the willingness to participate in medical research studies. J Natl Med Assoc 92(12):563–572

Song PH, Reiter KL, Weiner BJ et al (2013) The business case for provider participation in clinical trials research: an application to the national cancer institute's community clinical oncology program. Health Care Manage Rev 38(4):284–294. https://doi.org/10.1097/HMR.0b013e31827292fc

The Rockefeller Archieve Center (2018) The Rockefeller Foundation: a digital history health. https://rockfound.rockarch.org/yellow-fever. Accessed 7 May 2018

Twycross A, Shorten A (2014) Service evaluation, audit and research: what is the difference? Evid Based Nurs *17(3):65–66*

Wade DT (2005) Ethics, audit and research: all shades of grey. BMJ 330:468–471

Wilkinson AM (1991) The scientist's handbook for writing papers and dissertations. Prentice Hall, Englewood Cliffs/New York

World Health Organization (2001) World Medical Association Declaration of Helsinki Ethical Principles for Medical Research Involving Human Subjects. Bull World Health Organ 79(4):373–374

World Health Organization (2005) Handbook for Good Clinical Research Practice (GCP) Guidance for Implementation. http://apps.who.int/medicinedocs/documents/s14084e/s14084e.pdf. Accessed 14 May 2018

World Health Organization (2018) New training started on conducting clinical research during disease outbreaks news: http://www.who.int/tdr/news/2017/training-on-conducting_clinical_research-during-dx-oubreaks/en/. Accessed 14 May 2018

World Health Organization (2020) Coronavirus disease (COVID-19). https://www.who.int/emergencies/diseases/novel-coronavirus-2019/question-and-answers-hub/q-a-detail/coronaviruse-disease-covid-19 . Accessed 17 October 2020

World Medical Association Declaration of Helsinki (2013) Ethical Principles for Medical Research Involving Human Subjects. JAMA 310(20):2191–2194

Chapter 5
Safety Management

Introduction

Safety is an abstract concept with a broad spectrum; it means different things to different industries (Li and Guldenmund 2018). In the healthcare context, safety can specifically be defined as *"the avoidance, prevention and amelioration of adverse outcomes or injuries stemming from the process of healthcare"* (Vincent 2010). Amelioration connotes enhancement of a healthcare system with an effective and practical response plan in the form of clinical and non-clinical interventions to support a patient who has been injured and the healthcare worker involved. Safety problems in health care have indeed extended beyond the developing countries of Africa; it is a global challenge. The idea of safety issues in health care seems to keep expanding as standards of care improve (Vincent and Amalberti 2015). Today safety therefore means more than avoiding adverse events and patient harms or other forms of damage. It encompasses persistent attempts to reduce errors of all kinds to patients and staff, reduce or prevent risk in the care process and services while pursuing high reliability as an essential component of high-quality care and services (Vincent et al. 2013).

There has been an increase in the use of more scientific and innovative methods to improve the standards of care and services, thereby ensuring care delivered to patients at all times will be the best and safest. As a result, many complications of health care (errors and adverse events harming patients) which were in the past regarded as inevitable consequences of medical intervention due to the nature of medicine and the environments in which medicine was administered (Sharpe and Faden 1998) are now classified as safety issues. There is ample evidence in the literature that some of the incidents and errors that lead to patient harm are actually preventable and, thus, unacceptable (Hofer and Hayward 2002; Cooper et al. 1978; Vincent et al. 2001; Wilson et al. 2005). In other words, these incidents and errors could have produced safe outcomes if they had been handled differently. This is true today as innovations in delivery care coupled with the public and regulatory pressure, especially in the developed countries, have led to better and more effective ways of addressing the problems (Vincent and Amalberti 2015), for instance, health-care-associated infections (HAIs), such as nosocomial and surgical wound infections (Burke 2003) and complications associated with foreign objects left in the body after surgery. Others include falls and traumas, infusion of incompatible blood, catheter-associated urinary tract infections, pressure ulcers, certain infusion-associated infections and mediastinitis after coronary-artery bypass grafting (Milstein 2009; Sullivan and Schoelles 2013; Chopra et al. 2013). Of paramount importance is the fact that many things that initiate or lead to human error can be changed, and many of these changes that can result in safety (work environment improvement, training and use of technology) are within the power of organisational management to make (Bogner 1994).

In Africa, the situation is no different, even on a larger scale. There is currently limited evidence of scientific evaluation of healthcare safety incidents in the literature in the region. Under this circumstance, the scale of the problem may be overgeneralised. However, the situation would certainly be worse when compared with what is happening in the developed countries, bearing in mind that "*human error is the inevitable by-product of the pursuit of success in an imperfect, unstable resources constrained world*" (Dekker 2002). Certainly, health care in Africa, "*there are millions of children and adult patients who may still be suffering from preventable and unacceptable patient harms as a result of counterfeit or substandard drugs, unreliable equipment and practices including inadequate infection control and poor healthcare environment*" (Ente et al. 2010).

In this chapter, safety in health care is explored and aspects of a healthcare system that make safety incident occurrence indispensable are explained. These include the nature of health care, its operations and activities and the fact that the system is operated and managed by humans who are naturally limited in various ways. A safety management system (SMS) and achieving the goal of effective management of safety incidents across the organisation on an ongoing basis is also explained. The components of the system for attaining this goal are elaborated. This includes detailed explanations of individual elements with two essential components, risk control and learning systems. The chapter also provides information on how to set up a system for reporting, monitoring and investigating safety incidents. The implementation of feedback obtained from incident investigation findings to improve an organisation's safety performance is also presented.

Safety in Health Care

Health care by its nature cannot operate in a safe zone for a sustained period for various reasons. Medicine, for instance, has the potential to cause harmful side effects. In addition, as explained by Woloshynowych et al. (2005), the healthcare system in which medications are administered is very complex with a range of activities. According to the author, many of these activities are mostly routine and highly susceptible to error, which can threaten a patient's safety. An example is surgical activity, which has a high level of uncertainty with unpredictable outcomes. Another area of safety concern is the way in which care is delivered. According to Vincent et al. (2013), care is usually delivered by trained professionals working in a multidisciplinary team, using different pieces of technology and operating in an environment governed by various laws and regulations.

Furthermore, the healthcare system is operated by human beings who are limited and therefore prone to making mistakes in certain circumstances by the very nature of the healthcare environment, structure and management (Gaba 2000). Concerns over safety as a result of human involvement in health care has led to an explosion of scientific research in the human factor, which is *"the study of the relationship between humans, the tasks that they perform, the equipment or tools they use to perform those tasks, and the environment in which they perform them"* (Catchpole et al. 2005). Reason's (1995) and Vincent et al.'s (2000) works have dealt extensively with this. As shown in Figure 5.1, from the work of both authors, factors that are known to trigger safety incidents in health care are broadly classified into active failures, workplace conditions and latent conditions. Active failures are errors, mistakes and violations committed by humans at the frontline such as clinicians at the point of care. Workplace conditions are made up of team communication, workload, equipment and individual knowledge and skills. Latent failures are related to management decisions including defences, barriers and safeguards. According to Vincent et al. (2013), these latent failures represent a unique challenge to safety in health care because they are always present in the system.

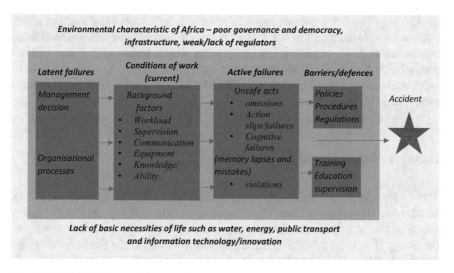

Fig. 5.1 Model of factors influencing human behaviour in healthcare settings in Africa (after Reason 1995, modified from Vincent et al. 2013)

As explained by the author, these latent failures may remain undetected for a period until they are brought to light when there a problem arises or error occurs. However, when any of these factors breaches barriers or defences, the outcome is an accident or adverse event. The barriers or defences could be in the form of human intervention (e.g. supervision and cross-checking activity) or administrative interventions (e.g. policies, procedures or regulations).

Fig. 5.1 shows a list of factors influencing human behaviour in healthcare settings in Africa. The inner layer shows factors that are noticeable in healthcare organisations in both developed and developing countries. The outer layer shows factors peculiar to developing countries, which present additional breeding grounds for safety issues in the region (Ente 2010). These include the prevailing political and socioeconomic factors, which according to the African Union Commission (2015) have manifested negatively in various forms across all sections. As shown in Figure 6.0 this manifestation is expressed in the form of weak governance, poor or absent modern infrastructure and a lack of adequate necessities of life such as water, sanitation, energy, transportation and information communication and technology. These factors will equally influence budget allocations to healthcare sector and certainly limit the resources alllocated to healthcare organisations and staff for safety and quality improvement (Yu et al. 2016).

In general, safety management in health care is still a new concept which requires a lot of scientific research. Healthcare safety is said to be dynamic in nature, a characteristic which makes it different from safety in other safety-critical industries. As explained by Vincent and Amalberti (2015), what is regarded as harm in the aviation industry, for instance, remains the same irrespective of what advances may occur in aviation technology and practice. But in healthcare, the application of technology and innovation to improve standards of care and services could actually lead to increases in the number of events treated as safety issues. A systematic and more proactive approach is therefore required to effectively measure and manage safety issues related to the nature of health care, its operations, environment and associated human factors using technology and innovation. This is to ensure that care is delivered reliably and safely to all patients in a healthcare system, which is the goal of safety management (Health Foundation 2018). This idea frames the concept of SMS presented in the next section.

Safety I and Safety II Concepts

The Safety I concept emphasises learning from incidents, mistakes and errors in health care. This allows lessons to be learned to prevent further occurrence of safety events and harm to patients, staff and organisational reputation. On the other hand, the Safety II concept advocates examining and learning from a good and safe performance achieved in health care and devising a method of sustaining such outcomes. As explained by Braithwaite et al. (2015), to attain a meaningful level of resilience in health care, both Safety I and Safety II must be embedded in the health-care safety and quality improvement practice. In effect, when unsafe or even dangerous incidents are being investigated to determine the root cause, positive or excellent outcomes should also be investigated to ascertain effective ways of sustaining these outcomes and even extrapolating the results to the wider organisation. However, as far as risk assessment goes, both Safety I and Safety II seek to assess and understand the contributory factors and conditions which can cause failures and malfunctions in the system. Safety II additionally makes allowances for the variability in environments where factors are difficult to monitor such as a busy accident and emergency department (Hollnagel et al. (2015). The Safety I concept is therefore a major component of this book.

Safety Management System in Health Care

Li and Guldenmund (2018) provide a description of a SMS, which is centred around three fundamental components: *safety*, *management* and *system*. Safety relates to accidents, adverse events, losses, errors and risks. Management is associated with organisational control and actions aimed at ensuring safety. System, on the other hand, refers to a systematic and proactive framework or model that relentlessly drives people to deliver logical safety management using risk management, system control and system improvement functions.

SMS is an organisation-wide integrated management system designed to achieve effective safety management across the organisation on an ongoing basis. It is widely used in many industries including offshore exploration (Sutton 2012), aviation (ICAO 2009) and nuclear power (IAEA 2009). The term management in SMS is the same concept of management that is applied to other disciplines and involves planning, organising, leading and controlling functions (Robbins and Judge 2012). The system in this case equally shares the same principle of a system where input is run through a process to produce output (waring 1996). This is the core principle of SMS, which explains the appearance of these key words in a description of SMS. The three purposes of SMS are preventing error, controlling risks that lead to errors and continuously improving the performance of the entire system (Li and Guldenmund 2018).

Safety management in the healthcare context is therefore the use of an integrated method or framework of principles, planning, process, activities and procedures to prevent the occurrence of accident, error, injury and harm to patients. It also involves controlling or minimising risks and continuously improving the system. In addition to preventing adverse events and harm to patients, controlling and reducing risks in future patient care processes and services, such a system must also comply with appropriate safety system management standards.

Elements of a Safety Management System

The characteristics of this system as described by the United States National Safety Council (2018) mean that it must be systematic and have an explicit and comprehensive process for safety risk management. It includes the capacity and capability to *"provide for goal setting, planning and measurements of performance against defined criteria"*. In addition to being comprehensive, it must also be well organised and incorporate the necessary organisational structures, accountabilities, policies, procedures and plans (ICAO 2009).

Another essential tool that is indispensable for good SMSs are lagging and leading indicators for measuring, monitoring and managing safety performance. These are also known as reactive and proactive safety measures respectively (Waring 1996). Lagging indicators which measure the end results of SMS processes, policies and procedures are designed to capture things that have already happened (Government of Alberta 2015). Specifically, lagging indicators are a reservoir of an account of incidents or problems that occurred in an organisation (e.g. mortality review, incident reporting and incident investigation system) which, when analysed, provide a means of reflecting on and learning from incidents. This reflection and learning lead to the identification of vulnerability in the system and actions to be taken to correct the problems. In the implementation of changes, caution must be exercised to ensure that such corrective actions not only improve safety but also introduce no new risks into the system (Vincent et al. 2013). On the other hand, leading indicators, such as safety management audit, safety cases, safety walk-arounds and safety culture surveys are the collection of information or signals about future safety performance. This information provides an essential insight for preventing harm before it happens and for the continuous improvement of the safety system. Leading indicators are risk identification, assessment and preventive tools which when used effectively can reduce the risk of harm and they involve proactive monitoring of services on an ongoing basis and in real time to prevent incident, injury and harm (Government of Alberta 205).

From Vincent et al.'s (2013) perspective, an effective SMS designed to measure, monitor and evaluate both healthcare workers and healthcare organisational safety performance with the aim of reducing risk and harm to patients and continuously improve care and services consists of the following elements:

- a safety policy,
- organisational arrangements to support safety,
- a safety plans,
- a means of measuring and monitoring safety performance,
- a means of reviewing safety performance and
- a feedback loop to improve safety performance.

Fig. 5.2 shows an ambitious attempt to adapt and customise a SMS model for a healthcare system from Hale (2005) by replacing individuals' sub-elements with that of Vincent et al. (2013). As shown in Fig. 5.2, the system is made of two broad

Fig. 5.2 Elements of a
SMS in health care.
(Adapted from Hale 2005;
Vincent et al. 2013)

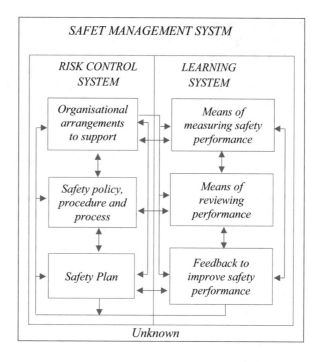

components, risk control and a learning system. In both systems, each element depends on the others and all are supported by the organisation. This entire component of the general system will have to be tested vigorously in real life and examined through scientific research to fine-tune it for African healthcare audiences and settings.

Risk Control System Components

One of the main purposes of any SMS is risk control (Li and Guldenmund 2018). A risk control system, as shown in Fig. 5.2, is made up of functions or tools that can help to proactively identify, assess and monitor risks, adverse events and other incidents that could present a threat to the safety of patients and staff. A risk control system also consists of elements that can be used to initiate an appropriate strategic safety plan for preventing or reducing the chance of identified risks or adverse events occurring.

As explained by Vincent et al. (2013), it is not possible to predict in advance all the possible risks in the process of care and services because the providers are a multidisciplinary team who use various clinical technologies and innovations. The risk control system components in effect aims at allowing for attempts to detect and manage the presence of conditions or vulnerabilities that might result in safety incidents within the system and to prepare an appropriate response in the event of expected or unanticipated risks. In the process, the system creates resilience in the face of unexpected adverse events or occasional and inevitable unforeseen safety failures before resulting in critical incidents or events.

A risk control system as shown in Fig. 5.2 is composed of the following components: organisational arrangement to support safety, safety policy, procedure and process and safety plans.

The Organisational Arrangements to Support Safety

Organisational support is central to the success of a risk control system and SMS. The organisation arrangement includes a well-organised and well-structured SMS across all departments. This includes adequate supervision at all levels to handle all stages of risk processes. These processes are identification, closed supervision required for investigation, implementation of corrective measures, planning and system auditing. Another indispensable function of organisational support is around manpower planning (recruitment, retention of staff and ensuring staff availability always). As emphasised by Hale (2005) for any SMS to be successful, the staff must be committed and motivated, communicate effectively within multidisciplinary team, competent and sufficiently funded. They must have skills and knowledge to deliver safe care and services in compliance with applicable safety policies and be able to respond appropriately in the event of unexpected.

However, in health care, there is an absence of in-house expertise in this discipline and this is a major challenge. There is a need for both clinical and non-clinical staff to be provided in-depth training in all aspects of safety management. This training should include how to proactively risk assess any process of care to be delivered before implementation. It is hoped that an initiative of this nature would allow risk in such a process to be identified and management response plans put in place in advance (Vincent et al. 2013). Moreover, these medical and non-medical staff should be "*seen as important partners in defining how to achieve safety*" but not "*as passive people who should follow the safety rules they are given*" (Hale 2005).

Organisational support for safety should also include allocation and committing of other limited resources such as money and protected time to staff for safety training. A culture that supports safety is another crucial issue that an organisation must focus on. The first of eight NPSA (National Patient Safety Foundation 2015) recommendations for achieving effective safety management and healthcare improvement is establishing and sustaining a culture that empowers and prioritises safety. The organisational arrangement to support safety should therefore embrace improving a culture of safety as an indispensable feature of the system for preventing or reducing errors (AHRQ PSNET 2018).

Safety Policy, Process and Procedure

The strategic decisions, actions and plans that are undertaken to achieve specific healthcare goals within a society are known as health policy (World Health Organisation 2018). Similarly, a formalised written policy for SMS will be an explicit written strategic decision, plans and actions that are undertaken to achieve specific SMS goals in an organisation. This fundamental SMS document must define the organisational vision on safety management and set targets and points of reference for the short, medium and long terms. It must also provide guidelines for acceptable practice in care, accountability on activities relating to safety and clearly define individual responsibility, communication and feedback strategy. Process unlike policy provides explicit written operation of a set of tasks that must be done and how they must be done to ensure adherence to the policy. The procedure, on the other hand, is an unambiguous detail of specific steps, plans and series of actions required to implement the process in compliance with the policy.

Policy, process and procedure are very important components of SMS as they cause staff to feel obliged to implement, monitor and evaluate safety programmes, including response initiatives. They constitute standardised practice across the organisation and reduce or eliminate variation in the practice of care (Vincent et al. 2013). These important components also facilitate compliance with recognised professional practices, serve as a resource for staff, especially new staff members, and reduce reliance on memory, which could cause human error (Irving 2014). As mentioned earlier, one of the advantages of lagging indicators is their ability to identify loopholes in policy, process and procedure, leading to a review of the current operation of SMS and structural improvements to it (Hale 2005).

Safety Plan

A safety plan should clearly define an organisation's mission, vision and objectives of safety management. The safety plan for any treatment should be designed based on a valid understanding of care standards and processes covering all possible risk scenarios that could cause harm. It is on the basis of the safety plan that risk identification and assessment, which are essential components of a risk management system, are specified (Li and Guldenmund 2018). As mentioned earlier, in practice it is difficult, if not impossible, to specify all the possible ways in which things could go wrong or a patient could be harmed in a particular care process due to the nature of health care and various patient conditions. In he light of this, creating an effective safety plan in health care will be very challenging. As explained by Vincent et al. (2013), if all patient care, services, processes and procedures are carefully and properly run through prospective and probabilistic risk assessment, it could provide critical information with a high degree of accuracy on what could go wrong and how potential risk could be effectively managed. This is extensively practised in the oil and gas industry, and the outcome of this assessment is referred to as a safety case.

A safety case is therefore a clear, comprehensive, documented body of evidence which presents a defensible argument that a system is acceptably safe to operate in each environment (Kelly 1998). A safety case "involves a structured, evidence-based argument showing the extent to which hazards have been detected and the associated risks controlled" (Dixon-Woods et al. 2014). In health care, since it is difficult to attain a level of absolute safety, a safety case could be viewed with the aim of reducing all "risks such that they are below a threshold of acceptability" in care and service to achieve a set outcome (Sutton 2012). The best practice would be to begin with less complex clinical cases and progress to complex ones as maturity and proficiency set in due to continuous practice.

Learning System Components

A learning system (Fig. 5.2) is an important component of a SMS. The elements are mainly lagging indicators which focus on learning from failure and non-compliance (Vincent et al. 2017). In other words, a learning system is composed of reactive elements or tools designed to provide insight into the effectiveness of healthcare organisation safety policy, procedures, training and other safety controls and defences. Learning systems in Hale's (2005) SMS will be made up of measuring and monitoring performance, the means of reviewing performance and a feedback loop to improve performance in Vincent et al.'s (2013) safety management model.

Means of Measuring and Monitoring Safety Performance

As discussed earlier, what is classified as safety issues in health care is not static as a healthcare system is both dynamic and complex in nature. It is therefore impossible to prescriptively define those relevant factors that will shape the safety of the system in the future, especially as some of those factors can only be partly specified in advance (Vincent et al. 2013). In addition, it is ubiquitous. When healthcare organisation is said to be safe, it is not clear whether it means it has execellent rating from regulators, it has a good culture, few patient complaints, few incidents, staff are able to manage workload effectively, etc. In Vincent et al.'s (2013) view, in an organisation, "*we might look back to past records of infection rates, surgical complications, evidence of delayed or missed diagnosis, examining trends over months or years. If these rates are stable or on a downward trend, we might infer that this is a safe organisation. However, our information may not be complete. For instance, we might not know if care is equally safe in all wards and departments or if the measures available adequately reflect care across the organisation. In addition, past performance is not a guarantee of future safety*" (Vincent et al. 2013).

In light of the foregoing explanation, the implication is that a healthcare organisation is said to be safe when it can always reliably deliver care to agreed-upon standards constantly across the entire organisation in all specialties. Of course, this is not limited to the safety of patients but that of staff as well, who in the course of their duties are daily exposed to considerable risks, including from handling dangerous chemicals and biological and radioactive substances, which could cause physiological damage to a person's health, or from being exposed to infectious diseases, such as coronavirus.

However, it is wrong to assume that if care is safe in an organisation today, then it will be safe tomorrow because of unstable features of the healthcare system (Vincent et al. 2013). In African healthcare systems, for instance, electricity which was running smoothly can suddenly change due to power cuts in the middle of a surgical operation, and such a power outage can undermine the safety of that operation in different ways. There could also be equipment breakdown, delays in diagnosis and a lack of the necessary clinical information to make decisions at the point of care due to poor healthcare record keeping. Moreover, staff shortage due to sickness could cause safety problems for car crash victims recently brought to the hospital. Another factor could be a sudden change in the mood of staff if, say, they had spent hours in traffic on their way to work or if they haven't received their paychecks yet, which could affect their attitude and behaviour at work.

Measuring and monitoring safety performance in health care should therefore be designed to ensure dynamic and adequate responses to fluctuations in the healthcare system that could violate the safety of patients and staff. The best way of achieving this is, first, by putting a system in place to enable safety to be always monitored and maintained by identifying and managing the known risks. This also includes a system that allows learning, adapting and responding swiftly to cope with those risks that remain unknown as they unfold. Finally, such a system must be able to address conditions that can degrade or render the current risk control measures obsolete and ineffective over a period (Safety Management International Collaboration Group 2013).

Sources of Information for Safety Performance Measurement

Currently there is no formal or scientifically validated SMS model designed for the health sector globally (Hales 2005, Li and Guldenmund 2018 and Vincent et al. 2013). However, Vincent et al. (2013) provided a framework that can provide information that captures a comprehensive and well-rounded picture of a healthcare organisation's safety. As shown in Fig. 5.3, this information can be classified into five dimensions based on the following questions: Has patient care been safe in the past? Are our clinical systems and processes reliable? Is care safe today? Will care be safe in the future? And are we responding and improving?

The framework was first used in England and Scotland (Chatbum et al. 2018), and it is now gradually gaining global recognition. The Patient Safety Institute in

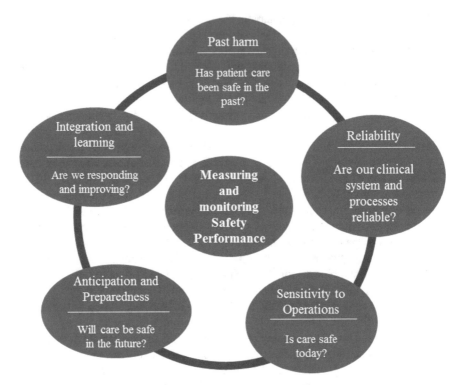

Fig. 5.3 A framework for measuring and monitoring safety performance (reproduced from Health Foundation 2016)

Canada is working on adapting and using it in the healthcare system there (Canadian Patient Safety Institute 2017). The explanation of the components of this framework is provided below.

Past Harm

In measuring and monitoring harm in health care, various patient harms suffered during hospitalisation are considered and various methods could be used to measure them. But there is no single means that can be used to capture the overall level of harm reliably and accurately in healthcare organisations (Vincent et al. 2014). This variation in harm makes its measurement and assessment in a healthcare SMS very complicated. However, some of the methods currently used in measuring and assessing harm in healthcare systems include systematic medical record review, mortality and morbidity review, incident reporting systems, auditing and the use of routine data. These methods may be used in combinations. The harms include treatment-specific harm, harm due to overtreatment, general harm from health care, harm due to failure to provide appropriate treatment, harm resulting from delayed and inadequate diagnosis, and psychological harm and feeling unsafe (Vincent et al. 2014).

Treatment-Specific Harm

This is a type of harm a patient suffers during a specific treatment or management of communicable disease, for instance, a patient who was receiving treatment for Lassa fever was given ribavirin. Instead of recovering, the patient experienced an adverse reaction from the drug. Surgical complications and wrong site surgery are both classified under this type of harm. As admonished by Vincent et al. (2014), the decision on whether harm is treatment-specific should be carefully examined in order not to be confused with a case of inherent risk of treatment. For instance, in African healthcare, infection control remains a struggle, and surgical-site infection due to poor pre-operative and post-operative management is found to be significantly higher in the region compared to what is experienced in high-income countries (Allegranzi et al. 2011). Harm to patients from this infection will be classified as inherent rather than treatment specific.

Harm due to Overtreatment

This is harm associated with the administration of more than one medication concurrently (polypharmacy) to patients with cardiovascular disease (high blood pressure), which is rated by the World Health Organization (WHO) as the world leading global killer, causing more than 75% of sudden unexpected deaths in Africa (World Health Organization 2018a). Spiritual healing and herbal medicines remain an option for patient treatment in some parts of Africa (Omonzejele 2008). Some patients who start treatment on these alternative routes often turn up in hospitals when such treatment fails to produce the expected benefits (Akinkugbe et al. 2010). These sets of patients may experience hazardous interactions of drugs administered in the hospital with the herbal medicine they had previously taken. Alternatively, the herbal medicine could render the drugs administered in hospital ineffective, thereby prolonging or worsening the patient's condition. There is also a chance that a patient will fall if given excessive sedation, leading to harm (Vincent et al. 2013). Another example of overtreatment in the region is *Clostridium difficile* (*C. difficile*) infection, which is suffered by many patients in the region because of prolonged or overuse of antibiotics (Seugendo et al. 2015).

General Harm from Health Care

HAI falls under this category. This is an infection that occurs in a patient during care in a hospital. This happens either because of the treatment a patient is receiving, such as surgical treatment, or from being in a hospital setting. This infection usually does not manifest at the time of admission but is experienced in the hospital or following discharge from the hospital (Nejad et al. 2011). For instance, Chikungunya is a mosquito-borne viral disease which patients can be infected with due to poor hygiene and sanitation in healthcare facilities. Patients can also suffer mental confusion known as delirium because of interventions like surgical operations and taking medication without food or not eating quality food in sufficient quantities. Others include wrong identification of patients, falls and harm due to equipment failure.

Harm due to Failure to Provide Appropriate Treatment

An appropriate treatment in health care is usually evidence-based. In Africa, a lot of diseases have received inadequate scientific research attention that would inform evidence-based treatment, including drugs and vaccines that could be used for treatment, for example, Lassa fever and Ebola virus disease (World Health Organization 2018b). Due to a poor culture of treatment compliance, patients can also suffer harm for not adhering to a treatment regime. There is also a problem associated with a lack of supervision and support. As reported by the World Health Organization (2018c) patients with tuberculosis require a standard 6-month course of four antimicrobial drugs administered with strong treatment adherence, under strict supervision, with support to patients to stop the disease from spreading. Failure to provide effective and rapid treatment to snake bite victims in the region is another example.

Harm Resulting from Delayed and Inadequate Diagnosis

Misdiagnosis, which occurs when a clinician diagnoses a person with the wrong medical condition, is common in Africa. Equally common is a missed diagnosis, which is a failure to diagnose or a delayed diagnosis, although both are unproven assumptions. Often in the region, the first thing patients and even some doctors think of when a patient has a fever is malaria. In some clinics, due to a lack of available and reliable diagnostic means (high-quality rapid diagnostic tests [RDTs]), doctors prescribe malaria drugs erratically even when international policy recommends and emphasises diagnostic testing to identify patients who have fever, but not malaria, in order to seek alternative diagnoses and provide appropriate treatment (World Health Organization 2018d). In some countries there are no national malaria control programmes for regular monitoring of the efficacy of antimalarial drugs in use to ensure that the chosen treatments remain efficacious (World Healthcare Organization 2018e). There is no adequate scientific research information on this either. Under this circumstance, a patient who is diagnosed with *Plasmodium vivax* malaria, for instance, may still be treated with chloroquine, even though *P. vivax* is resistant to the drug. This may lead to treatment failures and relapses.

Psychological Harm and Feeling Unsafe

In health care, adverse events can affect patients and members of staff both physically and psychologically. An example of harm in this category is an adverse event suffered by a patient for not taking a vaccine. As reported by Arevshatian et al. (2007) there has been considerable progress in immunisation in Africa, but routine immunisation coverage targets have still not been met. A study of measles vaccination shows a low vaccination rate, exposing these countries to measles outbreaks (Brownwright et al. 2017). Some of the challenges resulting in low vaccination is the lack of trust in health care, fear of being given fake (counterfeit or poor quality) medicines, insufficient public awareness, weak health care and lack of trust in the healthcare system. Another psychological consequence is clinical depression; for example, one patient developed it following a mastectomy as a treatment for breast cancer (Vincent et al. 2013).

Reliability

Reliability is another important component of measuring and monitoring safety performance under a learning system in a SMS. It is concerned with how a system consistently performs well over a period, in other words how often a system fails to achieve the defined outcomes over time (Vincent et al. 2014). According to the Institute for Healthcare Improvement (2004), reliability in health care is referred to "failure-free operations over time" and can be obtained where care is

- *effective*, as failure could occur by not providing evidence-based care;
- *patient-centered*, as failure could result from not ensuring all clinical decisions are guided by patient preferences, needs and values; and provided
- *in a timely manner,* as failure could result from not reducing wait times and delays in care.

In terms of measurement and monitoring of reliability in health care, it is more complex when compared to other industries such as production, engineering and aviation. In production, reliability has developed to the point where one can assume that products such as mobile phones and microwave ovens will work whenever they are used (Vincent et al. 2013). In computer software engineering, reliability is defined as *"the probability of a component, or system, functioning correctly over a given period of time under a given set of operating conditions*" (Storey 1997). The phrase *functioning correctly* in the preceding definition means working according to a given specification.

In both production and computer software, detailed specifications in terms of input, process and output are clearly defined. The reliability of products in both industries is assessed against this precisely defined specification and standardised process. This is unlike in health care since many processes in health care cannot be properly defined and specified as they usually evolve as opposed to being explicitly designed according to some predefined specification (Vincent et al. 2013). This implies that it is really complicated to define with precision what *functioning correctly* means at a specific moment in time for a patient as the model of treatment course emerges in hindsight when all facts are known (Burnett et al. 2011). Even in cases where protocols and guidelines for clinical care are available, it should be borne in mind that care can only be defined to some degree because it is difficult to specify and standardise treatment for a given condition. Clinicians are also expected to use their experience and expertise to judge and modify protocols or standard procedures in line with patient preferences. Moreover, there are occasions when guidelines cannot or should not be followed. For instance, patients with multiple conditions and problems cannot be easily treated according to strict guidelines, and, alternatively, patients themselves may simply decide against a course of treatment (Vincent et al. 2013). Under this circumstance, reliability can only be applied with variations provided it improves the outcomes or suits patient preference. But there are procedures, such as handover, monitoring of vital signs, hand hygiene compliance, prescription by doctors, timely administration of antibiotics before surgical operations, timely ordering of diagnostic tests and others, that are standardised, so the idea of reliability can be applied (Vincent 2010).

In a study by Burnett et al. (2012) on the reliability of clinical systems for supporting the delivery of care, the findings showed low reliability globally. According to the findings, in the UK 15% of patients' essential clinical information was missing at the point where the clinician made decisions, and essential equipment was missing or faulty in 19% of operations. In the African healthcare system, reliability will certainly be lower considering the poor quality of data reported in the system (Jha et al. 2010). Thus, it has been reported that clinicians in the region take decisions on clinical cases with little or no information from patient records or during equipment failure due to electricity outage.

Lastly the concept of reliability in health care must be carefully thought through as a result of difficulties in defining clearly and precisely many processes of care according to predefined specifications applicable in other industries. In terms of measurement and assessment, audit is currently the best method because it involves assessing compliance of care and services against standards and guidelines. Other methods are observation of critical behaviour and assessment of vital signs and risks (Vincent et al. 2013).

Sensitivity to Operations

Sensitivity to operations is another element of a learning system. It may be defined as alertness and responsiveness to all issues in care that threaten the delivery of quality care and staff safety. Sensitivity makes it possible to identify potential threats to patient safety early and to take action in advance before they mature to the extent of impacting patients adversely (Vincent et al. 2013). Sensitivity is often measured and assessed using methods such as whistleblowing policies and procedures, learning from complaints and safety walk-arounds. Others include employing designated patient safety officers, regular operational meetings, handovers and ward rounds, and briefings and debriefings (Vincent et al. 2013). Sensitivity could also be measured through day-to-day observations and informal conversations with clinical teams and interviewing patients (Weissman et al. 2008, Davis et al. 2013 and Berwick 2013), and real-time monitoring and timeliness of response and feedback.

The word *operations* in this context is different from surgical operations or procedures. This term as used here refers to functions of health care that can hinder quality and safe care. These functions in organisations could relate to patients, staff, organisations and environment. In other words, they are related to issues or problems that take place on a daily or hourly basis in the process of care and services. Examples include verifying patients' identity during admission and monitoring patients' vital signs and medication during treatment, as well as monitoring the team working with patients for signs of discord or fatigue and checking whether standards are being met. These are also related to how an organisation handles staff motivation, remuneration and supervision. It covers the environment in which care is delivered and whether equipment functions properly where equipment breakdown can easily be identified and even a sudden increase in the number of admissions can be effectively managed (Vincent et al. 2014).

Sensitivity to operations requires individual healthcare staff and their team to maintain a high degree of awareness, remain constantly alert and look out for problems that might affect care and take timely action against potential risks. Vincent et al. (2013) suggest that this should be handled in a manner similar to that of driving a car where one continuously monitors actions, attends to the environment and adapts to emergency situations.

Anticipation and Preparedness

Anticipation and preparedness constitute another critical component of a learning system. It involves thinking ahead, anticipating and assessing potential problems and hazards and taking strategic actions to mitigate the risks over time (Hollnage et al. 2006; Reason 1997). In health care, the ability to anticipate and respond to potential problems is important in the delivery of quality and safe care. Clinicians need to apply this when treating patients with complex and unstable conditions as this will allow thinking ahead and being prepared to adjust treatment as the patient's condition changes (Vincent et al. 2013). Anticipation and preparedness are already practised in a department like pharmacy where prescriptions are filled as checks are carried out to ensure correct medication is delivered to the right patient in the correct dosage with clear instructions. It is also practised by surgeons as they make predictions about likely problems to be encountered when preparing for operations, thereby enabling them to mentally prepare for what lies ahead during the operation. The WHO surgical checklist is designed to re-enforce this.

In health care, no specific information is considered adequate or inadequate for assessing future risks of problems in care and services. It is therefore essential that all actions and decisions be taken to be constantly reflected upon and questioned, even when things seem to be going well during operations (Vincent et al. 2014). The sources of information for reflecting on anticipation and preparedness include risk registers, human reliability analysis, safety cases, safety culture assessment and structured reflection.

Integration and Learning

Integration and learning elements provide feedback from learning derived from incidents and use it (feedback) to influence future operations. In health care the sources of incidents or safety information are numerous, for instance, such information could be obtained from clinical teams, wards and departments, including all levels of organisations, even at the executive and board level. Integration and analysis of this information from multiple sources across organisations can generate effective feedback for supporting organisational learning and sustainable improvements compared to a single source (Greene et al. 2012). Moreover, the accessibility of this information to patients and the public, about which they may give their opinion, can produce useful insights or feedback, which may be aimed at an individual member of staff, at a team, an entire department or an organisation. However, the challenge is how best to integrate the wide variety of safety-related data available, what weight to give to different types of information and the decision on the appropriate action to take on this safety information (Vincent et al. 2013).

The sources of safety information for the measurement and assessment of integration and learning are aggregate analyses of incidents, claims and complaints; feedback and implementation of safety lessons by clinical teams; information from regular integration; and reviews of clinical teams and general practice (Vincent et al. 2013).

Other Sources of Safety Performance Review Information

The other means of reviewing safety performance include the following.

Safety Audit and Survey

A safety audit is a tool used in safety-conscious industries to demonstrate that the existing SMS is sufficient to identify, control and prevent harm. A safety audit can be performed internally by appropriate staff within an organisation or externally usually by certified agencies. During the process, relevant records, policies, procedures and operations of the SMS are reviewed and compared with applicable standards for such a system. A safety survey, on the other hand, is an internal evaluation of operational procedures to ensure they are carried out satisfactorily in a safe manner. It can be performed by the staff in the organisation using questionnaires and interviews. Both tools are widely used in the aviation, chemical and production industries. In these sectors effectively managing risks forms part of the license to operate, and safety auditing of a SMS is specifically used to demonstrate to regulatory body a company's fitness to operate (Hales 2005).

Both safety audit and survey outcomes can help in identifying unsafe practices, which can be corrected, thereby preventing potential incidents and associated harms. The findings of these tools can also help in suggesting improvements on safety issues and confirming the system compliance with recommended safety regulations. Both tools will require a lot of scientific evaluation through high-quality research to be adapted and applied in the healthcare sector.

Medical Records and Other Administrative Data Sources

Another source of information for incidents that could be adapted to safety performance review is medical records, which is very important for continuity and improving patient care. As reported by Sari et al. (2007), a systematic case record review detects more incidents and adverse events than other sources, including incident reporting and learning systems. Other sources are administrative data, complaints, health and safety incidents, inquests, claims, clinical audits, routine data, observations of behaviour and informal conversations with patients and families (Vincent et al. 2013). In Olsen et al. (2007), the choice of data source or combination of data sources to be used for detecting risks and hazards should be carefully considered. The report added that the major aim should be how best to integrate and synthesise information from these diverse sources for effective feedback.

Means of Reviewing Safety Performance

As mentioned earlier, a SMS is a new concept in health care, and all aspects of the system are subject to scientific investigation for a better understanding of how each component should be measured and assessed. Such research will also shed light on how these components fit into the entire SMS in the healthcare context. Until then it will remain difficult to hold staff and management responsible for safety performance evaluation as applicable to other industries, such as the oil sector. A safety performance review in this sector is often evaluated against established safety policy, objectives, goals set in the organisational safety plan and clearly defined safety expectations. In health care, a safety performance evaluation is currently carried out through incident investigations, safety surveys and safety audits (Vincent et al. 2013).

How Incidents Happen

The knowledge of incidents and their occurrence often provides valuable guides to investigation and analysis. An understanding of the evolution of incidents is therefore essential in undertaking effective and systematic investigation. Incidents are known to be caused by series of errors, mistakes and violations because of underlying factors known as contributory factors. These factors must be taken into consideration during incident investigations. In health care, several system defences have been put in place to prevent incidents from occurring, and these defences are represented as slices of Swiss cheese in Reason's Swiss cheese model of accident causation (Fig. 5.4).

The organisational factors slice denotes organisational culture and principles (philosophy), policies, procedures and practices, or the four Ps of management

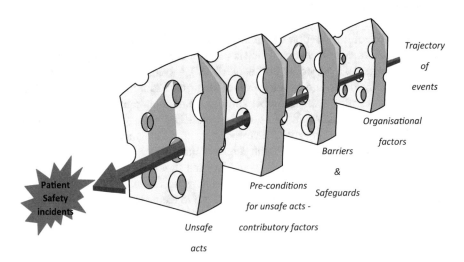

Fig. 5.4 Model of patient safety incidents. (Modified from Reason 2008 and Rothblum et al. 2002)

Fig. 5.5 Pathways to an incident. (Adapted from Reason 2008)

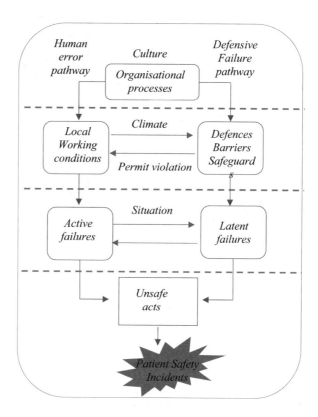

(Reason 2008), which puts safety and quality as the top priority in care and services. The second slice represents barriers and safeguards put in place to prevent incidents and improve the safety of a system. Examples include staff supervision, training and monitoring of staff, including administrative barriers such as rules, policies, regulations and procedures. No matter the strength of the barriers or safeguards, preconditions for unsafe acts (third slice), also known as contributory factors (such as staff motivation, knowledge, experience and ability of staff), can break the barriers or cause the safeguards to fail.

In Fig. 5.5, a scheme adapted from Reason (2008), the incident causal sequence runs from top to bottom, rather than from right to left, as in Fig. 5.4. This sequence is divided into four levels: culture, climate, situation and the incident itself. Of the four levels, organisational culture is the most important; it is a crucial factor that will always trump rules, standards and control strategies (Berwick 2013). Incident pathway is distinguished in human error and defensive failure with their origin from organisational processes. These include but are not limited to policymaking, resource allocation, goal setting, financing, managing, planning, organising and forecasting. These processes are all likely to be influenced by organisational culture and each in turn contributes to human error or defensive failure.

Climate relates to local circumstances, such as working conditions, including the workplace, local management, resources, workforce and defences existing within

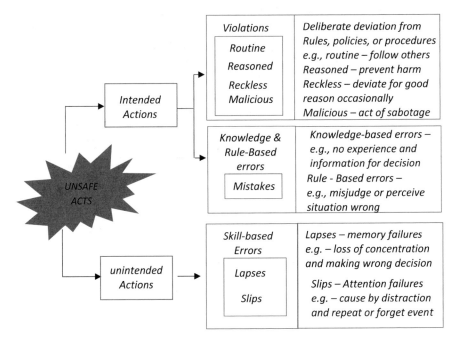

Fig. 5.6 Classification of unsafe acts. (Adapted from Adams 2008 and Rothblum et al. 2002)

the different locations. These also include barriers and safeguards, such as physical protection, innovative safety features, personal protection equipment, administrative controls (regulations, rules and procedures) and frontline operators (medical and non-medical staff). Another important feature of this scheme is the identification and association of the two main failures in the incident sequence to the incident pathways. These active failures, which are errors, mistakes and violations committed by humans in healthcare systems and latent failures, are clearly linked to failures in weaknessess in or the absence of defences, barriers and safeguards.

Human Errors and Their Causes

According to Reason (2008), there is no universally accepted definition of error; the most acceptable definition is that error involves some kind of deviation from upright (trip or stumble), from the current intention (slip or lapse) and from an appropriate action towards a given goal (mistake). Human errors that contribute to unsafe acts in health care are presented in Fig. 5.6 and classified under skill-based errors, knowledge- and rule-based mistakes and violations.

Skill-Based Errors

These are unintended deviations from procedures or plans of action which are so well learned that they are carried out almost automatically. These errors usually take place in the form of lapses and slips. Lapses occur when healthcare staff is distracted while performing a task or is in a hurry or working under duress, which results in memory failures. For instance, an experienced or skilled nurse might forget to complete a patient's drug chart after giving the patient medication because the staff was distracted by a power outage and then failed to complete the drug chart after the power was restored. This could lead to the patient's being given a double dose of the medication because a step (drug chart documentation) was missed in the procedure for drug administration. This nurse might even stand at the patient's bedside for one last action after the power is restored and forget what she had come there to do. Slips, on the other hand, have to do with attention failures, for instance, where a healthcare worker pushes the wrong button on equipment such as a patient monitor.

Knowledge- and Rule-Based Mistakes

Knowledge-based mistakes occur when a healthcare worker encounters a patient with a condition of which he has no experience or knowledge of or adequate understanding of how to handle it. This applies to conditions where there is no routine or rule provided for handling it. This could happen to a junior doctor or an experienced doctor who is faced with a completely novel situation. The decision taken at this point is made consciously based on the degree of knowledge, experience of the staff and available information, which could be inadequate at that point. For instance, a junior doctor who administers an antiepileptic drug (ADE) after misinterpreting a brain electroencephalogram (EEG) as showing abnormality during the patient's first epileptic seizure and without further detailed history from the patient's relatives.

In the clinical treatment of snake bite in a situation where a snake has been brought to the hospital, even an experienced doctor, if care is not taken, may confuse different venomous species, which could lead to wrong treatment. For instance, as described by Warrell (2010), a patient could be given antivenom for the case of hump-nose pit viper (*Hypnale hypnale*) bites instead of for saw-scaled viper (*Echis carinatus*). In this case, the availability of a catalogue of various types of snakes with their corresponding antivenom would have aided the clinician's decision-making, thereby preventing the mistake.

Rule-based mistakes, on the hand, occur when a healthcare professional encounters an unexpected patient, resulting in misjudgement on the part of the healthcare staff, who misapplies a good rule or applies a bad rule based on her perceptions. For instance, considering the management of a snake bite, there is specific venom for specific species of snake. If the snake is not taken to the hospital, the clinician will have to rely on information from the patient or eyewitnesses to identify the snake, which may give the clinician an incorrect understanding of the type of snake involved, leading to the patient's receiving the wrong antivenom. The perception of the clinician could equally be clouded by his/her inability to understand clearly the patient or patient-relative accents. The target audience or actions to be taken usually become apparent after analysis. For instance, safety issues relating to faulty equipment in the operating theatre could be a concern of a department or unit, while safety issues associated with wrong identification of patients during admission can be organisation-wide concerns. However, safety issues that have to do with the supply of counterfeit medicine cannot be easily addressed by an organisation but at the national level or even at the regional and international levels, as in the case of the Ebola virus outbreak.

Violations

As described earlier, errors occur when healthcare staff, despite their best intentions to provide evidence-based, safe and quality care by following the rules, still end up doing something wrong in care that almost or actually leads to patient harm. In contrast, a violation is when a healthcare worker deliberately deviates from rules, policies and procedures during patient care delivery. The reason for the violation could be that the staff wanted to take short-cuts around the system or because that is what others have been doing. For instance, a pharmacist may fail to spend enough time to counsel patients properly before dispensing medication to them.

In routine violations, a healthcare staff may fail to observe hand-washing protocol between patients as this will cause delay. A violation is said to be rationalized when deliberate deviation from protocol or procedure is for a good purpose. For instance, a healthcare worker may witness a car accident on the way to work involving a patient with suspected Lassa fever, rush to the scene and start treating the severely injured person disregarding infection control measures to prevent contact with the patient's blood and body fluids, that is, without wearing face protection such as medical mask or goggles and other protective clothing against blood products such as gloves. A violation is said to be reckless when the health worker is fully aware of the risk involved in each action and then goes ahead with the action anyway. For instance, in the clinical management of snake bite, the victim is expected to be monitored for at least 24 h and not within 1 or 2 h after admission. Malicious violation occurs if a clinician allows a snake bite victim to bleed and die because the relative could not afford a down payment of a certain amount requested instead of being treated immediately when the patient arrives at hospital.

Incident Reporting System

One means of enhancing incident investigation, feedback and learning outcomes of incidents is by building a database that captures every stage of some processes. It is important that incident reporting and management system be set up for reporting incidents that take place in an organisation. This is very important in reviewing safety performance. Electronic and computerised incident reporting and management systems will be preferred to manual record system.

An incident reporting and management system is widely acknowledged to be very beneficial in learning and education. Some of the limitations of this system, according to the literature, include a failure to detect many adverse events (Levinson 2012), ineffective analysis of reports and feedback due to unusually large volumes of incidents reported (Vincent et al. 2013), difficulties with funding and institutional factors including functionality of the information technology platform (Mitchell et al. 2016), and low reporting rates due to clinicians' busy schedules (Nucklos et al. 2007). However, such systems are still recognised as a major resource in improving patient safety in health care, which is why many countries have set up their own local and national incident reporting system (Vincent 2010).

Much emphasis is placed on redesigning a system to focus on and maximise the local learning process instead of solutions for the reporting safety issues (Leistikow et al. 2016). In response to this, Vincent et al. (2013) suggested that an incident reporting system should be called an "information analysis, learning, feedback and action system" to cover the multiple functions of the system. These functions include capturing incidents and providing feedback after processing and analysis. Hale (2005) suggested that such a "learning system should be designed from the output end, by asking the questions: what can we change, what do we need to learn to decide whether to make such a change, and, hence, what information do we need to collect?" Moreover, according to Levinson (2012), the system can be optimised and the importance of safety from received feedback reinforced by encouraging multidisciplinary inputs and effective engagement of clinicians at all levels and hospital boards.

In addition, a good incident reporting and learning system must be easy to use and user-friendly, with well-designed fields to capture relevant information required to answer all safety-related questions in line with the system's purpose and incident investigation goals. It must have relevant in-built functions for data integrity checks to promote data reliability (completeness, consistency, integrity and accuracy), security and confidentiality. The system classification scheme (taxonomy) must support analysis and reporting. It must enable incident investigators to update data with relevant details as things unfold during investigation. Investigators must also be able to run queries and reports such as safety solutions in the form of feedback, as the need arises.

The WHO has also made revolutionary contributions aimed at facilitating the development and management of such systems as well as the extraction and communication of useful knowledge. These contributions include the development of Draft Guidelines for Adverse Event Reporting and Learning Systems, a Conceptual Framework for the International Classification for Patient Safety and a Global Community of Practice for Reporting and Learning Systems (Larizgoitia et al. 2013). The WHO has also identified key data features (Table 5.1) that can provide minimal meaningful learning from patient safety incidents (World Health Organization 2014). However, healthcare organisations are encouraged, in addition

Table 5.1 Key data features of incident reporting system

Data set	Attributes
Incident identification	Identification of person, where and when and agent involved Patient or person involved in incident anonymously identified to respect privacy and confidentiality Date and time incident occurred – date format - DD/MM/YYYY and time 12-h format Where – physical environment or location that incident took place Product, device, equipment or any other element involved in incident with the potential to influence it
Incident type	Descriptive term for clear identification of type of incident (e.g. clinical incident, non-clinical incident, near-miss incident and workplace incident). Classification should be based on a common nature group or shared or agreed-upon features
Incident outcomes	Impact upon a patient, staff member or organisation wholly or partially attributed to an incident patient outcomes – impact upon patient which is wholly or partially attributed to an incident staff outcomes – impact upon staff wholly or partially attributed to incident organisational outcomes – impact upon organisation wholly or partially attributed to an incident
Resulting actions	Actions resulting from an incident: ameliorating action, which is an action taken to compensate for any outcome after an incident preventing action which is action taken to reduce, manage and control any future occurrence
Reporter	Person who collects and writes information about the incident profession and role of reporter at time of incident must be documented.

Adapted from World Health Organization (2014)

to making use of the data sets on Table 6.2, to collect any other relevant information based on their requirements.

Incident Investigation

Incident investigation is an essential tool for safety performance review and assessment as there will always be a chance for unplanned, unintended or unexpected events or incidents to occur during care and service delivery. The reason for this is that health care, like other safety-conscious industries, cannot foresee or track with certainty all potential incidents in all their operations in advance and proactively put in place preventive measures to prevent their occurrence (Vincent et al. 2013).

The two main types of events or incidents that always occur are sentinel events or actual incidents and near misses. Actual incidents or sentinel events are incidents that took place and led to patient harm. Near misses, on the other hand, are incidents that almost took place and resulted in no harm to patients because they did not actually happen. Investigation of both incidents and near misses are very important as it can unveil the underlying, at times hidden, causes of such incidents or near misses. In Leistikow et al. (2016), the expression incident investigation is necessary because incidents are merely "symptoms" pointing to the underlying diseases, and an investigation will help to reveal the diseases and provide insight into the appropriate treatment. Moreover, research shows that systematic incident investigation and analysis has enormously increased the understanding of both causes and prevention of harm (Vincent et al. 2017).

Incident investigation is therefore an essential element in any organisation's safety management strategy. This is because it will illuminate the strategy's strengths and weaknesses by identifying the cause or the presence of conditions that could lead to incidents and offer learning opportunities for safety improvement. It is essential during an investigation to consider why unsafe acts occur. An in-depth systematic incident investigation can lead to the identification of contributory factors which are preconditions for incidents. In light of the triggers of incidents coupled with the human limitations which are responsible for the errors discussed above, it is important that healthcare staff be assured that the investigation not be aimed at finding fault or blaming or shaming the perpetrators but rather to address underlying safety contributory factors that led to the incidents.

Basic Elements of a Good Incident Investigation

In traditional incident investigation, the cause of incidents is usually attributed to material failures and equipment malfunctions, making them the centre of the investigation (Rothblum et al. 2002). In health care there is a shift from this traditional method to systems thinking. Systems thinking in incident investigation encourages the view that incidents are mostly caused by underlying dynamic interactions between multidisciplinary teams, various tasks, the ever-changing landscape of medical technology and innovation, and working conditions, including management, and the regulations and policies that are in place within and across all levels of the entire healthcare system (Jun 2017). In all the factors of causality of an incident just enumerated, the staff members who make up the multidisciplinary team are central. The best approach is one that will encourage their cooperation as it will certainly yield a meaningful outcome that when implemented can strengthen the SMS and improve overall safety.

In addition to a good incident reporting and learning system and other sources of incident reports which are necessary to support incident investigation, other factors are necessary for a successful investigation. These are a clear understanding of the purpose and scope of the incident investigation, investigators who are appropriately trained in incident investigation techniques, and an open and fair safety culture. All these factors must be carefully thought through to achieve reasonable success in any investigation. They and others are covered in the next section.

Understanding the Purpose and Scope of Incident Investigations

It is important that the purpose and scope of an incident or near-miss investigation be clearly defined at the early stage of the investigation. Among other benefits, this will give an idea of the time and resources that will be required for the investigation. The main purpose of any incident investigation is to provide insight into the strength and vulnerability of the SMS and suggest interventions to improve its reliability (Vincent et al. 2017). In addition, the findings may also be used to meet the need to explain and support the families of the harmed patient in fulfilment of the healthcare organisation's moral responsibility and duty of care (Gallagher et al. 2007).

The scope of an investigation defines the area to cover in patient care and treatment. It also specifies how far back the investigating team could go to source for witnesses and evidence. According to Vincent et al. (2017), the scope that will be beneficial in providing rich and quality information to support organisational strategy for the SMS is the one that will cover the analysed safety of a patient's journey over a wider time frame, taking into consideration psychological and social issues and communication with care providers. This should also include close examination of safety issues and contributory factors at different time points in the patient's journey. The study also emphasises the need to "be more proportionate and strategic in analysing safety issues, seek to understand success and recovery as well as failure, consider the workability of clinical processes as well as deviation from them and develop a much more structured and wide-ranging approach to recommendations".

Incident Investigation Team

Incident investigation is more effective when it is carried out by a multidisciplinary team. A team of three to four whose members can demonstrate competence, honesty and cultural sensitivity is recommended. Other qualities and skills of the team are authority and credibility with an objective attitude and good organisational skills. At least one member of this team must be fully trained and experienced in investigation and analysis activities (Adams 2008). These include experience using data collection tools such as interviews, witness statements and carrying out equipment and environment assessment, including layout and position of equipment. Knowledge and experience in reviewing of documents (e.g. incident reports, guidelines, policies, procedures, medical and clinical data, test and scan results, training records, emails, letters, memos) are very useful too. The use of incident investigation analysis tools such as Root Cause Analysis tools, Fishbone, Spider diagrams and WHY techniques is also essential.

Partnerships with patients and families should be encouraged in incident investigation. In the view of Vincent et al. (2013), the involvement of patients and their families in identifying, defining, analysing and prioritising safety issues will provide additional useful information not available to healthcare professionals and expand the horizon of safety to cognitive and emotional needs in patient care. The confidence that patient contributions in this respective will be equally useful is based on their already demonstrated ability to accurately identify adverse events that eluded healthcare professionals' notice. This includes their ability to provide insight into service- and quality-related problems associated with doctor-patient relationship, such as a lack of respect, rudeness and violations of confidence (Lang et al. 2016). Another reason is the perspective patients and families have have brought to the measurement of adverse events (Phillips et al. 2006 and Wetzels et al. 2008).

Open and Fair Safety Culture

The previously mentioned investigation team can only be successful in its endeavours as incident investigators in an open, fair, friendly and welcoming atmosphere or culture, that is, a culture based upon the principles of fairness that promotes transparency and discussion. This is a culture where the ultimate goal of an investigation is to seek information on the contributory factors resulting in incidents and the circumstances of the incident. This is to enable lessons to be learned and steps taken to identify the weakness in the SMS. It is only in such conditions that strategic preventive and remedial safety measures can be designed and implemented to prevent the re-occurrence of similar events and provide a framework for consistency on the SMS (Adams 2008).

An open and fair safety culture is essential during an investigation. This will drive out fear and enable all staff to be treated professionally, equally and respectfully not based on tribalism or who the staff know or in relation to the hospital at the management level or in government. It will enable staff to serve as a resource for safety rather than a potential cause of incidents or problems (Jun 2017). This thought will allow staff to be supported during incident occurrence because their emotional needs will be associated with the fear of ridicule, loss of face and other negative feelings. This support will secure the cooperation of both staff member who were directly involved in the incident under investigation and those who will be contacted as witnesses to speak freely if they are interviewed or give statements with a detailed account of events which led to the incident.

However, without such support, which can only be obtained in an open and fair safety atmosphere, where staff feel they will be hung out to dry after an incident, they will be unlikely to participate effectively in any meeting or grant honest interviews. This can lead to a lack of quality data and, hence, an undesirable investigation outcome (Adams 2008).

As shown in Fig. 5.7, during an investigation, the focus is on addressing key questions necessary in identifying the root causes. These questions are what happened, how it happened, why it happened and where and when it happened. These questions are designed to elicit information to initiate and promote learning and solution development. As illustrated in Fig. 5.7, an investigation begins with the assessment of immediate actions and events, then progresses to the identification of unsafe acts that took place, aspects of human behaviour that contributed to the incident and contributory factors.

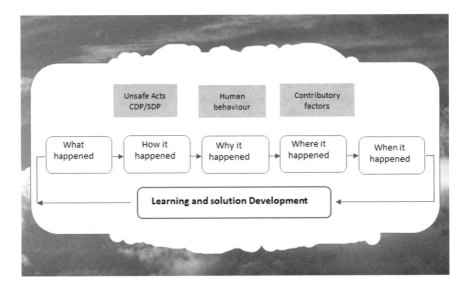

Fig. 5.7 Incident investigation in an open and fair safety atmosphere

Unsafe Acts

The unsafe acts in Fig. 5.7, which are classified in Fig. 5.6, could fall under care delivery problems (CDPs) and service delivery problems (SDPs). CDP failures are those directly related to the provision of care, for instance, a patient reacts to a blood transfusion without the knowledge of the nurse on duty because the nurse was busy with other patients due to staff shortage. SDP failures, on the other hand, are directly related to care provision, for instance, faulty equipment due to failure in the voltage stabiliser.

Human Behaviour

It is important to take into consideration during an investigation human abilities and limitation which can contribute to errors and adverse incidents. For instance, people are good at pattern discrimination and recognition but limited in memory capacity, visual perception and ability to perform arithmetic quickly and accurately. Their performance is equally influenced by many factors including their environment, organisation, technology, skills and experience, stress, motivation and others.

Contributory Factors

The situations associated with increased risk of human errors and unsafe acts are referred to as contributory factors. The classification of preconditions or influencing contributory factors for human errors and unsafe acts are presented in Table 5.2.

Table 5.2 Contributory factors

Factor types	Influencing contributory factors	Examples
Institutional context	Political and economic factors, regulations	Poor or inconsistent policies, corruption leading to mismanagement of funds allocated to healthcare sector, tribal sentiments
Organisational and management factors	Financial resources and constraints, organisational structure, policy standards, safety culture	No unit or department in charge of quality and safety in health care, no existing or poor protocol or clinical guidelines to follow
Work environment factors	Staffing level, workload, lack of equipment, poor power supply	Continual power failure during care, lack of essential equipment
Team factor	Poor leadership, poor communication, team structure	Poor communication between staff, influence of "godfather" with team
Individual (staff) factors	Knowledge and skills, competence, physical, mental and physiological health	Lack of knowledge and experienced staff in different specialties, lack of motivation due to irregular disbursement of payroll paychecks, poor training and education programme
Task factors	Task design and clarity of structure, availability and use of protocol, availability of diagnostic equipment	Non-availability of tested protocol or procedure for tasks, no diagnostic equipment
Patient factors	Condition (complexity and seriousness), language and communication, personality, social factor	Distressed patient, language problems, poor patient–clinician relationship
Technology and innovation	Availability of suitable technology and innovative treatment methods	Non-availability of basic technology and experienced staff to use tools in daily application

Adapted from Vincent et al. (2013)

Feedback to Improve Safety Performance

Feedback is the last component in the learning system under in a SMS (Fig. 5.2). It is an important component as effective feedback can show the extent to which incident investigation findings have been implemented to achieve significant safety improvements (Rothblum et al. 2002). Any learning system without feedback is destined to fail in a short space of time as learning is only complete when there is evidence of practice changes (Hale 2005). Feedback can provide information for assessing whether the goals of implementing a SMS, which are to improve and sustain an organisation's safety performance, over time have been met. Feedback is an essential enabler of incident investigation. As explained by Rothblum et al. (2002), "*nothing dulls an investigator's enthusiasm more than to be working hard to capture useful data only to get the feeling that it's going down some deep, dark hole*". Effective feedback from an incident reporting system is indispensable if healthcare organisations are serious about safety and quality improvement through learning from errors, mistakes and failures in the delivery of care and services (Benn et al. 2009). It is therefore necessary that findings from collecting, analysing and interpreting safety-related data be communicated to appropriate staff at regular safety performance management review meetings. This is to aid decision-making on specific actions required to address the deficiencies or further improve the system (Aderson and Kodate 2015).

Feedback Routes and Timeline

Feedback from incident reporting can be acquired via different routes and on various response timelines. Once patient incidents are captured in the system, the reports are immediately screened, classified into types, assigned severity and stored, and it is at this stage that the feedback route and response time are determined (Wallace et al. 2006). As explained in this paper, incident reports with probable high severity and immediate risk to patients and staff are fast-tracked through rapid and immediate feedback for actions to be implemented as quickly as possible to avoid further harm. In the African healthcare setting, urgent feedback actions could be communicated to a targeted audience through email, meetings, verbal messages and telephone calls. Other mechanisms that could be used include publications such as posters, newsletters and bulletins. Workarounds and debriefing could also be used. Recommendations to address the problem or concern will depend on the outcome of the findings from the incident and could include improving staffing levels and skill mixes, replacement of equipment, training or the introduction of a standard operating procedure or updating an existing one, for example.

Unknown Elements

The unknown elements of the SMS shown in Fig. 5.2 are due to the constantly changing nature of safety in health care (Vincent and Amalberti 2015). So those elements of safety in the system that are yet to be brought to light fall under this section. In addition, a SMS is designed to prevent, reduce and control risk in health care rather than making the healthcare system risk-free. This is because risks are measures of the probability and consequence of uncertain future events, a chance of an undesired outcome (Yoe 2011). Now considering the nature of a healthcare system, its operations and environment with associated human factors, it is therefore impossible to predict the occurrence of risk in a healthcare system with accuracy and certainty. As a result, there are bound to be some safety issues in the system that are not known at present so cannot be represented in the system.

Conclusion

Delivery care and services which are safe to both patients and staff are indispensable in today's health care. To accomplish this, taking into consideration the nature of health care and its operation requires staff, patients and service users who must always remain alert, engage continuously in safety management and research studies aimed at assessing the impact of safety on different areas of care and find better and innovative ways of delivering care safely while continuously improving the system. However, currently, even in industries where SMSs are operational, there is still no sufficient evidence on the effectiveness of different elements of such systems (Shannon et al. 1997). Specifically, in health care the situation is such that currently there is no formal or scientifically validated SMS model designed for the health sector globally (Li and Guldenmund 2018; Vincent et al. 2013). In Hale (2005), the assessment of the current SMS across different settings including health care, the system "is still on pre-scientific stage of development in many aspects" and therefore require more high-quality research from a range of industries for a better understanding of its structure, functions, culture and politics.

SMS as presented in this chapter is therefore an ambitious attempt which is likely to arouse opposition, as was the case in the early stage of the system in the avation sector (Hale 2001) due to the limited scientific evidence on the effectiveness of the different elements. But it is hope that it will generate new and interesting research questions on safety management system in healthcare and facilitate its (SMS) acceptance in the sector. It is also important to note that testing and validation of this system to meet the safety goals and objectives of a complete system of the healthcare sector will not be smooth and easy but is rather bound to be problematic (Hale et al. 1997).

In health care in Africa, much work needs to be done in some areas to lay a foundation for building an effective SMS based on the African context. The first task should be in connection with culture, as emphasised by Berwick (2013). Building an appropriate culture is very crucial and ranks first among rules, standards and control strategies in the field of safety. African health care desperately needs the right culture, which is a culture which embeds just principles into attitudes, behaviours and practices including the design of legislation, regulation, standards, policies and systems. The just culture referred to here is a culture which encourages an open culture (transparency and discussion), a reporting culture (raising concerns) and a learning culture (learning from mistakes). This means a punitive culture based on assigning blame and meting out punishment must be avoided as it contributes to creating a culture of fear, in the sense that when people see what happens to others and if what they see is perceived to be unjust, this will generate fear and lead to a reluctance to report or raise concerns and, consequently, a loss of opportunities to learn. Moreover, a no-blame culture is undesirable as well as it can breed a complacent or casual attitude, which could also impact safety due to a lack of accountability and subsequent abuse of privilege or trust (Royal Pharmaceutical Society 2018).

Currently in the region there is no comprehensive reporting and learning system. It is therefore not clear how patient safety incidents are recorded and investigated and the outcomes used to inform education and learning. The WHO emphasises the importance of this system, provides guidelines for setting one up with clear objectives and explains how to protect to patients' confidentiality and privacy (World Health Organization 2005), but the current safety culture in the region is not yet amenable to the idea of implementing such a system. It is only in an atmosphere of the so-called right culture that such a system and related risk management can be established. The right culture will likewise help in laying the groundwork for a solid scientific foundation of safety in health care in the region, but for now it operates based on assumptions and extrapolations from the experiences of countries outside the region.

References

Adam S (2008) Systematic Incident Investigation Part 1. Paper presentation at lecture on understanding quality, MSc in Quality and Safety in Healthcare, Imperial College London, 11 March 2010

Aderson JE, Kodate N (2015) Learning from patient safety incidents in incident review meetings: organisational factors and indictors of analytic process effectiveness. Safety Sci 80:105–114

African Union Commission (2015) Agenda 2063: the Africa we want. Final report. ISBN: 978-92-95104-23-5. African Union Commission, Addis Ababa

Agency for Healthcare Research and Quality (AHRQ) Patient Safety Network (AHRQ PSNet) (2018) Patient safety primer: culture of safety. https://psnet.ahrq.gov/primers/primer/5/culture-of-safety. Accessed 14 Feb 2018

Akinkugbe OO, Lucas AO, Onyemelukwe GC et al (2010) Nigeria health review 2010: non-communicable diseases in Nigeria – the emerging epidemics. Health Reform Foundation, Nigeria

Allegranzi A, Nejad SB, Combescure C (2011) Burden of endemic health-care-associated infection in developing countries: systematic review and meta-analysis. Lancet. 377:228–241

Arevshatian L, Clements CJ, Lwanga SK et al (2007) An evaluation of infant immunization in Africa. Is a transformation in progress. Bull WHO Past Issues 85 (6): 421 – 500. http://www.who.int/bulletin/volumes/85/6/06-031526/en/ . Accessed 14 Mar 2018

Benn J, Koutantji M, Wallace L et al (2009) Feedback from incident reporting: information and action to improve patient safety. Qual Saf Health Care 18:11–12

Berwick DM (2013) A promise to learn – a commitment to act. Improving the safety of patients in England. Department of Health, London

Bogner MS (ed) (1994) Human error in medicine. Lawrence Erlbaum Associates, Hove

Braithwaite J, Wears RL, Hollnagel E (2015) Resilient health care: turning patient safety on its head. Intl J Qual Health Care 27(5):418–420

Brownwright TK, Dodson ZM, van Panhuis WG (2017) Spatial clustering of measles vaccination coverage among children in Sub-Saharan Africa. BMC Pub Health 17(957):4961–4969

Burke JP (2003) Infection control – a problem for patient safety. *N Engl J Med* 348(7):651–656

Burnett S, Cooke M, Deelchand V et al (2011) Evidence: how safe are clinical system? Primary research into the reliability of system within seven NHS organisation. Health Foundation, London

Burnett S, Franklin BD, Moorthy K et al (2012) How reliable are clinical systems in the UK NHS? A study of seven NHS organisation. BMJ Qual Saf 21:466–472

Canadian Patient Safety Institute (2017) Introduction of the measuring and monitoring of safety (Vincent) framework to Canada. http://www.patientsafetyinstitute.ca/en/toolsresources/pages/measuring-and-monitoring-of-safety-vincent-framework.aspx . Accessed 12 Mar 2018

Catchpole KR, Godden PJ, Giddings AEB et al (2005) Identifying and reduction errors in the operating theatre. Patient Safety Research Programme – Research Contract PS 012. FINAL REPORT 1.0. Queen's Printer and Controller of HMSO 2005, London

Chatbum E, Macrae C, Carthey J et al (2018) Measurement and monitoring of safety: impact and challenges of putting a conceptual framework into practice. BMJ Qual Saf 27:818–826

Chopra V, Anand S, Hickner A et al (2013) Risk of venous thromboembolism associated with peripherally inserted central catheters: a systematic review and meta-analysis. Lancet 382(9889):311–325

Cooper JB, Newbower RS, Long CD et al (1978) Preventable anaesthesia Mishaps: a study of human factors. Anaesthesiology 49:399–406

Davis RE, Sevdalis N, Neale G (2013) Hospital patients' reports of medical errors and undesirable events in their health care. J Eval Clin Pract 19(5):875–881

Dekker SW (2002) The Field Guide to Human Error Investigation. Ashgate, Aldershot

Dixon-woods M, Martin G, Tarrant C et al (2014) Safer clinical systems: evaluating findings learning from the independent evaluation of the second phase of the safer clinical system programme. The Health Foundation, London

Ente C (2010) Human factor and patient safety. Paper presented at the first quarter 2010 Seminar of the Society for Healthcare Quality (SQHN) Nigeria, Lagos, 11–12 February 2010

Ente C, Oyewumi A, Mpora OB (2010) Healthcare professional understanding and awareness of patient safety and quality of care in Africa: a survey study. Int J Risk Safety Med 22:103–110

Gaba DM (2000) Structural and organisational issues in Patient Safety: a comparison of health care to other high-hazard industries. Calif Manage Rev 43:83–102

Gallagher TH, Studdert D, Levinson W (2007) Disclosing harmful medical errors to patients. N Engl J Med 356(26):2713–2719

Government of Alberta (2015) Leading Indicators for workplace health and safety: a user guide. http://work.alberta.ca/documents/ohs-best-practices-BP019.pdf. Accessed 1 Aug 2018.

Greene SM, Reid RJ, Larson EB (2012) Implementing the learning health system: from concept to action. Ann Intern Med 157(3):207–210

Hale A (2001) Regulating airport safety: the case of Schiphol. Safety Sci 37(2-3):127–149

Hale A (2005) Safety management, what do we know, what do we believe we know, and what do we overlook? Safety Science Group, Delft University of Technology, Netherlands

Hale AR, Heming BHJ, Carthey J et al (1997) Modelling of safety management system. Safety Sci 26(1/2):121–140

Health Foundation (2018) Safety management. http://patientsafety.health.org.uk/area-of-care/safety-management. Accessed 15 Oct 2018

Hofer TP, Hayward RA (2002) Are bad outcomes from questionable clinical decisions preventable medical errors? A case of Cascade Iatrogenesis. Ann Internal Med 137:327–333

Hollnage E, Woods DD, Leveson N (2006) Resilience engineering. Concepts and principles. Ashgate, Aldershot

Hollnagel E, Wears RL, Braithwaite J (2015) From safety-I to safety-II: a white paper. The Resilient Health Care Net: Published simultaneously by the University of Southern Denmark, University of Florida, USA, and Macquarie University, Australia. https://www.england.nhs.uk/signuptosafety/wp-content/uploads/sites/16/2015/10/safety-1-safety-2-whte-papr.pdf . Accessed 9 May 2020

Institute for Healthcare Improvement (2004) Improving the reliability of health care. http://www.ihi.org/resources/Pages/IHIWhitePapers/ImprovingtheReliabilityofHealthCare.aspx. Accessed 16 Mar 2018

International Atomic Energy Agency (IAEA) (2009) The management system for nuclear installations: safety guide. N0: GS-G-3.5. IAEA, Austria

International Civil Aviation Organisation (ICAO) Safety Management Manual (2009) Doc 9859, Safety Management Manual (SMM) (2nd edn). https://www.icao.int/safety/fsix/Library/DOC_9859_FULL_EN.pdf . Accessed 8 Jan 2018

Irving AV (2014) Policies and procedures for healthcare organisation: a risk management perspective – PSQH. https://www.psqh.com/analysis/policies-and-procedures-for-healthcare-organizations-a-risk-management-perspective/#. Accessed 15 Feb 2018

Jha AK, Prasopa-Plaizier N, Larizgoitia I et al (2010) Patient safety research: an overview of the global evidence. Qual Saf Health Care 19:42–47

Jun GT (2017) System thinking – a new direction in healthcare incident investigation. https://www.youtube.com/watch?v=5oYV3Dqe0A8 . Accessed 18 Feb 2018

Kelly TP (1998) Arguing safety – a systematic approach to managing safety cases. Dissertation, University of York

Lang S, Garrido MV, Heintze C (2016) Patients' view of adverse events in primary and ambulatory care: a systematic review to assess methods and the content of what patients consider to be adverse events. BMC Family Pract 17:6. https://doi.org/10.1186/s12875-016-0408-0

Larizgoitia I, Bouesseau M, Kelly E (2013) WHO efforts to promote reporting of adverse events and global learning. J Public Health Res 2(3):168–174

Leistikow I, Mulder S, Vesseur J et al (2016) Learning from incidents in healthcare: the journey, not the arrival, matters. *BMJ* 10(1136):2015–004853

Levinson DR (2012) Hospital incident reporting system do not capture most patient harm. Report no: OEI-06-09-00091. US Department of Health and Human Services, Washington, DC

Li Y, Guldenmund FW (2018) System management systems: a broad overview of the literature. Safety Science 103:94–123

Milstein A (2009) Ending extra payment for "never events" – stronger incentives for patients' safety. N Engl J Med 360(23):2388–2390

Mitchell I, Schuster A, Smith K et al (2016) Patient safety reporting: a qualitative study of thoughts and perceptions of experts 15 years after 'To Err is Human'. BMJ Qual Saf 25:92–99

National Patient Safety Foundation (NPSA) (2015) Free from harm. accelerating patient safety improvement fifteen years after to Err is. Human - report of an expert panel. NPSA, London

National Safety Council (2018) Elements of an effective safety management system. http://www.nsc.org/Measure/Pages/elements-of-an-effective-safety-management-system.aspx. Accessed 7 Jan 2018

Nejad SB, Allegranzi B, Syed SB et al (2011) Health-care-associated infection in Africa: a systematic review. Bull World Health Organ 89:757–765

Nucklos TK, Bell DS, Liu H et al (2007) Rates and types of events reported to established incident reporting systems in two US hospitals. Qual Saf Health Care 16:164–168

Olsen S, Neale G, Schwab K et al (2007) Hospital staff should use more than one method to detect adverse events and potential adverse events: incident reporting, pharmacist surveillance and local real-time record review may all have a place. Qual Saf Health Care 16(1):40–44

Omonzejele PF (2008) African concepts of health, diseases, and treatment: an ethical inquiry. Explore J Sci Heal 4(2):120–126

Phillips RL, Dovey SM, Graham D et al (2006) Learning from different lenses: reports of medical errors in primary care by clinicians, staff, and patients. J Pat Saf 2:140–146

Reason J (1995) Understanding adverse events: human factors. Quality Health Care 4:80–89

Reason J (1997) Managing the risks of organisational accidents. Ashgate, Aldershot

Reason J (2008) The human contribution: unsafe acts, accidents and heroic recoveries. Ashgate, Surrey

Robbins SP, Judge TA (2012) Organisational behaviour, 15th edn. Prentice Hall, Englewood Cliffs

Rothblum A, Wheal D, Withington S et al (2002) Improving incident investigation through inclusion of human factors. Working group 1-HFW2002. United States Department of Transportation, Houston

Royal Pharmaceutical Society (2018) Medicines, ethics and practice, 42nd edn. Royal Pharmaceutical Society, London

Safety Management International Collaboration Group (2013) Measuring safety performance guidelines for service providers. https://www.skybrary.aero/bookshelf/books/2395.Pdf. Accessed 6 Mar 2018

Sari AB, Sheldon TA, Cracknell A et al (2007) Sensitivity of routine system for reporting patient safety incidents in an NHS hospital: retrospective patient case note review. BMJ 334(7584):79. https://doi.org/10.1136/bmj.39031.507153.AE

Seugendo M, Mshana SE, Hokororo A (2015) Clostridium difficile infection among adults and children in Mwanza/Tanzania: is it an underappreciated pathogen among immunocompromised patients in Sub-Saharan African. New Microb New Infect 8:99–102

Shannon H, Mary J, Haines T (1997) Overview of the relationship between organisational and workplace factors and injury rates. Safety Sci 26(3):201–217

Sharpe VA, Faden AI (1998) Medical harm. Historical, conceptual and ethical dimensions of iatrogenic illness. Cambridge University Press, Cambridge

Storey N (1997) Safety-critical computer system. Addison-Wesley, London

Sullivan N, Schoelles KM (2013) Preventing in-facility pressure ulcers as a patient safety strategy: a systematic review. Ann Intern Med 158(5 Pt 2):410–416

Sutton I (2012) Offshore safety management – implementing a SMS programme. Elsevier, Amsterdam

The Health Foundation (2016) A framework for measuring and monitoring safety: a practical guide to using a new framework for measuring and monitoring safety in the NHS. The Health Foundation, London

Vincent C (2010) Patient safety, 2nd edn. Wiley, Chichester

Vincent C, Amalberti R (2015) Safety in healthcare is a moving target. BMJ Qual Saf 24(9):539–540

Vincent C, Taylor-Adams S, Chapman E et al (2000) How to investigate and analyse clinical incidents: clinical risk unit and association of litigation and risk management protocol. BMJ 320:777–781

Vincent C, Neale G, Woloshynowych M (2001) Adverse events in British hospitals: preliminary retrospective record review. BMJ 322(7285):517–519

Vincent C, Burnett S, Carthey J (2013) The measurement and monitoring of safety – drawing together academic evidence and practical experience to produce a framework for safety measurement and monitoring – Report N0: ISBN 978-190646-44-7. Health Foundation, London

Vincent C, Burnett S, Carthey J (2014) Safety measurement and monitoring in healthcare: a framework to guide clinical teams and healthcare organisations in maintaining safety. BMJ Qual Saf 23(8):670–677. https://doi.org/10.1136/bmjqs-2013-002757

Vincent C, Carthey J, Macre C et al (2017) Safety analysis over time: seven major changes to adverse event investigation. Implement Sci 12(151):1–10

Wallace LM, Koutantji M, Spurgeon P et al (2006) PSRP feedback from incident reporting systems PS028. Department of Health Patient Safety Research Programme, Final report. Imperial College London, London

Waring A (1996) Safety management system. Chapman and Hall, London

Warrell D (2010) Snake bite. Lancet 375(9708):77–88

Weissman JS, Schneider EC, Epstein AM et al (2008) Comparing patient-reported adverse events with medical record review: do patients know something that hospitals do not? Ann Intern Med 149(2):100–108

Wetzels R, Wolters R, van Weel C et al (2008) Mix of methods is needed to identify adverse events in general practice: a prospective observational study. BMC Family Pract 9:35. https://doi.org/10.1186/1471-2296-9-35

Wilson RM, Runciman WR, Gibberd RW (2005) The Quality in Australian Health Care Study. Medical Journals of Australia 163:458–471

Woloshynowych M, Roger S, Taylor-Adams S (2005) The investigation and analysis of critical incidents and adverse events in health care. Health Care Technol Assess 9(19):1–143.iii. https://doi.org/10.3310/hta9190

World Health Organisation (2005) WHO draft guidelines for adverse event reporting and learning system. World Health Organisation, Geneva

World Health Organisation (2014) Working paper – preliminary version of minimal information model for patient safety. Report no: WHO/HIS/SDS/2014.7. World Health Organisation, Geneva

World Health Organisation (2018) Health topics health policy. http://www.who.int/topics/health_policy/en/. Accessed 16 Feb 2018

World Health Organisation (2018a) Programmes cardiovascular disease. http://www.who.int/cardiovascular_diseases/en/. Accessed 13 Mar 2018

World Health Organisation (2018b) Media Centre Ebola virus disease. http://www.who.int/mediacentre/factsheets/fs103/en/. Accessed 15 Feb 2018

World Health Organisation (2018c) Media centre tuberculosis. http://www.who.int/mediacentre/factsheets/fs104/en/. Accessed 13 Mar 2018

World Health Organisation (2018d) Media Centre WHO releases new malaria guidelines for treatment and procurement of medicines. http://www.who.int/mediacentre/news/releases/2010/malaria_20100308/en/. Accessed 14 Mar 2018

World Health Organisation (2018e) Programmes overview of malaria treatment. http://www.who.int/malaria/areas/treatment/overview/en/. Accessed 14 Mar 2018

Yoe C (2011) Primer on risk analysis: decision making under uncertainty. CRC Press, New York

Yu A, Flott K, Chainani, et al (2016) Patient safety 2030. NIHR Imperial Patient Safety Translational Research Centre, London

Chapter 6
Quality Management

Introduction

Quality management is fundamental to systematic improvement in the safety and quality of a healthcare system. Thus, in spite of the complexity of a healthcare system, the uncertainty of some of its operations and the inherent nature of medicine to cause unwanted and harmful side effects explained in the first chapter of this book, evidence suggests that it is still possible to provide consistent, high-quality medical care to all patients (Kohn et al. 1999). Moreover, even with the challenges posed by the nature of the healthcare environment, its structures, organisations and management (Gaba 2000), ample research evidence shows that safe and quality care can still be achieved (Chassin and Galvin 1998; Schuster et al. 1998; Kohn et al. 1999; Institute of Medicine 2000). In the Institute of Medicine National Roundtable on Health Care Quality as reported by Chassin and Galvin (1998), quality was identified as a problem causing harm to very large numbers of patients. According to the report, once it was established that quality in health care could be precisely defined and measured with a degree of scientific accuracy, a solution was sought through an integrated systematic approach and continuous innovative actions. The solution includes prioritising quality improvement (QI), developing systems to monitor and evaluating care and service performance. This solution has led to re-engineering and restructuring of systems of healthcare delivery, redesign of professional medical education and training. It has also encouraged peer review, incentivising of competition among healthcare organisations and good performance for patient benefits (McIntyre et al. 2001; Loeb 2004). Improving the quality of healthcare is therefore a common objective shared by proponents of improving healthcare system safety worldwide irrespective of its history, structure, resources, accountability and priority (Leatherman and Sutherland 2007).

In Africa there is a growing consensus both at the international and national level that healthcare systems in the region must be improved, but no consensus has been

© The Author(s), under exclusive license to Springer Nature Switzerland AG 2022   137
C. Ente, M. Ukpe, *Essentials for Quality and Safety Improvement in Health Care*,
https://doi.org/10.1007/978-3-030-92482-9_6

established on how best to achieve this (Heiby 2014). To date there is no systematic evidence about quality of care and services in the region and its socioeconomic impacts. The literature on the evolution of QI in the region is very scant despite the fact that the WHO recognises quality of care as essential for improving health outcomes and efficiency and strengthening healthcare systems in resource-poor countries (Leatherman et al. 2010). Currently, evidence of the effectiveness of interventions for QI in the region is either scanty or flawed due to poorly designed research. However, neglect of healthcare processes has been identified as the main issue for low performance in the health systems in the region (Heiby 2014). Insight into the current strategies for QI in the region and other developing countries has also been reported, but it is very patchy. These include traditional methods, such as training and supervision, which are generally limited in rigour and as a result have limited impacts (Bosch-Caplanch and Garner 2008; Rowe et al. 2010; Carlo et al. 2010). Other interventions according to the literature are audit and feedback and staff meetings (Siddiqi et al. 2005; Hashim et al. 2013). In developed countries modern and scientific approaches based on evidence and proactive systems are used to improve quality. These include disease surveillance and self-management. Others are Lean manufacturing, Plan-Do-Study-Act (PDSA), Experience-based co-design (EBCD), and Failure Mode and Effects Analysis (FMEA). These methods have led to tremendous improvements in quality of care and economic benefits (Øvretveit 2009) in developed nations. But research still shows the adoption of these interventions in health care in Africa remains sporadic (Leatherman et al. 2010; Hashim et al. 2013).

This chapter aims to encourage healthcare professionals in the region to continuously assess their practice using modern and scientific approaches as this could reveal areas where further improvements are required. Specifically, it urges professionals in health care to ponder whether their care and services are delivered safely, efficiently, effectively, timely, equitably and whether their integrated care is delivered in a person-centred manner (Institute of Medicine 1990; Edwards et al. 2008; World Health Organization, Organisation for Economic Co-operation and Development, and The World Bank 2018). To achieve this aim, the chapter covers the seven core quality dimensions. It will also cover elements of quality and how they could be measured including evidence of poor-quality care and socioeconomic implications.

Furthermore, interventions and techniques in QI which could be adapted and developed in new quality initiatives in the African healthcare context are elucidated. The evidence of effectiveness of these interventions and techniques is also provided. The chapter also provides some of the barriers in Africa that may need to be overcome in order to enjoy the benefits of advancement in clinical practice and value associated with successful implementation of these tools.

As expressed by Heiby (2014), it is hoped that healthcare workers and those involved in healthcare management will be motivated by quality of care and in turn make it a norm in healthcare service and ensure the model of a learning organisation is fully embedded in the culture of African healthcare systems. Finally, it is also hoped that the resources provided in this chapter will encourage research in quality management in health care in the region among healthcare workers, focusing specifically on identifying the aspects of organisational, cultural, technological, and environmental factors that affect quality of care and services in the region. Moreover, researchers should publish their findings as this will help to reduce the gap in QI literature in the region.

Quality in Health Care

There is growing demand for improving safety and quality in health care in the face of increasing complexity of technology, political influence, and cultural, social and institutional factors (Jamison et al. 2006). Delivering quality health services is essential to universal health coverage (UHC) (World Health Organization, Organisation for Economic Co-operation and Development, and The World Bank 2018). In terms of definition, QIs are defined differently by various people in different settings. But emphasis on all the definitions is on change which brings about improvement, with understanding that all improvements require change but not all changes lead to improvement. Making changes in the most effective way that can result in improvement involves systematic examination of the system to be changed. It requires the use of appropriate methods, tools and factors that best facilitate improvement based on sound scientific knowledge and best clinical skills (Speroff et al. 2004).

According to the Institute of Medicine (1990), quality is defined as "*the degree to which health services for individuals and populations increase the likelihood of desired health outcomes and are consistent with current professional knowledge*". High-quality health services entail reducing harm and wasting resources while providing the right care, at the right time, responding to the service users' needs and preferences. In order to achieve quality and to ensure that care and services delivered to patients in local populations meet the seven core quality dimensions, healthcare staff, especially clinicians, are expected to have a clear understanding of their practice, what they are doing and whether there are better ways of delivering care and services (Manias 2011). The seven core dimensions according to the World Health Organization, Organisation for Economic Co-operation and Development, and The World Bank (2018) are safety, effectiveness, patient-centredness, efficiency, timeliness, equitability and integration of care (**Table 6.1**).

Elements of Quality in Health Care

Advanced knowledge and understanding of the measurement of three fundamental elements of quality, namely structure, process and outcomes (SPO), are very important in effective evaluation of care and service (World Health Organization 2000). In Reeve et al. (2015)) SPO is referred to as Donabedian's three seminal domains of

Table 6.1 The seven dimensions of quality

Dimension of quality	
Safe Avoiding harm or injury to patients from care that is intended to help them, including medication, surgery, health-care-associated infection	**Timely** Reducing wait times and sometimes harmful delays for both those who receive and those who give care, including safe transition into and out of the hospital system
Effective Providing services based on scientific knowledge, high-quality training, guidelines and evidence and which produce a clear benefit; ensuring clinical pathway is followed	**Efficient** Providing care that makes best use of available resources for optimal benefit and avoiding waste, including waste of equipment, supplies, ideas and energy
Person-centredness Establishing a partnership between practitioners and patients to ensure care provided respects patients' needs, preferences and values and that all clinical decisions are guided by patient values	**Equitable** Providing equal care regardless of patient traits such as gender, ethnicity, geographic locations and socioeconomic status; services should reflect evidence on the potential health benefits of the treatment only
Integration of care Ensuring care provided across healthcare facilities are coordinated. Putting in in place care plans and evaluating support plans that cover all the different elements of care that a patient needs –connecting all required related care and service departments or agencies that patients will need	

Adapted from World Health Organization, Organisation for Economic Co-operation and Development, and The World Bank 2018; Institute of Medicine 1990)

health service evaluation. This is in line with Donabedian's proposal that there are relationships between structure, process and outcome based on the suggestion that good structure should promote a good process, and a good process should in turn promote a good outcome.

Structure

Structure covers the physical environment and settings in which care and services are delivered. It is the settings in which the care takes place, including infrastructure, tools and technology. It also covers the resources of the organisation that provides care including financing of care. It may also include administrative and related processes that support and direct the provision of care. It also encompasses things such as the adequacy of facilities and equipment, staffing and the qualifications of clinical staff, administrative structure, level of funding, payment scheme and incentives (World Health Organization 2000; Weinerman 1950). Measurement of structure, such as staff shortages, lack of medications and other essential facilities which are easily obtained, is often the most common criterion used in developing countries to assess quality of care. The assumption is always that given a proper structure, good quality of care will be delivered, but according to Donabedian (2005), this is not the case as a strong correlation between structure and outcome or structure and process is yet to be established. On the other hand, structures by themselves seldom improve the health of a population (World Health Organization 2000).

Process

Process is another element for assessing quality. It is the interaction between healthcare professionals and patients during care and service delivery, including activities carried out. The activities during the interaction are documented and afterwards transformed into health outcomes (World Health Organization 2000). In the process measurement, the impact of the use of technology as well as whether care delivered was evidence-based is considered. In the measurement of process as quality of care, the following criteria are considered and documented: completeness, accuracy and timeliness of care. Clinical history, physical examination, diagnostic tests, justification of diagnosis and therapy offered and technical competence in the performance of diagnostic are also documented. Other criteria include therapeutic procedures such as surgery as well as preventive management in health and illness including coordination and continuity of care (Donabedian 2005).

Even though evidence-based clinical research has increasingly shown the process measures that can lead to better health outcomes, measuring process is still very challenging especially in developing countries (World Health Organization 2000). Process as another element of assessing quality therefore requires a great deal of attention to specify relevant dimensions, values and standards to be used in evaluation. The absence of reliable measurement tools, lack of reliable measurement criteria and the private nature of the doctor-patient consultation pose a serious barrier to the efficient assessment of process (Peabody et al. 2004).

Outcomes

An outcome is the result or impact of care. It is measured in terms of recovery, restoration of function and of survival. It is an important element in evaluating the effectiveness and quality of care. Outcomes demonstrate the power of medical science to achieve a certain result under any given set of conditions as well as the degree to which the most current evidence-based medicine has been applied (Donabedian 2005). Outcomes encompass health status, death or disability. It also covers morbidity and mortality of patients, patient satisfaction or patient responsiveness to the healthcare system (World Health Organization 2000). The choice of outcome as a criterion for quality care must be carefully made bearing in mind its associated limitations. For instance, outcomes such as death can easily be measured, but others, such as patient satisfaction and attitudes, social restoration and physical disability and rehabilitation, are difficult to clearly define and measure. In addition, it is possible to choose an outcome which is irrelevant, such as choosing survival as a criterion for success in a situation which is not vital but likely to result in suboptimal health (Donabedian 2005).

Quality Management System in Health Care

A quality management system designed to improve care and services in health care usually incorporates quality planning, quality control, quality assurance and QI (East London NHS Foundation Trust 2021). An effective quality management system is that which is built based on advanced knowledge and understanding of when and how to use each of the four components and create a balance across them (Shah 2020). In addition to planning, control, assurance and improvement elements, a quality management system requires a learning system. This is a measurement system which enables evaluation to be conducted for a better understanding of what is and what is not working, create appropriate evidence and share knowledge. The success of a quality management system also depends on leadership support, learning culture, skills and other factors that enable improvement (Jones et al. 2021).

Elements of Healthcare Quality Management System

A quality management system in health care comprises four principles: quality planning, quality control, quality assurance and QI.

Quality Planning

Quality planning involves understanding the needs of patients, service users and the population and designing interventions, structures and processes based on evidence to meet those needs.

Quality Control

Quality control requires putting a good system in place to continually evaluate and manage care and service quality and monitor performance in real time comparing the outcomes with agreed standards or benchmarks.

Quality Assurance

This involves the auditing of care and service to check whether agreed standards or requirements are met, including re-auditing where necessary to confirm compliance. This can also involve the use of surveys, inspections of standards and review of clinical incident reports.

Quality Improvement

This involves the use of a systematic and applied approach involving specific methods and tools to continuously improve the quality of care, services and outcomes for patients and service users. This is presented in subsequent sections with various QI approaches and interventions.

Quality Improvement in Health Care

QI is a part of an overall quality management system. QI in health care is a systematic and applied approach to solving a problem employing specific methods, tools and techniques using the time, permission, skills and resources provided to resolve the problem with the aim to improve quality of care processes, pathways and services (Jones et al. 2021). It is a process of obtaining and sustaining excellent outcomes is in line with the needs and expectations of patients and other service users through the combination of evidence-based medicine and advanced clinical skills (Speroff et al. 2004). It means achieving better patient experience and outcomes by employing evidence-based, systematic change methods and strategies to change care providers and organisational behaviour so they support QI (Øvretveit 2009). In Batalden and Davidoff's (2007) view, in addition to incorporating scientific evidence, making changes must be recognised as a crucial part of everyone's job, every day, in all parts of the healthcare system. Based on this view, the authors now define QI as a "*combined and unceasing effort of everyone – healthcare professionals, patients and their families, researchers, payers, planners and educators – to make changes that will lead to better patient outcomes (health), better system performance (care) and better professional development (learning)*".

According to Sainfort et al. (2001), QI should go beyond improving the quality of care and patient safety. It should be extended to improving the entire healthcare setting with the aim of making the environment better and establishing a healthy workplace. According to the author, a healthy workforce in a safe workplace with good ergonomic design and better working conditions can help to reduce stress, thereby resulting in good performance. The understanding and use of QI are therefore important for any healthcare staff and anyone who is interested in improving healthcare quality and patient safety as it has the potential to create a service capable of ensuring "*no needless deaths; no needless pain or suffering; no helplessness in those served or serving; no unwanted waiting; no waste; and no one left out*" (Berwick 2010).

Principles of Quality Improvement

Prior to the application of any QI technique or intervention, it is important to understand the core underlying principles (**Table 6.2**) that are common to most methods, tools or approaches currently being used in health care. All of the principles are high interrelated with the others, and the order is important, although they can be organised differently within a project. Data collected during care and services are what is used to make the case for QI. This is a major determinant of the success of any QI approaches or methods. High-quality data are therefore a very influential element for addressing the essentials. Considering the quality of data in the developing countries of Africa, the application of any of the approaches will be challenging.

Table 6.2   6 Essentials of QI principles

Essential components of quality improvement principles	
Component	Explanation
Identify an opportunity for improvement or a problem	The issues with care and services that require QI can be obtained in various ways including observation, demand from internal customers – board of directors, healthcare managers, clinicians and other employees – and external customers – patients, public, etc. Insight into the problem is based on information obtained from the data
Organised team	There is a need to select a leader and have representatives from all areas in an organisation involved with improvement. The most successful team should be made up of frontline staff supported by QI facilitators with experience in QI methods, approaches, tools, techniques and change implementation strategies and management
Understand current process and systems within organisation	Existing data are essential in assessing whether there are care or service quality issues. Understanding of why such issues or problems exist will require understanding of the current process. One of the ways to do this is to represent the process in a flowchart or mapping tool which will show each step in the process. This will help to identify whether the process or service is standardised, detect variation and eliminate waste or delays. This understanding will be equally helpful in developing a data collection plan
Choose a tool to make changes	Identify steps or variable in process that will have the greatest impact on the entire process and decide on QI tool or method, e.g., PDSA cycles
Implement, evaluate and measure impact of change	The action related to the key process variable is implemented, and more data are collected and evaluated. After implementation of improvement strategy, the team need to determine whether the change has the desired impact; if so, the step is taken to make the action a permanent part of the process
Establish a mechanism for monitoring and support	It is important that a means of monitoring the process on an ongoing basis is put in place so as to maintain the observed improvement and ensure the process or service does not slip back to its initial level of unacceptable performance

Adapted from Health Foundation (2013) and Carey and Lloyd (2001)

Quality Improvement Approaches and Methods in Health Care

Historically, the approaches and methods used in improving quality in the healthcare sector today were initially developed for industrial use and have now been adapted for use in health care, for instance, for production quality control which emerged in the early 1920s. The system was further developed in Japan in the 1940s and 1950s, pioneered by US experts Joseph Juran and W Edwards Deming and the Japanese expert Kaoru Ishikawa (Jones et al. 2021). But the adapted version of the industrial QI methods used in the healthcare sectors today are notably the concepts developed by Don Berwick (Health Foundation 2013). However, evidence-based QI effectiveness and application in health care are gaining momentum with the increasing interest in improvement science (The health Foundation 2011). In the developed nations the body of knowledge about implementing and sustaining the concept of quality and QI in health care has been built into healthcare systems over the years, but this principle is yet to be fully embedded throughout healthcare organisations in the developing nations of Africa.

In Carey and Lloyd's (2001) view, effective techniques involve considering the entire output of the processes of care or services as what provides the basis for action, and they must specifically aim at reducing the variability in the process and shifting the process in the desired direction. The Health Foundation (2013) suggests broader areas to be addressed using the techniques. These include addressing variation in organisations of services or processes which often lead to inefficiency, waste and increased waiting times, reducing variation in clinical practice or processes such as variation from an established evidence-based best practice, which often results in error and harm, as well as poor outcomes for patients. In addition, it is also suggested that additionally, the physical environment in which care is delivered must also be considered. This is important as it will help to assess whether the environment was designed to reduce error and promote patient safety and best practice. However, in circumstances where a variation is considered normal, operation must stay within controlled limits.

There are various QI approaches, methods or tools which have been adapted from other industries for use in the healthcare sector. But as pointed out by Health Foundation (2013) findings, no single method is better than others, and some methods may be used simultaneously. These approaches include the following.

Plan-Do-Study-Act

PDSA (Fig. 6.1) is one of the improvement methods adapted from industry to healthcare settings to assess whether an intervention applied to a process of care produces an improved outcome. PDSA provides a framework for designing a QI intervention (Plan), implementing a change from the intervention on a small scale (Do), evaluating the results (Study) and implementing or altering the intervention accordingly (Act) to improve the system (Jamison et al. 2006). This method uses scientific, structured, iterative and experimental methods to determine whether changes resulting from the study intervention are actually an improvement. The PDSA improvement technique involves testing an intervention on a small scale, observing the impact of tests on other elements and reviewing whether the proposed change in the area actually leads to an improvement before extensive implementation is planned (Speroff and O'Connor 2004). It is popular in healthcare settings and is a simple QI tool that can be used by virtually anyone (Reed and Card 2016).

PDSA is attributed to the work of William E Deming, which evolved from Walter A Shewhart's statistical method for quality control in production called the Shewhart cycle (Shewhart 1939). Upon reviewing the Shewhart cycle, Deming stressed the importance of the constant interaction of the design of products, production, sales and research when considering the quality of products and services. The outcome of this review was initially known as the Deming wheel or Deming cycle but later became known as Plan, Do, Check and Act (PDCA). Furthermore, PDCA was again reviewed, and C, which stands for *Check*, was replaced with *Study*. This is because the word *check* was considered to be limited and inaccurate as it was considered to connote *to hold back*. The word *study* was preferred as it supports learning and improvement, which is the core principle of the process (Moen and Norman 2010). In Taylor et al. (2014), the main difference between PDCA and PDSA is the fact that the former process is a quality control cycle for dealing with faults within a system, while the latter is a process intended for iterative learning and improving a process.

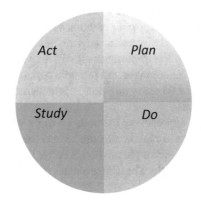

Plan	Plan a change or test aimed at improvement
Do	Carry out the change or test (preferably on a small scale)
Study	Examine the results. What did we learn? What went wrong?
Act	Adopt the change, abandon it or run through the cycle again

Fig. 6.1 PDSA cycles

Use of PDSA Cycles in Health Care

PDSA is widely considered an important method in healthcare QI initiatives (Reed and Card 2016; Walley and Gowland 2004). According to Baxley et al. (2011), PDSA has been successful as a component of QI within health care in specialties such as infection control, diabetes care, surgery, mental health and critical care.

The choice of PDSA in health care stems from the fact that it is a scientific method which promotes small-scale testing and iterative approach. It provides the capability for rapid assessment and flexibility to make changes obtained from feedback, thereby leading to the development of fit-for-purpose solutions. The benefits of small-scale testing are enormous, for instance, it enables learning from one cycle to be used to inform the next cycle and provides users with the freedom to act and learn. It also reduces risk to patients and provides useful opportunities to build evidence for change and engagement of stakeholders as confidence in the intervention grows. Moreover, it presents a pragmatic scientific approach to testing changes in a complex system.

The iterative nature of the testing and evaluation approach makes PDSA a useful QI method for reviewing care interventions essential for delivering high-quality and high-value care (Taylor et al. 2014). Other features of PDSA which make it a better choice in healthcare QI are its simplicity, flexibility and adaptability. These features allow PDSA to be applied to any problem irrespective of size, whether as part of a national or local QI initiative. Another strength of the PDSA methodology is the ability to produce outcomes which can be quickly assimilated for learning and immediately reveal whether an intervention works in a complex social healthcare setting. This enables adjustments to be made where necessary to achieve and sustain the desired improvement (Reed and Card 2016).

As explained in Berwick (1998), even in circumstances where the PDSA cycle fails to deliver the expected outcome, this failure can generate valuable information for building knowledge which could provide insight on what actual success would have provided. In Reed and Card (2016), what is referred to as failure in PDSA could reveal a QI goal that would be impossible to attain, realistic constraints and other related issues to be addressed to achieve an expected outcome. According to their report, these issues could vary from minor changes to the current care process, including major issues buttressing the organisation, or they could be completely new problems outside the scope of the originally identified problems.

The PDSA Cycle as a Component of Clinical Quality Improvement

In clinical QI, there are three initial questions to be answered: First, what are we trying to accomplish? Second, how will we know if the change is an improvement? Finally, what changes can we make that will result in improvements (Fig. 6.2).

These three questions are addressed under a four-stage cycle of plan, do, study and act. These stages are explained below.

Plan: The Plan stage is where a change aimed at the improvement of any clinical area is identified and the objectives to be achieved are set. In other words, a hypothesis or research question is formulated at this stage, including predictions about what will happen and why. The relevance of the objective to the organisation and health care must be taken into consideration. In this cycle, questions as to who, what, where and when to carry out the work to attain the formulated objective are defined. A test plan is also developed identifying the data that need to be collected.

Do: The Do is where the Plan stage is tested or executed. The study protocol is developed at this stage, and the information source and means of data collection are also developed (a data source could include clinical information systems, patients notes, interview, questionnaires and observations). The outcomes of this test are well documented with all problems and unexpected observations. Data analysis equally begins at this stage.

Study: The outcome from the Do stage is examined in the Study stage. This involves completion of data analysis and interpretation of the outcome. It is at this

Fig. 6.2 PDSA clinical improvement model

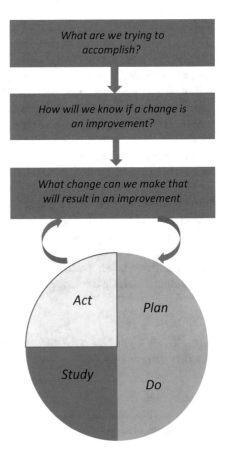

stage that effort is made to identify whether the expected objective has been met and lessons (positives or negatives) to be learned identified. A summary and reflection on the lessons learned are produced.

Act: At this stage, the intervention to be introduced is assessed as to whether it will result in significant improvement in care and patient outcomes. The strategy of change is identified, and the next step is also defined, which could be a repetition of a similar plan or a completely different one.

Designing and Implementing Effective PDSA Quality Clinical Improvement

Research evidence (Lomas et al. 1991; Dopson et al. 1994) shows that the implementation of research evidence or a new intervention aimed at improving clinical practice involves a complex change process of interplay and interdependence of many factors. In McCorMack et al. (2002), the implementation of such an intervention is a dynamic function and simultaneously a "relationship between *evidence* (research, clinical experience and patient preferences), *context* (culture, leadership and measurement) and *facilitation* (characteristics, role and style)".

For effective implementation of the PDSA outcome, close attention must be paid to the design, implementation, barriers and enablers within the intended local implementation settings identified at the earliest stage. This step will enable the influential components that could compromise the effectiveness of this method of quality methods in the environment to be identified and proactive measures planned. The knowledge and understanding of the principles of PDSA which are helpful in its design and implementation is covered in the next section.

Knowledge and Understanding of Principles of PDSA

One of the salient principles of the PDSA methodology worth considering during design and implementation is its similarity to a scientific experimental method. In Speroff and O'Connor (2004), the Plan, Do, Study and Act stages correspond to formulating a hypothesis, collecting data to test this hypothesis, analysing the data, interpreting the results and drawing a conclusion. The implication of this is that the design, implementation and reporting of PDSA should comply with principles that underpin scientific experimentation. Each cycle must therefore follow a framework, systematic and rigorous standards, and principles. While considering the methodological rigour that will guarantee the highest scientific quality of the outcome, such rigour must be carefully balanced against the scale or size of the problem. Emphasis should be placed on the design that will allow sufficient information necessary to reach useful conclusions to be obtained. This information must be useful enough to suggest the next steps to be taken (Berwick 1998).

Based on the foregoing explanation, considerable knowledge and skills may be required to design and implement PDSA successfully. Some of these include critical appraisal, process mapping and FMEA. Others are skills in interviewing, stakeholder engagement, data analysis and reporting. These knowledge and skills will certainly help in acquiring a better understanding of the issue and justification that the area identified for improvement is relevant and fits into organisational priorities and that the organisation will be willing to commit the required resources to carry out the improvement. In addition to human resources, materials, financial and time resources are also required.

Secondly, a combination of some of the aforementioned knowledge and skills will help in conducting investigations and reviewing existing evidence of the use of PDSA at early stages of design to ensure the problem to be solved is correctly understood. It will help to decide whether the problem can be solved with only PDSA or in combination with other QI tools.

The knowledge, understanding and skills mentioned in this section will be found to be very useful in data management, monitoring and documentation, as discussed in the next section.

Data Management, Monitoring and Documentation

As PDSA is scientific method used in implementing and testing the effects of proposed interventions in patient care, it will require effective data management, monitoring and documentation at every stage of development, design and implementation. These activities will prove decisive in achieving the overall aims and objectives of projects. This is because they will

- lead to early and timely identification of problems and challenges (internal and external threats) that will be encountered and provide insights on both the problems and challenges. This will include how best to resolve them through ongoing assessment and feedback from brief interviews with the team involved in the implementation and evaluation of the intervention;
- support scientific quality. The primary purpose of PDSA is to learn, reflect and provide useful recommendations for the next step. In situations where the expected outcome is not achieved, PDSA will help to determine whether this was due to poor implementation or whether the proposed intervention was successfully implemented but only less effective; and
- provide a reservoir of knowledge to support the organisation's quality agenda and spread the learning to other healthcare organisations.

Research recognises the relevance of using guidelines in the PDSA methodology to capture information related to series of interdependent steps and key principles in applications (Walshe 2009). Furthermore, methodological scientific rigour and its application and reporting increase the scientific legitimacy of the PDSA (Taylor 2003). Methodological scientific rigour provides succinct standards for the critical appraisal of PDSA QI protocols and publications (Speroff et al. 2004). Table 6.3 provides guidelines on some of the parameters to be documented in a typical PDSA project. The guideline is not a final and validated product, so it could be reviewed and improved over time in the course of its application.

Effective monitoring is indispensable, and this will be best done by developing monitoring indicators for each stage. This can be in the form of a checklist or questionnaire, which will permit the project team to collect data for performance evaluations. More specifically, monitoring will provide important information on whether the project is progressing according to plan.

Other Quality Improvement Approaches and Methods

In this section, other tools and techniques for QI are discussed briefly. These are experience-based co-design, statistical process control (SPC), Lean manufacturing, business process re-engineering (BPR), Six Sigma, total quality management (TQM) and FMEA.

Experience-Based Co-design

This method is drawn from participatory design and user experience to bring about QI in healthcare organisations (Donetto et al. 2015). EBCD enables staff and patients (or other service users) to co-design service and care pathways in partnership. The stages in EBCD include setting up a project, obtaining data on staff experiences through observational fieldwork and in-depth interviews, and gathering patient and carer experience through observation and filmed narrative-based interviews. Other stages are showing staff an edited film of patients' views about their experiences of services, bringing staff, patients and carers together in a first co-design event to identify priorities for change and reviewing events (Bate and Robert 2007; King's Fund 2011)

Statistical Process Control

SPC is a branch of statistics and a versatile tool for QI. SPC can help different stakeholders in a healthcare system manage change and improve patient outcomes (Thor et al. 2007). It combines rigorous time series analysis methods with graphical presentation. This method of data presentation makes it easy to understand findings even to a lay decision maker. In this SPC presentation, variation can easily be

Table 6.3 Guidelines for data management, documentation and monitoring of PDSA for effective design and implementation

Study and team details	
Project title	Insert project title
Specialty	Document area of care affected
	List policy or standard operating procedure related to problem
Design	
Aims and objectives	Identify problem project is trying to address or resolve
	Identify suspected root cause
	Document how it is related to organisational priorities
	Justify if it is not tied to organisational priorities
	State aim clearly
	State questions to address
	State predicted outcomes or expectations
Design and development team	QI department team
	Clinical and specialty team
	Management team
	Champion/facilitator
Staff team skills and knowledge	Is PDSA only sufficient for the project or is it going to be used with other QI methods? List associated QI if applicable
	Identify skills and knowledge required for project from problem identification and design to implementation, evaluation and reporting
	Identify training needed for staff
Target population and method of data collection	Define target populations
	Design and document detailed data collection to verify or assess problem and its extent
	Document sources of data, e.g. case record review, survey and interview
	Document criteria to be used to demonstrate problem
	Define timeline and how to assess progress
	Document evidence of problem's existence and impact
Finding and verifying causes	Document data analysis and findings
	Design additional data collection on causes if required, including use of interviews and questionnaire for subject cause data
	Document criteria used in demonstrating each cause
	Identify how each cause impacts the problem
Proposed intervention	Identify management's feasibility limit on the proposed solutions, for instance, the funding they are willing to allocate to the problem
	if required, extend willingness to make change if new staff or re-organisation is required
	Present proposed solution to relevant team and document feedback
	Document selected solution
Implementation	
Implementation, evaluation and monitoring	Design and document implementation and evaluation plan
	Define criteria to evaluate proposed intervention
	Define and document steps to make proposed intervention operational
	Identify and document what will be classified as success
	Identify indicator to monitor solutions

(continued)

Table 6.3 (continued)

Study and team details	
Outcome	
Expected and unexpected outcome	Document whether aims and objectives have been met and to what extent
	Identify and document surprises
	Identify and document next steps to take
	Document conclusion

identified. As a result, it can help in determining whether changes made led to improvements. SPC uses control charts to manage healthcare processes. These kinds of charts are used to routinely analyse data sets and show boundaries for acceptable variation in the process. One of the benefits of using control charts is that they do not require as much data as traditional statistical analysis, which relies on large aggregate data sets (Benneyan et al. 2003).

Lean

Lean, also known as Lean production, Lean enterprise, and Lean thinking, is another QI tool. It was adapted from automobile manufacturers, where it is used in managing production processes. Lean is used for QI in health care. It allows staff to systematically review their practices and workplace and take decisive action to eliminate activities that do not add value to care and services. Lean steps comprise accurate evaluation of the process of care and services, identification of every step in the process and specification of the values desired by customers (internal and external). Other steps are distinguishing value-added steps from non-value-added steps and eliminating waste so that every step can add value to the entire process of care and services (Institute for Healthcare Improvement 2005). As summarised by Nave (2002), Lean uses five steps in improving quality: identifying value, a value stream, flow, pull and perfection. Lean methodology can be used to better match demand to capacity, develop flexibility to respond to unavoidable variation, and avoid "batching", that is, too much work in some areas and too little in others (Womack and Jones 2007).

Business Process Re-Engineering

The term *business process re-engineering* is often used interchangeably with process improvement, business transformation, process innovation and business process redesign. As defined by leading experts in the field, BPR is *"analysis and design of work flow and processes within and between organisations"*, *"a methodological process that uses information technology to radically overhaul process and thereby attain major business goals", "overhauling of business processes and organisation structures that limit the competitiveness, effectiveness, and efficiency of the organisation" and "fundamental analysis and radical redesign of business processes to achieve dramatic improvements in critical measures of performance"* (Grover et al. 1993). BPR is very important in health care because it offers the opportunity to consciously rethink why care and service are delivered in a certain way, rather than tampering, fine-tuning or speeding up what is already in place (Grover and Malhotra 1997).

Six Sigma

This is a systematic process-focused strategy for business improvement. It can be used to improve care process, eliminate waste, reduce costs, and enhance patient satisfaction (van den Heuvel et al. 2006). Six Sigma focuses on reduction of variation to improve the entire process and resolve problems associated with business. It uses five steps namely define, measure, analyse, improve and control known as DMAIC to gain complete understanding of the problem. Then employ statistical tools to understand the variations of a process and elements influencing the process. Once the fundamental and most important cause of the defects or problem is detected, data is analysed, solution is developed and implemented. The outcome is then judged whether the changes are beneficial or another change is necessary. Once it is confirmed the changes resulted in improvement, it is monitored to avoid the occurrence of unexpected changes (Nave 2002).

Total Quality Management

TQM is another QI method. It is also known as Continuous Quality Improvement (CQI). The focus of this approach is on quality and the role of people within an organisation to develop changes in culture, process and practice. It applies to the entire organisation, including factors such as leadership, customer focus, evidence-based decision-making and a systematic approach to management and change (Health Foundation 2013).

Failure Mode and Effects Analysis

In health care, most of the methods used to assess risk and analyse adverse events are retrospective in nature. In the field of engineering, FMEA has been used to pro-actively analyse risk in a process, and this method has recently been used in health care (Fletcher 1997; Apkon et al. 2004). The National Center for Patient Safety of the US Department of Veterans Affairs adapted FMEA to the healthcare setting, resulting in a version known as Healthcare Failure and Effective Analysis (HFMEA). HFMEA is a five-step process which uses a multidisciplinary team to proactively evaluate care and service process. The steps consist of defining the topic, organising an interdisciplinary team, graphically describing the process flow of the topic, conducting a hazard analysis and constructing a decision tree to identify and assess potential vulnerabilities. FMEA uses worksheets to record assessments, including proposed actions and outcome measures (DeRosier et al. 2002). HFMEA can be used to prospectively correct latent system errors before they lead to adverse events (Linkin et al. 2005). It can also be a valid tool for proactive analysis of prescription and adminstration process of chemotherpy (van Tilburg et al. 2006).

Quality Improvement Interventions

Interventions cover techniques, programmes, methods and tools employed in health care to introduce changes that make care and services better for patients and which could also result in productivity increases and financial benefits (Øvretveit 2009). There are various interventions designed to improve quality in health care. The key to making an informed choice about quality-enhancing interventions with successful implementation is advanced understanding and knowledge of the evidence on the interventions' use and effectiveness (World Health Organization, Organisation for Economic Co-operation and Development, and The World Bank 2018). Moreover, it is important to understand which interventions are most likely to result in positive returns on investment. Thus, the evidence must therefore detail the investment and operational costs of implementation as well as the change in revenue and costs that will result from the intervention (Kilpatrick et al. 2005). QI interventions and programmes for health care in Africa discussed in this section include regulatory (Sutherland and Leatherman 2006), clinical governance strategies and programmes (Scally and Donaldson 1998) and interventions related to QI initiatives recommended by the WHO for the Africa region (World Health Organization 2003).

Legislation and Regulatory Interventions

Regulatory interventions in healthcare QI cover various aspects, including target-setting, which means defining the level of performance to attain, and standards-setting, which means defining the level of performance expected from the healthcare organisation being regulated (Sutherland and Leatherman 2006). Legislation can help in the establishment of a new or empowering an existing national body, payment reform, licensing and registration of healthcare professionals, facilities and organisations (World Health Organization, Organisation for Economic Co-operation and Development, and The World Bank 2018). In the developing countries of Africa, regulations can still play a huge role in ensuring quality, the safe and effective use of medicines, vaccines and medical devices and eliminating substandard and out-dated medical products. The governments of some countries have put in place leg-islation and regulatory bodies to ensure healthcare organisations are appropriately resourced to deliver an agreed-upon standard of high-quality care. However, to see more desirable results from the efforts and interventions covered in this section, urgent action is required to review and restructure the legal and judicial system to strengthen and provide a capacity for surveillance and enforcement in the system. In countries in the region with a strong legal system, the following regulatory inter-ventions can prove productive in improving the quality of care and ensuring that minimal accepted standards of care and services are attained.

Professional Regulation

Professional regulation is one of the most commonly used interventions and involves putting a system in place to control entry into the medical profession and officially register healthcare professionals who are licensed to practice. Registration and licensing under the management of professional licensing bodies ensures continu-ing professional development over a lifetime of practice, in line with the Institute of Medicine's (2000) recommendation. Regulation can actually influence behaviour in the delivery of a healthcare service (Brennan and Berwick 1996). The fundamental objectives of professional regulation include fostering continuing professional development, enhancing skills including knowledge and experience, setting stan-dards of clinical competence for practice, identifying the competence of individual professionals and ultimately improving the quality of care and assuring patients and the public about the competence of those in the professions responsible for their care (Sutherland and Leatherman 2006).

Accreditation

This consists of an onsite evaluation involving the assessment of the healthcare organisation's compliance with pre-established performance standards and verifica-tion of the organisation's improvement activities (Sutherland and Leatherman 2006). The evaluation is usually carried out by trained peer reviewers from an exter-nal body, usually a non-governmental organisation (NGO) such as the Joint Commission International, which has accredited some healthcare organisations in Africa (Joint Commission International 2018). Accreditation, which is usually con-ducted every 2 to 3 years, is a widely used external oversight for standards-based QI in health care (World Health Organization 2003). It is usually designed to promote continuous improvement within participating organisations with standards set to a level considered to be optimal and achievable (Sutherland and Leatherman 2006).

Research shows that accreditation programmes improve the process of care provided by healthcare services (Alkhenizan and Shaw 2011), and it has been confirmed by Sutherland and Leatherman (2006)) that accredited or certified organisations generally provide a higher quality of care.

Inspection

Inspection is an external oversight process where experts from regulatory bodies make visits to healthcare organisations to evaluate their performance. It is aimed at checking compliance with professional standards and outcomes for patients and other service users. It also includes assessing the competence of professional staff, the capacity of facilities and workers and the presence of resources to maintain and sustain a safe and high-quality healthcare environment. Standards accessed during an inspection can help to identify structural elements that are foundational for quality, such as clean water sources, reliable power and backup capacity, adequacy of skilled workers, clear management responsibilities, complete medical records and accountability (World Health Organization, Organisation for Economic Co-operation and Development, and The World Bank 2018). Visits may be announced or unannounced, and satisfactory inspections often result in certification with penalties and sanctions imposed on organisations for non-compliance (Sutherland and Leatherman 2006).

Clinical Governance

The concept of clinical governance, as healthcere quality strategy, is one in which heathcare organisations are expected to take responsibility for continually improving the quality of their care and services and safeguarding high standards of care by creating a healthcare environment where a desirable level of performance can be consistently achieved (Scally and Donaldson 1998). As recounted by (Ente 2010), the successful integration of clinical governance QI initiatives, which has positively impacted the way care is delivered and tremendously improved the quality of care and services in the National Health Service (NHS) in the UK, can produce a similar outcome in healthcare organisations in the developing countries of Africa. Some of these clinical governance components, which have been extensively discussed in previous chapters in this book, are audit and feedback, standards and guidelines, incident reporting, and research and development. Others are discussed in what follows.

Patient, Family and Carer Engagement

"*Patient engagement refers to the process of building the capacity of patients, families and carers, as well as healthcare providers, to facilitate and support the active involvement of patients in their own care, in order to enhance safety, quality and people-centredness of health care service delivery*" (World Health Organization 2016). Patient engagement can inform the patient and provide education and policies, including enhancements in service delivery and governance (Bombard et al. 2018). It is associated with a better patient experience and adherence to treatment, which may contribute to better outcomes (Jha et al. 2008; Glickman et al. 2010). Effective engagement and empowerment of patients, families and carers can also enhance the accountability of the healthcare professionals and healthcare organisations involved and improve the doctor–patient relationship. The healthcare professionals in the region will therefore have to explore how best to engage and empower their patients, families and carers and decide on the scope, extent and nature of their involvement, including the impact of sociocultural factors in the process through the use of focus groups, surveys and interviews.

Healthcare Information Communication and Technology System

The impact of a healthcare information communication and technology system (HICTS) on QI in health care is enormous. As summarised by Alotaibi and Federico (2017), this includes clinical decision support (CDS) systems, which have a range of in-built functions, such as notifications, alerts and reminders, patient-specific clinical summaries, documentation templates, investigation and diagnostic functions for enhancing decision-making and clinical workflow. Computerised physician order entry (CPOE), for instance, is an important component of QI with a CDS tool that can promote safe, efficient and evidence based care including ability to create electronic record order sets and reduce the rate of medical errors (Wright et al. 2012). A patient data management system (PDMS) helps to reduce prescribing time while increasing the time spent on direct patient care and reducing the occurrence of medical errors. A study by Jamal et al. (2009) shows HICTSs also increase clinicians' adherence to guidelines. These and many other HICTS products, too numerous to mention, could be implemented across healthcare organisations in the developing countries of Africa but will require, first and foremost, improvements in the necessary infrastructure, such as Internet access and a reliable power supply (Ali et al. 2011). Secondly, healthcare workers must have the vital literacy skills needed to operate these systems and have the ability to obtain basic health information required to make appropriate healthcare decisions during treatment; patients, on the other hand, must be literate enough to follow medical instructions and read and comply with prescriptions (Sampson et al. 2013).

Teamwork and Collaboration

In modern health care, with medicine and health care increasing in complexity, high-quality care is increasingly dependent on high-quality and effective collaboration between multidisciplinary teams of clinical, non-clinical and allied healthcare professionals (Wright and Hill 2003). Effective teamwork involves the combination of different functions and people working together in a way that enhances the performance and quality of the team and is often associated with the quality and safety of care delivery systems (Rosen et al. 2018). Collaboration, on the other hand, is made up of common features including the sharing of ideas for improvement, interactive testing of actions leading to improvement and mutual learning across multiple healthcare organisations. For instance, the Ethiopian Hospital Alliance for Quality, which was a national collaborative sponsored by Ethiopia's Federal Ministry of Health, included 68 hospitals, of which 44 showed a 10% improvement in a 10-point measure of patient satisfaction (Linnander et al. 2016).

WHO Africa Region Initiatives

WHO Africa Region interventions of quality care improvement in health care are incorporating into the training programmes of all healthcare staff the knowledge, skills and attitudes required to deliver quality care, offering incentives and establishing a national quality of care programme.

Education, Training and Supervision of Workforce

The introduction of training programmes aimed at imparting and developing knowledge, skills and attitudes in healthcare workers required to deliver quality care is one of the initiatives to encourage continuous improvement of the quality of care and service in Africa (World Health Organization 2003). This is also a core component of clinical governance. Healthcare professionals are expected to keep their knowledge and skills up to date throughout their working life by taking part regularly in educational activities which further develop and enhance their skills, competence and performance (Wright and Hill 2003). These are the most common interventions to improve the quality of health care in low- and middle-income countries such as Africa, although effective supervision in the region can be hindered by poor coordination, inadequate management skills, ineffective management teams, lack of motivation, health worker resistance, supervision workload, incomplete implementation of project interventions and loss of leadership (Rowe et al. 2010).

Incentive Programmes

Incentives programmes are a WHO regional initiative to encourage continuous improvement of the quality of care and service in Africa (World Health Organization 2003). Incentives, which may be financial or non-financial, are designed to enhance behaviours and motivate and encourage individuals, teams, departments or organisations to perform well and improve their outcomes (Abduljawad and Al-Assaf 2011). Reputational (non-financial) incentives capture how recipients are viewed by others, while financial incentives reward recipients with additional income for achieving the defined performance target; both are often combined in initiatives to improve quality of care (Allen et al. 2018). This intervention can also be used in the developing countries of Africa to encourage healthcare staff to strive for better performance, but, as Scott et al. (2011) warned, such programmes should be designed, evaluated and implemented with caution. They must be customised, well focused, suitable to the culture and setting of the organisational environment and worthwhile to attract interest and encourage participation (Abduljawad and Al-Assaf 2011).

Morbidity and Mortality Reviews

Morbidity and mortality reviews are a QI strategy which could be built into the components of the national QI programmes in the region recommended by WHO.

Morbidity and mortality review processes usually enhance understanding of quality-of-care problems associated with patient deaths (Kobewaka et al. 2017). These reviews represent a collaborative learning mechanism and transparent review process for clinicians to examine their practice and identify areas of improvement, such as patient outcomes and adverse events, without fear of blame (Higginson et al. 2012). Morbidity and mortality reviews are used to bring together clinical staff to review, for learning purposes, what contributed to complications for a patient during treatment or that resulted in death (Higginson et al. 2012). Such reviews promote active recognition of mistakes or errors and provide an opportunity to learn as well as to identify the required process improvement. These reviews lead to improved collaboration and communication, aid team-based learning and result in changes in record keeping and governance relevant to patient safety (Francois et al. 2016; Higginson et al. 2012).

Conclusion

High-quality care is dynamic in nature. Darzi (2018) described it as a moving target, so any healthcare system that stands still is bound to fall back. Thus, the only solution is to embrace the challenge and accelerate change that can effectively guarantee the longevity of present and future healthcare systems. In a World Health

Organization, Organisation for Economic Co-operation and Development, and The World Bank (2018) report, this means developing an integrated approach whereby stakeholders, namely governments, hospital management, healthcare workers, patients and the public, can work together with a sense of urgency to achieve high quality of health care and services for the benefit of patients and the community. It is hoped that this chapter has provided an insight into how to initiate and execute a successful QI project.

Various interventions and techniques exist for QI in health care, but, as revealed in this chapter, these interventions and techniques vary in their effectiveness and cost in different settings and contexts (Øvretveit 2011). It is therefore important for the key actors in the region, especially local healthcare workers, to study the conditions or factors that may influence the implementation of their proposed QI products before committing further resources to their design and development. A better understanding of the products can provide useful insight into the process, quality and administrative issues that may be encountered (Berwick 2008). This will also enable the key actors to determine how an intervention could be systematically set up to renovate care and service delivery, educate and train staff and assess the system for further improvement (Chassin and Galvin 1998).

Quite often, when it comes to improving the quality of health care in the region, attention is usually immediately given to acquiring more equipment and introducing new treatments; this is a mistake. Experience shows such decisions are often taken without detailed knowledge of how the equipment functions or its proper use. This has often led to newly acquired equipment being locked away and wasted in some hospital facilities in the region. Today research shows that the greatest opportunity for QI lie not in new equipment and the discovery of new treatments but rather on effective and efficient use of existing therapies and resources (Pronovost et al. 2004).

To this end, achieving a high quality of care and service in the region will require a different mindset and a change in habits among healthcare workers. The new approach will require a renewed effort by staff to honestly question their practices, whether it is evidence-based, and learn collaboratively. In a situation where a change is required, they must contemplate whether such a change will lead to QI in their practice (Berwick 1996, Blumenthal 1996; Plsex 1999). Developing and sustaining QI in health care in the region will also require cultural change to ensure shared values and beliefs, organisational support and a structure capable of coordinating and monitoring performance, including the provision of and incentivise for QI. It will also require well-trained staff in various relevant activities such as data collection, analysis, interpretation and change implementation (Dixon-Woods et al. 2012).

References

Abduljawad A, Al-Assaf AF (2011) Incentives for better performance in healthcare. Sultan Qaboos Uni Med J 11(2):201–206

Alkhenizan A, Shaw C (2011) Impact of Accreditation on the Quality of Healthcare Services: a Systematic Review of the Literature. Ann Saudi Med 31(4):407–416. https://doi.org/10.4103/0256-4947.83204

Allen T, Whittaker W, Kontopantelis, E et al (2018) Influence of financial and reputational incentives on primary care performance: a longitudinal study. Br J Gen Pract. https://bjgp.org/content/68/677/e811

Alotaibi YK, Federico F (2017) The impact of health information technology on patient safety. Saudi Med J 38(12):1173–1180. https://doi.org/10.15537/smj.2017.12.20631

Apkon M, Leonard L, Probst L et al (2004) Design of a safer approach to intravenous drug infusion: failure mode effects analysis. Qual Saf Health Care 13(4):265–271

Batalden PB, Davidoff F (2007) What is "quality improvement" and how can it transform healthcare? Qual Saf Health Care 16(1):2–3

Bate P, Robert G (2007) Bringing user experience to healthcare improvement: the concepts, methods and practices of experience-based design. Radcliffe Publishing, Oxford

Baxley EG, Bennett KJ, Pumkam C et al (2011) "PDSA-ADHD": a newly reported syndrome. JABFM 2(6):752–757

Benneyan JC, Lloyd RC, Plsek PE (2003) Statistical process control as a tool for research and healthcare improvement. Qual Saf Health Care 12(6):458–464

Berwick D (1996) A primer on leading the improvement of systems. BMJ 312(7031):619–622

Berwick DM (1998) Developing and testing changes in delivery of care. Annal Internal Med 128:651–656

Berwick DM (2008) The science of improvement. JAMA 299(19):1182–1184

Berwick D (2010) No needless framework. Institute for Healthcare Improvement, Boston

Blumenthal D (1996) The role of physicians in the future of quality management. New England J Med 335(17):1328–1331

Bombard Y, Baker GR, Orlando E (2018) Engaging patients to improve quality of care: a systematic review. Implement Sci 13:–98. https://doi.org/10.1186/s13012-018-0784-z

Bosch-Caplanch X, Garner P (2008) Primary health care supervision in developing countries. Trop Med Int Health 13(3):369–383

Brennan TA, Berwick DM (1996) New rules: regulation, markets, and the quality of American health care, BMJ 312:1108. https://doi.org/10.1136/bmj.312.7038.1108

Carey RG, Lloyd RC (2001) Measuring quality improvement in healthcare: a guide to statistical process control applications. New York, American Society for Quality

Carlo WA, Goudar SS, Jehan I et al (2010) The first breadth study. Newborn-care training and perinatal mortality in developing countries. N Engl J Med 362(7):614–623

Chassin MR, Galvin RW (1998) The urgent need to improve health care quality. Institute of Medicine National Roundtable on Health Care Quality. JAMA 280(11):1000–1005

Darzi A (2018) The Lord Darzi review of health and care: final report, Institute for Public Policy Research (IPPR). https://www.ippr.org/research/publications/better-health-and-care-for-all. Accessed 16 July 2018

DeRosier J, Stalhandske E, Bagian JP et al (2002) Using health care failure mode and effect analysis: the VA National Center for Patient Safety's prospective risk analysis system. J Comm J Qual Improv 28(5):248–267

Dixon-Woods M, McNicol S, Martin G (2012) Ten challenges in improving quality in healthcare: lessons from the Health Foundation's programme evaluations and relevant literature. BMJ Qual Saf 21(10):876–884. https://doi.org/10.1136/bmjqs-2011-000760

Donabedian A (2005) Evaluating the quality of medical care. The Milbank Q 83(4):691–729

Donetto S, Pierri P, Tsianakas V et al (2015) Experience-based co-design and healthcare improvement: realising participatory design in the public sector. Design J 18(2):227–248

Dopson S, Mant J, Hicks H (1994) Getting research into practice:facing the issues. J Manage Med 8:8–12

East London NHS Foundation Trust (2021) ELFT's quality management system. https://qi.elft.nhs.uk/elfts-qualitymanagement-system. Accessed 2 July 2021

Edwards PJ, Huang DT, Metcalfe LN et al (2008) Maximising your investment in HER. Utilising EHRs to inform continuous quality improvement. J Healthc Inf Manag 22(1):32–37

Ente C (2010) Incorporating patient safety practice into the Nigerian healthcare system; whose responsibility? Paper presented at the 2nd conference of the Society for Healthcare Quality (SQHN) Nigeria, Lagos, 6 July 2010

Fletcher CE (1997) Failure mode and effects analysis. An interdisciplinary way to analyse and reduce medication errors. J Nurs Admin 27(12):19–26

Francois P, Prate F, Vidal-Trecan G et al (2016) Characteristics of morbidity and mortality conference associated with the implementation of patien safety improvement initiatives: an observational study. BMC Health Serv Res 16:35. https://doi.org/10.1186/s12913-016-1279-8

Gaba DM (2000) Structural and organisational issues in Patient Safety: a comparison of health care to other high-hazard industries. Calif Manage Rev 43:83–102

Glickman SW, Boulding W, Manary M et al (2010) Patient satisfaction and its relationship with clinical quality and inpatient mortality in acute myocardial infarction. Circulat Cardiovas Qual Outcomes 3(2):188–195

Grover V, Malhotra MK (1997) Business process reengineering: a tutorial on the concept, evolution, method, technology and application. J Operat Manage 15(1997): 193 – 213.

Grover V, Teng JTC, Fiedler KD (1993) Information technology enabled business process reengineering: an integrated planning framework. Omega 21(4):433–447

Hashim MJ, Prinsloo A, Mirza DM (2013) Quality improvement tools for chronic disease care – more effective processes are less likely to be implemented in developing countries. Int J Health Care Qual Assur 26(1):14–19

Heiby J (2014) The use of modern quality approaches to strengthen African health system: a 5-year agenda. Int J Qual Health Care 26(2):117–123

Higginson SJ, Walters R, Fulop N (2012) Mortality and morbidity meetings: an untapped resource for improving the governance of patient safety? BMJ Qual Saf 21(7):576–585

Institute for Healthcare Improvement (2005) Going lean in health care. Institute for Healthcare Improvement, Boston

Institute of Medicine (1990) Crossing the quality chasm: a new health system for the 21st century. National Academy Press, Washington, DC

Institute of Medicine (2000) To err is human: building a safer health system. National Academy of Sciences, Washington, DC

Jamal A, McKenzie K, Clark M (2009) The impact of health information technology on the quality of medical and health care: a systematic review. Health Inform Manage J 38(3):26–37. https://doi.org/10.1177/183335830903800305

Jamison DT, Breman JG, Measham AR et al (eds) (2006) Disease control priority in developing countries: disease control priorities project, 2nd edn. Oxford University Press, Washington, DC. https://www.ncbi.nlm.nih.gov/books/NBK11728/. Accessed 2 July 2018

Jha AK, Orav EJ, Zheng J et al (2008) Patient's perception of hospital care in the United States. New England J Med 359(18):192–1931

Joint Commission International (2018) JCI-Accredited Organisations. https://www.jointcommissioninternational.org/about-jci/jci-accredited-organizations/. Accessed 8 July 2018

Jones B, Kwong E, Warburton I (2021) Quality improvement made simple - what everyone should know about health care quality improvement. The Health Foundation, London.. https://doi.org/10.37829/HF-2021-I05

Kilpatrick KE, Lohr KN, Leatherman S et al (2005) The insufficiency of evidence to establish the business care for quality. Intl J Qual Health Care 17(4):347–355

King's Fund (2011) The patient-centred care project: evaluation report. The King's Fund, London

Kobewaka DM, Van Walraven C, Turnbull J (2017) Quality gaps identified through mortality review. BMJ Qual Safety 26:141–149

Kohn L, Corrigan J, Donaldson M (1999) To err is human: building a safer health system, Institute of medicine report. National Academy Press, Washington, DC

Leatherman S, Sutherland K (2007) Designing national quality reforms: a framework for action. Intl J Qual Healthc 19(6):334–340

Leatherman S, Ferris TG, Berwick D et al (2010) The role of quality improvement in strengthening health systems in developing countries. Int J Qual Health Care 22(4):237–243

Linkin DR, Sausman C, Santos L et al (2005) Applicability of healthcare failure mode and effect analysis to healthcare epidemiology: evaluation of the sterilisation and use of surgical instruments. Clin Infect Dis 41(7):1014–1019

Linnander E, McNatt Z, Sipsma H et al (2016) Use of a national collaborative to improve hospital quality in a low-income setting. Intl Health 8(2):148–153

Loeb JM (2004) The current state of performance measurement in health care. Int J Qual Health Care 16(1):i5–i9

Lomas J, Enkin M, Anderson GM et al (1991) Opinion leaders versus audit feedback to implement practice guidelins. J Am Med Assoc 265:2202–2207

Manias E (2011) Measuring safety and quality in health care: classic methods paper. Intl J Nursing Stud 48:347–358

McCorMack B, Kitson A, Harvey G et al (2002) Nursing theory and concept development for analysis. J Adv Nurs 38(1):94–104

McIntyre D, Rogers L, Heier E (2001) Overview, history, and objectives of performance measurement. Health Care Financ Rev 22(3):7–21

Moen R, Norman C (2010) Circling back: clearing up the myths about the Deming cycle and seeing how it keeps evolving. Qual Progress 42:23–28

Nave D (2002) How to compare six sigma, lean and the theory of constraints: a framework for choosing what's best for your organisation. American Society for Quality

Øvretveit J (2009) Does improving quality save money? A review of evidence of which improvements to quality reduce costs to health service providers. Health Foundation, London

Øvretveit J (2011) Understanding the conditions for improvement: research to discover which context influences affect improvement success. BMJ Qual Saf 20(1):18–23

Peabody J, Luck J, Glassman P et al (2004) Measuring the quality of physicians practice by using clinical vignettes: A prospective validation study. Ann Internal Med 141(10):771–780

Pronovost PJ, Nolan T, Zeger S et al (2004) How can clinicians measure safety and quality in acute care? The Lancet 363(9414):1061–1067

Reed JE, Card AJ (2016) The problem with plan-DO-study-act cycles. BMJ Qual Saf 25(3):147–152

Reeve C, Humphreys J, Wakerman J (2015) A comprehensive health service evaluation and monitoring framework. Evaluat Program Plann 53:91–98

Rosen MA, DiazGranados D, Dietz AS (2018) Teamwork in healthcare: key discoveries enabling safer, high-quality care. Am Psychol 73(4):433–450. https://doi.org/10.1037/amp0000298

Rowe AK, Onikpo F, Lama M et al (2010) The rise and fall of supervision in a project designed to strengthen supervision of integrated management of childhood illness in Benin. Health Policy Plann 25(2):125–134

Sainfort F, Karsh BT, Booske BC et al (2001) Applying quality improvement principles to achieve healthy work organisations. Jt Comm J Qual Improv 27(9):469–483

Sampson UK, Amuyunzu-Nyamongo M, Mensah GA (2013) Health promotion and cardiovascular disease prevention in sub-Sharan Africa. Progr Cardiovas Dis 164(5):344–355

Scally G, Donaldson LJ (1998) Clinical governance and the drive for quality improvement in the new NHS in England. BMJ. 317(7150):61–65

Schuster MA, McGlynn EA, Brook RH (1998) How good is the quality of health care in the United States? Milbank Q 76(4):517–563

Scott A, Sivey P, Ouakrim DA et al (2011) The effect of financial incentives on the quality of health care provided by primary care physicians. Cochrane Database of Systematic Reviews.. https://doi.org//10.1002/14651858.CD008451.pub2

Shah A (2020) How to move beyond quality improvement projects. BMJ 370:m2319. https://doi.org/10.1136/bmj.m2319

Shewhart WA (1939) Statistical method from the viewpoint of quality control, U.S. Department of Agriculture, reprinted by Dover

Siddiqi K, Newell J, Robinson M (2005) Getting evidence into practice: what works in developing countries? Int Qual Health Care 17(5):447–453

Speroff T, O'Connor GT (2004) Study designs for PDSA quality improvement research. Q Manage Health Care 13(1):17–32

Speroff T, James BC, Nelson EC et al (2004) Guidelines for appraisal and publication of PDSA quality improvement. Q Manage Health Care 13(1):33–39

Sutherland K, Leatherman S (2006) Regulation and quality – a review of the evidence. The Health Foundation, London

Taylor MJ, McNicholas C, Nicolay C et al (2014) Systematic review of the application of the plan-do-study-act method to improve quality in healthcare. BMJ Qual Saf 23:290–298

The Health Foundation (2011) Evidence scan: improvement science. Health Foundation, London

The Health Foundation (2013) Quality improvement made simple – what everyone should know about healthcare quality improvement. Health Foundation, London

Thor J, Lundberg J, Ask J et al (2007) Application of statistical process control in healthcare improvent: systematic review. Qual Saf Health Care 16(5):387–399

Van den Heuvel J, Does RJ, Bogers AJ (2006) Implementing Six Sigma in The Netherlands. Jt Comm J Qual Patient Saf 32(7):393–399

van Tilburg CM, Leistikow IP, Rademaker CMA et al (2006) Health care failure mode and effect analysis: a useful proactive risk analysis in a pediatric oncology ward. Qual Saf Health Care 15(1):58–63

Walley P, Gowland B (2004) Completing the circle: from PD to PDSA. Int J Health Care Qual Assur Inc Leadersh Health Serv 17(6):329–358

Walshe K (2009) Pseudoinnovation: the development and spread of healthcare quality improvement methodologies. Int KJ Qual Health Care 21:153–159

Weinerman ER (1950) Appraisal of Medical Care Programs. Am J Pub Health 40:1129–1134

Womack J, Jones D (2007) Lean solutions: how companies and customers can create value and wealth together. Simon and Schuster, London

World Health Organisation (2000) World health report 2000 health systems: improving performance. World Health Organisation, Geneva

World Health Organisation (2003) Quality and accreditation in health care services – a global review. World Health Organisation, Geneva

World Health Organisation (2016) Patient engagement: technical series on safer primary care. World Health Organisation, Geneva

World Health Organization, Organisation for Economic Co-operation and Development, and The World Bank (2018) Delivering quality health services: a global imperative for universal health coverage. World Health Organization, Organisation for Economic Co-operation and Development, and The World Bank, Geneva. Licence: CC BY-NC-SA 3.0 IGO

Wright J, Hill P (2003) Clinical governance. Elsevier Science Limited, Philadelphia

Wright A, Feblowitz JC, Pang JE et al (2012) Use of order sets in inpatient computerised provider entry systems: a comparative analysis of usage patterns at seven sites. Int J Med Inform 81(11):733–745. https://doi.org/10.1016/j.ijmedinf.2012.04.003

Chapter 7
Evaluation

Introduction

Integral to achieving meaningful improvements in safety and quality in health care using the essentials covered in this book is the provision of appropriate methods for continuous assessment of their implementation and the outcomes. This assessment will enable healthcare professionals and other stakeholders involved to determine whether their implementation is progressing or went as planned and whether the changes introduced by the interventions are producing the desired outcomes. Evaluation is the most effective means to achieve this as it often generates information that could be used to improve an intervention. This information generally reveals whether the goals or objectives of an intervention are being met and how different aspects of an intervention are functioning, which is crucial in a continuous improvement process. In the event that the objectives of interventions are not met, information generated through evaluation will help to establish how it can be improved in future (Siriwardena 2009). Evaluation can also provide new information or new insights about an intervention that was not anticipated (Westat et al. 2002). Evaluation is, therefore, another essential component of safety and quality improvements in health care.

Historically, evaluations date back to 2000 B.C. and the Chinese civil servant evaluation system, as reported by Westat et al. (2002). Thus, evaluation has been around for some time now, and there is ample evidence in the literature showing that a robust and quality evaluation can provide information about not only whether an intervention worked but also why and how, thereby making it possible to share knowledge, replicate interventions and develop new ones (Health Foundation 2015). Also, the evaluation of healthcare interventions is essential to inform future decisions and generate information which could be used to compare observed outcomes with what would have been the case if the intervention had not been implemented (Clarke et al. 2019).

There is little information in the literature on evaluation as an improvement method and its application in Africa despite the report by Jabot et al. (2014) that evaluation constitutes a valuable approach to improving health promotion in the region. As a result, in this chapter evaluation will be discussed with the aim of encouraging healthcare staff and stakeholders in Africa to reflect on how to use it to assess, enhance and improve the performance and effectiveness of their interventions designed and implemented to improve safety and quality of care. However, as explained by Westat et al. (2002), evaluation is very broad and varied in its definition and means various things to various people. Therefore, comprehensive information on evaluation is beyond the scope of this book. It is important to emphasise that what will be covered in this chapter are the salient points of evaluation, with the intention of motivating and helping healthcare workers in the region to design and carry out evaluation and explore the topic further. In view of this, this chapter will therefore cover the purpose of evaluation, types of evaluation and the main components of the evaluation process, which are designing and planning, conducting and reporting. It will also present the benefits of evaluation in healthcare settings, including the challenges of organising and carrying out evaluations in the region.

Evaluation

Evaluation is a scientific, rigorous and objective assessment of the effectiveness of an ongoing or completed project, practice or intervention. The design, implementation and outcome are scrutinised to determine its relevance and the extent to which its proposed objectives have been met. Evaluation also refers to the process of determining the merit, worth, significance or value of an activity, policy, programme, project or intervention (Scriven 1991). As explained by Menon et al. (2009), evaluation can apply to many things including strategy, topic, theme, sector or organisation.

Evaluation, in comparison with audits and research as presented in Table 4.2 in Chap. 4, generates information used mainly to define and judge achieved results and inform decisions. An audit generates information to advise on delivery of best care and service, while research generates information to derive generalisable new knowledge or produce and test hypotheses. Unlike an audit, in evaluation there is no reference to standards, and in terms of research, ethical review is not mandatory but required only when part of the evaluation involves interviewing patients and the use of patient identifying data. All aspects of evaluation must be conducted in compliance with data protection regulations and confidentiality. However, evaluation is a kind of research and all evaluation work can be described as research, but not all research aims to evaluate something (NHS Institute for Innovation and Improvement 2005). In addition, unlike both audits and research, evaluation is less about strict protocols and routine day-to-day management but rather emphasises practical assessment of the implementation and impact of intervention since it is conducted in a spirit of discovery rather than management and monitoring (Health Foundation 2015).

Purpose of Evaluation

There are different types of evaluation, but the essence of all evaluations is to help develop a better understanding of how an intervention, practice, care, service or policy is working (Clarke et al. 2019). The primary aim of an evaluation, therefore, is to determine how things have changed after an intervention (Public Health England 2018). Evaluation will help to ensure that not only has the change resulted in improvements but also that the improvements attained are as effective as expected and are the right improvements. Evaluation is therefore about examining whether one is doing the right thing and doing it properly (NHS Institute for Innovation and Improvement 2005).

The evaluation finding can be used not only for improvements and decision-making but for enlightenment and persuasion (Shadish et al. 1990), in the sense that it can be used as evidence-based information or feedback to share with the stakeholders demonstrating how they are working to improve the quality of care and service and change practice for the better. This can be shared with patients to show that the healthcare system is credible, reliable and safer, thereby encouraging, enlightening and persuading or influencing them to use the system. The finding can also be shared with the healthcare sponsors and funders, for instance the government, to solicit funding for further development of the existing or new interventions.

Types of Evaluation

There are two major kinds of evaluation, formative and summative evaluations. In evaluation design, either a formative or a summative evaluation can be used depending on what one is expected to achieve. It is also possible to design an evaluation that has summative and formative components to address whether an intervention or a project is bringing about improvements and why it produces specific outcomes (NHS Institute for Innovation and Improvement 2005).

Formative Evaluation

A formative evaluation is usually conducted during the developmental stage of an intervention and continues throughout the life of the intervention with the aim of providing information for initial assessment, monitoring and fine-tuning the intervention (Westat et al. 2002). A formative evaluation can help to determine what is working in an intervention, whether the intervention is bringing about improvements and explore how it has worked in a particular healthcare environment (Health Foundation 2015). Formative evaluations can be classified into implementation and progress evaluations. An implementation evaluation, also known as a process evaluation, is used to assess whether an intervention is being organised and conducted as planned. A progress evaluation, on the other hand, is used to assess progress or to investigate whether an intervention is meeting the desired goals. In addition to information on whether targeted progress is being met, a progress evaluation can also provide insight into unexpected developments in the intervention (Westat et al. 2002). The major questions that could be raised during a formative evaluation include the following: What have we learnt? What were the enablers and barriers to change? And how did the improvement initiative change over time? (NHS Institute for Innovation and Improvement 2005).

Summative Evaluation

A summative evaluation, also known as an outcome evaluation, is undertaken after the completion of an intervention. The purpose of a summative evaluation is to assess the intervention's impact and to determine whether it has been successful in achieving its stated goals. It can help to demonstrate whether the intervention worked and met its objective, point out the level of improvement attained and whether it was completed within the time frame and whether it was cost effective using information collected about the outcomes, processes and its activities (Westat et al. 2002). The main questions in a summative evaluation include the following: Did the improvement exercise achieve its objective? What improvements did the improvement exercise create? And what benefits did the improvement exercise deliver compared to what it cost? (NHS Institute for Innovation and Improvement 2005).

Evaluation Design and Planning, Conducting and Reporting

In this chapter, a standard operating procedure (SOP) will be used to demonstrate the design, conduct and reporting of an evaluation. As background information, in this book the use of SOPs is advocated as one of the essential components required to improve patient safety and quality of care in the Africa healthcare setting. The evaluation that will be described in this chapter will be based on the assumption that 12 months after successful development and implementation an intervention (SOP) should generate considerable information to check whether the application of SOPs actually leads to patient safety and quality improvement in health care in Africa. It will also be helpful to know the difficulties of putting SOPs into practice in the region. On account of this, both impact and process evaluations will be used. The impact evaluation will determine whether the intervention (SOP) is delivering the objectives set and producing the expected outcomes. The process evaluation, on the other hand, will clarify the way in which an intervention (SOP) was implemented and managed. It will also provide insight into the driver and obstacles for change resulting from the intervention and what could be learnt from the exercise (NHS Institute for Innovation and Improvement 2005).

Evaluation Planning and Design Process

The evaluation of a SOP 12 months after development and implemented as discussed previously fits into Plan-Do-Study-Act (PDSA) model of improvement, discussed in Chap. 6 of this book, and an evaluation design made of both formative and summative elements will be used to generate relevant information to gain valuable learning and knowledge on the impact and process of this improvement intervention (SOP). In the attempt to explain the evaluation planning and design process of the proposed intervention, a logic model of the intervention and evaluation questions including measurable outcomes, evaluation plan and evaluation team will be covered.

Logic Model of SOP Intervention

A logic model of the SOP intervention is represented in Fig. 7.1 below. It shows a systematic and visual relationship between the resources invested (inputs) in the intervention, the activities carried out (outputs) and the benefits expected

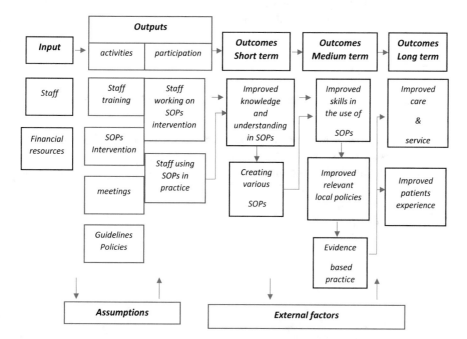

Fig. 7.1 A logic model for SOP intervention for safety and quality improvement

(outcomes). A logic model, also known as a conceptual model, helps in planning, describing, managing and communicating the evaluation of an intervention. It varies in design, components and description, can be represented using a flow chart, a map or a table and as a rule must be presented on one page (Centers of Disease Control and Prevention 2018). The other characteristics of a logic model to be considered during its design are that it should be appropriate in its level of detail, easy to modify, easy to relate to and useful in clarifying intervention activities and expected outcomes (Leviton et al. 2010). A brief description of the components of such a model are provided in what follows.

Assumptions

To achieve meaningful improvements in safety and quality in health care, it is important to address the use of evidence-based practice as opposed to anecdotal evidence of healthcare professionals to create basic clinical processes that underpin quality and safe care. As evidence-based medicine is not widely practiced in healthcare settings in Africa, it is assumed that the practical knowledge and understanding of developing and implementing SOPs will be an invaluable asset. The reason for this assumption is that such knowledge and understanding will help healthcare staff in the region to distil, for instance, the latest guidelines developed by the World Health Organization containing recommendations for clinical practice or public health policy into simple and easy-to-follow procedures (in the form of SOPs) for local use in making informed decisions on whether to undertake specific interventions or clinical tests or other measures, including where and when to do so, thereby improving patient safety and quality care and service.

Inputs

The resources considered important for developing and implementing SOPs include the following:

- A designated team possibly from the proposed safety and quality department (SQD) discussed in Chap. 1 of this book,
- Staff from both clinical and non-clinical areas requiring SOPs with relevant in-depth knowledge and skills,
- Management staff,
- Staff time and
- Financial resources.

Outputs

The outputs in this example will comprise both the activities which the participants or staff will undertake and participants or staff that will undertake those activities. The activities include

- staff training on the development, implementation and use of SOPs;
- SOP development, implementation and use of SOPs in practice;
- meetings and
- review and extraction of information from relevant guidelines and policies.

   The participants include

- staff who engage in the SOP development and implementation of SOPs – those who design and implement the SOPs, clinical and non-clinical staff who review the SOPs and management staff who sign off on them off, and others;
- staff using the SOPs in daily operations.

Outcomes

The aims and objectives of the use of SOPs in healthcare settings in Africa will lead to

- improved knowledge and understanding of the development and implementation of SOPs and encourage the application of SOPs in practice and
- evidence-based practice, resulting in improved patient safety and quality care and improved patient experiences.

External Factors

Different kinds of external factors may influence an intervention in health care in Africa. The factors could be political, economic, environmental, technological or workforce related. This also includes the influence of contextual factors, healthcare staff and management response to the intervention, which is unknown.

Evaluation Questions and Measurable Outcomes

The logic model also assists in creating evaluations and developing measurable outcomes or criteria to evaluate. In a healthcare setting like that in Africa, where poor-quality routine information is widely reported as the biggest threat to research, it is important to assess at the early stage of evaluation question formulation whether there will be sufficient and reliable information to address the proposed questions. The fact that additional or specific data may be required from the stakeholders, for instance patients and staff of the organisation, for the evaluation must also be considered at the early stage and planned for in advance taking into consideration the inadequate resources that may be experienced. In the final analysis, the evaluation questions to be developed must be adequate, credible and achievable and identify what is valuable and useful information in the intervention. Taking into consideration these characteristics, the key evaluation questions for this intervention could include the following:

- **What is your experience?** This question will illuminate the evaluation process and set the stage for other questions. It will help stakeholders state and explain the challenges faced in creating and implementing the SOP as well as the processes used to overcome those challenges.
- **How many SOPs have been developed and implemented?** This question will lead to the listing of specific SOPs created with the department or the areas where they are used. This will provide a measurement of the knowledge and skills gained and the enthusiasm, aspirations and confidence expressed by the staff in translating their experience, knowledge and skills into practice.
- **What are your thoughts about the outcomes?** This is another key evaluation question aimed at measuring or assessing the output. In developing and implementing the intervention, SOPs in this case, the expectation was that care and service delivery would change and improve. This question is therefore about the effectiveness or impact evaluation of the intervention. Additional questions that could be used to explore this include the following: What change have you observed in the care and services since the implementation of the intervention? Do you think the results are associated with the intervention? Please provide specific examples. These questions will also shed light on the participants' satisfaction.
- **Does the intervention achieve its goals or objectives?** This is one of the most important evaluation questions. It will be used to probe whether the intervention has succeeded or failed in meeting the intended objectives. This can be measured in terms of changes to specific policies and practices. More useful information on this could be gained by asking further questions such as the following: What are your observations about the success or failure of the intervention? Do you feel the success or failure to meet the objectives of the intervention is due to implementation strategies or other factors?
- **How do patients and other service users feel about the intervention?** The expectation is that patients should feel safe. As Maxwell (2020) reported, evidence shows that patients' feedback on their experience can shape services to better meet patient needs. In a situation where patients' observations or experience contradicts what is reported on the outcomes of the intervention, the report could be a valuable source of reflection and be used to recommend further improvements. Other questions that could be used to examine patients experience include the following: What is your experience on the medical team's assessment? Were you given enough information about your illness and its cause and an adequate explanation of the medicines given and the side affects you may experience? Did you feel the medical staff took your consent seriously? How

would you rate the experience of the care and service received during this visit compared with previous ones? (Iversen et al. 2014; Pettersen et al. 2004)

- **How do the costs and benefits compare?** This is very important in health care in Africa as the system is strapped for resources. The likely questions to probe into the cost-effectiveness include whether there are any more cost-effective alternatives to the intervention that might achieve the same objectives and intended results and whether there are more cost-effective ways of achieving the intervention being evaluated. Both cost-benefit and cost-effective analyses should be examined to avoid wasting resources. Information generated through these questions could provide insight into whether resources and activities were sufficient and necessary during the evaluation or whether either the resources and activities or evaluation objectives were adjusted to meet the limitations of the resources (Leviton et al. 2010). The questions could also provide insight into social and economic impacts on the organisation.
- **Does it meet required standards?** The intervention first and foremost was introduced for care and service to be delivered to agreed standards. This questionnaire will help to explore adherence to specific standards and, where applicable, specific examples provided. It will help to answer the question of whether evidence-based practice has been achieved.
- **What further improvements are required?** This question is important as it is used to seek suggestions for further improvement.
- **Should the intervention be discontinued?** This question could be used to obtain further information on the usefulness of the intervention.

However, it is important to note that the preceding questions do not constitute an exhaustive list of evaluation questions that could be asked in an intervention of this nature. As suggested by Marsh and Glendenning (2005), as is common in any evaluation question, these questions could be re-framed differently or changed depending on the specific learning one intends to derive from the exercise.

Evaluation Plan

Once the key evaluation questions and the need to evaluate the intervention have been agreed upon, it is necessary to carry out an assessment to determine the tools and amount of time the evaluation team will require to provide satisfactory answers to the questions (World Health Organization 2013). The outcome of this assessment is often best represented using an evaluation plan, which is a very important component in the evaluation planning and design process. An evaluation plan helps in the decision-making on the allocation of resources for the evaluation. The plan includes evaluation questions which represent what must be known about the intervention and provides information on how this will be known, which is the indicator for outcome measures; how to collect data about the outcome measures, which are the data source and method; when the data will be collected, that is, the duration or time frame; and who will do this, which team will be responsible for the evaluation.

Table 7.1 Evaluation plan for SOP intervention for safety and quality improvement

Evaluation questions	Outcome measures	Data source/ methods	Duration	Responsibility
What is your experience?	Could be measured in terms of the cost of the intervention in terms of time, resources and ease of accessing resources, whether human (seeking assistance from other staff, especially senior staff responsible for decision-making), material (such as obtaining relevant guidelines that could be used and referenced in the SOPs) or financial (ease of accessing funds for consumables) or the knowledge, skills and understanding gained in the process	Interview, focus group and review of relevant documents	3–10 days depending on number of participants to be contacted	Staff on proposed SQD team or staff in other departments in charge of similar roles
What do patients and other service users observe about the intervention?	Participant satisfaction, change in practice and policies	Interview, focus group, questionnaire survey and review of documents	3 weeks to 2 months	Staff on proposed SQD team or staff in other department in charge of similar roles

Table 7.1 below shows an example of an evaluation plan for the intervention. As shown in the plan, although all the evaluation questions should be included in the plan, only two are listed in this case for demonstration purposes.

Evaluation Team

An evaluation can be carried out by an in-house team or an external team. In the evaluation of an intervention presented in this chapter, it is assumed that the evaluation will be conducted by an in-house team with members of staff from the proposed SQD. The team should work out together the resources that will be required to carry out the evaluation, for instance, time, budget, participants and others. There must be an evaluation manager on the team to coordinate the process and spread the workload to make it manageable. An evaluation is dynamic in nature in the sense that some adjustment may be required, for instance there may be changes in the initial schedule for interviews or focus groups, so the manager should lead in formulating the review evaluation plan and make the necessary adjustments. The evaluation team leader, with the help of other members of the team, is responsible for analysing the data and compiling the findings and recommendations, including circulating the findings. The success of an evaluation also depends on the level of support and cooperation from the relevant multidisciplinary team at all levels, especially those from the management and other stakeholders.

Conducting Evaluation

Quality information which is relevant and suitable to address the evaluation questions adequately is the lifeblood of any evaluation. This section is about obtaining such useful information which, when analysed, generates reports capable of sufficiently answering the aforementioned evaluation questions formulated for the SOP intervention. Secondary data often collected for administration and other purposes will be reviewed and analysed during the evaluation. These data include patient records, hospital policies and SOPs, reports, staff rotas, training records and minutes of meetings. In addition, primary data, which are data collected directly from hospital staff and their patients through the use of interviews, questionnaires, focus groups and observations, will also be used. This section will cover evaluation design, methodology, with the corresponding range of data collection tools and techniques, and data analysis. It will also highlight some of challenges that could be faced in a healthcare setting in Africa, which will impact the use of these tools, with a reflection on which of the tools could be suitable to apply in the region.

Evaluation Design

Evaluation design describes the model that is used in gathering impartial evidence on results that can be attributed to the intervention (Minister of Public Works and Government Services 1998). In terms of the features of evaluation design, there exist many variations and there is no one right evaluation design. However, crucial in developing the design is that it must be appropriate for the evaluation purpose and questions, the nature of the intervention, the context in which it is implemented and the availability of data (Coly and Parry 2017). Central to evaluation design, therefore, is the selection of a methodological approach and data collection tools.

Types of Evaluation Design

Evaluation designs which can be used to collect credible data that can be transformed into the required information for generating valid evaluation outcomes can be broadly categorised into experimental and observational designs.

Experimental Designs

Experimental design is the most rigorous method of establishing causal relationships between interventions and the outcomes of interest. In an experimental design study, the investigator has control over who receives the intervention or service and who does not in order to determine the effect of the intervention, particularly decisions concerning the assignment of participants to different intervention groups. The use of a control or intervention group and randomisation in experimental designs eliminates threats to internal validity. The major weakness of the experimental design is that it is difficult to implement. Experimental design is broadly divided into randomised controlled, quasi-randomised and non-randomised trial/quasi-experimental study (Deeks et al. 2003). In randomised controlled studies, participants are randomly assigned to the intervention or control group and followed up over time to assess any differences in outcome rates. Randomisation with allocation concealment ensures that on average known and unknown determinants of the outcome are evenly distributed between groups.

Quasi-Randomised

In this kind of study, participants are assigned to the intervention or control group by the investigator. The assignment in this case is not through actual randomisation as is done using criteria such as date of birth or ethnicity or hospital number. Quasi-randomised experiments take creativity and skills to design, are cheaper and more practical and produce highly accurate findings compared to an experimental design study with randomisation (Westat et al. 2002).

Non-randomised Trial/Quasi-Experimental

In this type of study, the investigator has control over the assignment of participants to groups not through randomisation but through criteria such as patient or physician preference.

Observational Designs

In an observational design, unlike in experimental design, there is no randomisation of participants. The investigator observes and explores the effects of the intervention on health outcomes but does not intervene or manipulate the data or observations to find associations between the intervention and the outcomes (Coly and Parry 2017). Examples of observational studies according to Deeks et al. (2003) are discussed in the following sub-sections.

Controlled Before-and-After Study

This is also called a pre-post study. It is used to measure outcomes in a group of participants before the introduction of an intervention and again afterwards. The group that receives the intervention (i.e. the intervention group) and the group that did not receive the intervention (i.e. the control group) are both observed.

Historical Cohort Study

This kind of study is designed to compare a group of participants receiving an intervention in one period with a similar group who did not receive the same intervention. Participants are not studied concurrently.

Case-Control Study

This is a study that compares participants with a specific outcome (case) with participants from the same population but without the outcome (control). Both groups are then exposed to a given intervention and compared.

Cross-Sectional Study

This is designed to collect information on interventions (past and present) and current health outcomes for a defined population at a particular point in time to examine the relationship between the outcomes and exposure to interventions.

Cohort Study

In this study design, a defined group of participants (the cohort) is followed over time to examine the relationship between different interventions received and subsequent outcomes. Participants are studied either prospectively (a prospective cohort study recruits participants before any intervention and follows them into the future) or retrospectively (a retrospective cohort study identifies participants from past records describing the interventions received and follows them from the time of those records).

Case Series Study

In this study, observations are made on a group of participants receiving the same intervention, before and after the intervention, but no comparison is made with a control group.

Evaluation Methodology

Evaluation methodology deals with the techniques for data collection and analysis. A wide variety of methods can be used in the evaluation methodology, but the choice should depend on the nature of the data, availability of the source and cost effectiveness; the ability to address the evaluation questions using credible evidence (i.e. data which are reliable and of high quality); and the types of analysis to be conducted to produce valid results which can adequately address the evaluation (World Health Organization 2013).

The two main methods of data collection are qualitative and quantitative. The combination of both methods will be used in the evaluation discussed in this chapter. The advantages of using both methods, according to Raine et al. (2016), is that by combining them, one can obtain a better understanding, present different perspectives and address the quality, validity and reliability of the entire evaluation process. In addition, the use of both methods can produce comprehensive information on the intervention, for instance, it would enable the use of a focus group to gain a deeper understanding of the meaning of the results than may be obtained from questionnaires (Andrew and Halcomb 2009).

Quantitative Methods

Quantitative methods are used in observing or investigating things that are specific and measurable or quantifiable. These methods generate numerical or quantitative data, that is, data which can be measured and expressed or represented numerically as percentage, gender, age, rate or ratio. Measurement by quantitative methods is said to be objective in nature, that is, the data generated on what happened are based on facts or theory not on personal judgement (World Health Organization 2013). These data, which are usually collected using a predefined standard and structured, can be described accurately and confirmed irrespective of source. This kind of data is useful in describing general trends or distributions or to test a theory or hypothesis about the relationships between things, including cause and effect (Black 1999). These methods, which are effective in measuring what happened, could provide insight into whether the intervention of SOPs discussed in this chapter leads to improved care and service and is cost effective. The major quantitative data collection tool is the questionnaire, although such numerical data can also be collected through statistics and structured interviews (NHS Institute for Innovation and Improvement 2005).

Questionnaires

Questionnaires are important data collection tools for collecting quantitative data from a targeted group or population (Belisario et al. 2015; Edwards et al. 2002). They can be constructed in many ways and always consist of two key components: questions and answers or responses. In most questionnaires, close-ended questions are used. In this type of question, the participants or respondents are expected to provide answers by selecting from a limited set of possible responses or a range of predetermined answers such as A, B, C or "All/None of the above". The response or answers can also take the form of a rating scale of given items from 1 to 4, such as agree, disagree, strongly agree and strongly disagree. They can also be designed using open-ended questions where participants can provide free-form answers with sentences, lists and stories. The use of open-ended questions in questionnaires could provide deeper insight into the intervention being evaluated (Westat et al. 2002).

Questionnaire Administration

Questionnaires can be disseminated using a paper-based method where the questionnaire is sent via post (in the mail) to participants. It can also be administered in person or electronically using emails and online links (Bälter et al. 2005; Hardré et al. 2012). The traditional mail or post method of questionnaire administration has already been used successfully in the region by Janca et al. (1995)), specifically in Nigeria, Senegal and Zimbabwe. However, this method has a very low response rate, is time consuming as it might require sending out reminders and must be simple in design and presented in a clear and self-explanatory form. On the other hand, it is cheap and anonymous; the latter feature makes this method effective in handling sensitive, embarrassing or upsetting topics. The in-person method of questionnaire administration is not good for managing sensitive topics and where a large geographical area is to be covered. It is expensive and time consuming but it is very useful in leading participants through appropriate sections in the questionnaire, explaining what is required where necessary and helpful for overcoming disability and language problems (Public Health England 2018).

In online administration, the questionnaire can be completed on the Internet on a platform such as Qualtrics, Survey Monkey and Alchemer, or an electronic copy of the questionnaire is sent to participants through email. It is important that the platform chosen be supported by the information and communications technology (ICT) department and comply with the data protection policy of the organisation. Online questionnaires require electronic devices such as computers, smartphones and tablets. This method will also need a good Internet connection and some degree of ICT knowledge and skills to set up.

Belisario et al. (2015) reported on a "Comparison of self-administered survey questionnaire responses collected using mobile apps versus other methods" and stated that online administration could maximise scalability and ease of administration to a wide geographical area, enabling completion in the participants' own time. Online administration speeds up data collection and improves data completeness while reducing costs compared to the traditional paper method. According to Hardré et al. (2012), although the quantity of generative data was higher in web-based administration compared to other methods, there was no significant difference in overall quality in terms of completeness, coherence and correctness of the data.

In general, a well-designed questionnaire is a very versatile tool with the advantages of collecting descriptive data from a large geographical area of target population and on a wide range of topics, including sensitive ones. According to Belisario et al. (2015), it is less resource-intensive to implement compared to other data collection methods. Apart from where data are generated through open-ended responses, generally data produced from questionnaires can be easily analysed using various computer applications (Bryman and Cramer 1997).

On the other hand, a questionnaire does not often generate adequate information on context, so the data generated may provide a general picture but lack depth (Westat et al. 2002). The design, conduct and interpretation of a good-quality questionnaire require some degree of expertise. The choice of questions and scale of questionnaire must be carefully considered (Dell-Kuster et al. 2004), and the roll-out of a survey or questionnaire and the interpretation or analysis of the results must be carried out in a manner that ensures the reliability and validity of the findings as this may adversely impact the outcome (Rattray and Jones 2007).

Qualitative Methods

Qualitative methods are used in collecting data on participants' experiences, feelings, attitudes and perceptions. Data are generated using methods which are subjective and descriptive in nature and suitable for addressing questions related to why and how things happened (Shah and Corley 2006). These data are important in gaining insight into participants' beliefs, motives and behaviours (World Health Organization 2013). In addition, qualitative methods can be helpful in exploring how the participants' feelings account for the differences in the outcomes that may have been obtained (Willig 2008). Qualitative methods of data collection include interviews, focus groups and observations.

Interviews

An interview is one of the qualitative methods of data collection. Its design consists of open-ended questions to encourage detailed answers from participants rather than a yes or no response. In conducting an interview, it is best practice to start with questions which are natural, understandable and easy to answer and then proceed to more difficult or sensitive ones. This style is adopted to put participants at ease and allow them to build up confidence and rapport; it often generates rich information that subsequently develops the interview further (Gill et al. 2008). The use of an interview protocol or a topic guide is also important during the interview as it can help the interviewer to achieve consistency and pose relevant questions adapted to the demand and experience of the participants as the need arises (Pedersen et al. 2016).

There are three kinds of interview, namely unstructured, semi-structured and structured. The unstructured interview is an informal interview that uses specific interview questions formulated on site or during the interview session as opposed to being organised and preplanned. For instance, a question such as "Can you tell me about your experience with developing and applying SOPs in the hospital?" which could help to generate in-depth information on participants' attitudes, perceptions and perspectives and highlight areas of specific interest. Further questions could then be asked by members of the evaluation team seeking additional information required for better understanding and decision-making. A semi-structured interview is an interview that uses a predetermined list of interview questions in addition to some probe or follow-up interview questions based on the response of the participants. Thus, a semi-structured interview does not strictly follow predetermined questions from a list. For instance, a question such as "What influence does the African social context have on SOP development and implementation?" could identify key areas to explore followed up by additional questions to seek more details on the response or interesting comments from the participants. The structured interview uses predetermined interview questions. In this type of interview, participants are not allowed to deviate from the questions apart from seeking clarifications of the meaning of the question asked (Chua and Ke 2017; Gill et al. 2008).

Interview Methods

The methods of conducting interviews include in person, by telephone and via an online platform. The in-person or face-to-face interview is flexible; it enables control over the interview environment and aids in establishing a rapport with the participant(s). A face-to-face interview makes it possible to capture visual cues such as spontaneous personal and observable interactions, including emotion and body language, verbal and non-verbal signals and responses to interview questions (Deakin and Wakefield 2014). However, the face-to-face interview is expensive; it may be limited by geographical coverage and time constraints associated with travelling.

The telephone interview is effective in handling intimate and sensitive topics as it allows the participants to feel relaxed during the session (Novick 2008). It offers effective cost and time management because it does not involve travelling (Heath et al. 2018) Also, in support of the use of telephone interviews in the region is the report by Watkins et al. (2018)) that mobile phones are providing solutions for improving access to healthcare information and services in low- and middle-income countries. It must be remembered that this depends on good phone connections and networks able to carry signals to remote areas. However, the telephone interview lacks the ability to observe participants, resulting in the loss of contextual and non-verbal information and difficulties in establishing a rapport, follow-up and interpretation of responses (Groves 1990; Novick 2008).

An online interview involves the use of the Internet and can be conducted using platforms like Skype, Zoom and Microsoft Teams, as well as via email. The platforms allow face-to-face communication with the opportunity to observe body language and other non-verbal communication, which can reveal key messages about the participants' intentions, emotions and much more, as expressed in the proverb "Actions speak louder than words". It is essential that any platform utilised must be supported by the ICT department and comply with the data protection policy of the organisation. In an online interview using email, participants do not have to be present at the same time but can respond to the interview questions sent to them at their convenience (Hershberger and Kavanaugh 2017). As an email interview does not require participant or evaluator presence at the same prespecified time, it is potentially more acceptable to those who might decline or be unable to participate in spoken interviews but willing to answer questions sent to them electronically (Duffy et al. 2005).

Online interviews offer low-cost interaction without the need to travel and can make it possible to gain easy access to remote locations (Joseph et al. 2013). However, they require a good Internet connection, which represents a real barrier in some parts of Africa with low Internet access (James and Busher 2009). Mobile health (mHealth), which refers to healthcare practices supported by mobile devices such as mobile phones, laptops and tablets in the region, is equally influenced by other factors which could affect an online interview. These factors include language barrier, gender discrimination in the use of electronic devices and poverty issues (Odendaal et al. 2020), as well as poor digital infrastructure and low digital literacy (Watkins et al. 2018).

Focus Groups

Focus groups are used in collecting data through discussions between a group of participants and a moderator or a facilitator who guides, monitors and records the discussion using a topic guide (Morgan 1998). The use of a topic guide can help to achieve consistency and support the moderator in posing relevant questions and adapting to the needs and experiences of the participants as necessary (Pedersen et al. 2016). The group is said to be a *focus* group in the sense that it involves collective activities, such as the examination of documents and debating a particular set of questions (Kitzinger 1994). In focus groups, unlike in interviews, emphasis is placed on discussion and interaction among group members instead of on questions and answers; at the same time, it capitalises on group dynamics (Chua and Ke 2017).

Focus groups are useful in creating a rich understanding of participants' experiences and beliefs on a given topic. Groups also generate information on their collective views and the meanings that lie behind those views. Focus groups help in understanding how and why different groups of participants have differing views and provide a platform to challenge each other's views (Gill et al. 2008). The interactions shine a spotlight on the participants' behaviours, attitudes and body language that would likely remain unknown otherwise. The usefulness of focus groups in evaluation includes identifying and defining problems in intervention development and implementation, identifying intervention strengths, weaknesses and recommendations, and identifying the impacts and outcome of the intervention (Westat et al. 2002). The main problem of focus groups is that they generate complex data which can be difficult and time-consuming to transcribe and analyse. They could be challenging to use in discussions which involve sensitive and embarrassing topics (Public Health England 2018).

Observation

Observation, as the name implies, is a qualitative data collection technique which is used to collect data through observing. Observation is defined differently by several authors; however, in this chapter, observation will be viewed within the context of ethnography involving the need to carefully study and gain a better understanding of people within their natural environment (Baker 2006). Observation can be used in formative and summative evaluations. A formative evaluation helps to determine whether or not an intervention is being delivered or operated as planned, whereas a summative evaluation is used to determine whether or not an intervention has successfully met the desired aims and objectives (Westat et al. 2002).

Observation can elucidate workers' behaviour in a healthcare setting and provide information which is important in understanding how social context influences the workers' behaviour and how their behaviour in turn influences the social context (Shah and Corley 2006). Direct observation of operations and activities can develop a holistic perspective, in other words, it helps in creating an understanding of the context within which an intervention operates and provides an opportunity to collect data on a wide range of behaviours. Observation can capture a great variety of interactions. It can openly explore evaluation topics, clarify how an event may fit into or be affected by a sequence of events and bring to light issues that staff may be unaware of or that they are unwilling or unable to discuss honestly in an interview or focus group as a result of a negative safety culture (Minister of Public Works and Government Services 1998; Westat et al. 2002). According to Walshe et al. (2011), observation is useful for understanding the actions, roles and behaviours of people and how these can alter in response to situations and over time. It also makes a significant contribution to understanding care and service structures and processes. However, it can be expensive and time-consuming and can also affect the behaviour of participants. The selective perception of observers may distort data, so observation requires training and expertise to be carried out successfully (Westat et al. 2002).

Tools and Techniques for Data Collection in Healthcare Setting in Africa

The choice of data collection tools and techniques must be carefully thought through, taking into consideration the advantages and challenges of their application in health care in Africa, as discussed in the previous section. Questionnaires, interviews, focus groups and observations are all valuable tools and techniques that will be used to obtain data about the intervention discussed in this chapter. Data that could also be generated from routine information collected about a SOP intervention, to demonstrate changes following implementation, may also be reviewed and analysed.

Questionnaire administration must be carefully considered in African healthcare settings. Online survey administration should be considered in areas where participants may have the facilities and adequate knowledge and skills required to operate devices. In addition, such areas must have reliable Internet access, which is indispensable to the successful delivery of a web-based questionnaire study in any settings (Bälter et al. 2005). Even mail or post survey administration could be problematic in some areas where there is no secure postal system.

For the traditional face-to-face interview and telephone interview methods, the latter may be suitable in healthcare settings in African regions with poor public transport networks and facilities (James 2014). The face-to-face method is useful in leading participants through questions, explaining what is required where necessary and aiding in overcoming any disability and language problems that might arise.

To adequately address the evaluation questions proposed in this chapter, an ethnographic field study could be used. This will involve considerable hours of direct observation of healthcare professionals and non-medical staff in their natural environment (both clinical and non-clinical areas, for instance, offices, wards, clinics, laboratory, radiology department and other areas using the SOPs in question). This should be done carefully while silently watching what happens, attentively listening to what is said, taking notes with minimal interference with the subjects' work to avoid distraction or interruption to staff daily duties and placing less burden on them. Follow-up through informal and formal discussions could also be used, and such meetings could be scheduled at a different time. During these sessions, clarification questions will be asked and relevant documents requested and reviewed to gain a better understanding of the rationale behind their behaviours, tasks and processes observed (Hammersley and Atkinson 2007). It is very important that efforts be made to ensure the data collected are of high quality.

It is essential to make staff feel like they are part of the evaluation; to achieve this, the initial invitation to participants to take part in the study should detail why data are being collected and how the data result will be used. Data should be collected from as many participants as possible because the validity of the evaluation findings will depend not only on how the participants were selected but also on the extent to which data were successfully collected from those staff and patients selected as participants for the study. The implication of this is that participants who did not respond to the initial invitation to participate in the study should be followed up with. This may mean sending the questionnaires out two or three times or rescheduling interviews or observations several times (Westat et al. 2002). It should be taken into account that interviews and focus groups not only are for obtaining information about a given intervention but could also provide information on participants' degree of commitment and understanding of the intervention. Sources of secondary data, patient records, policies and standard operation procedures, reports, staff rotas, training records and minutes of meetings to be reviewed and analysed for the evaluation should be identified as early as possible, and permission for access must be obtained in advance.

Another area that would require advance planning is resource use. The evaluation activities, people and time allocated should be carefully planned. There should be adequate office space, facilities and stationery for meetings, review of records and documents, interviews and focus groups, and it should be decided in advance whether the interview or focus group will be recorded and how the records will be transcribed and analysed. The issue of confidentiality should also be addressed at an early stage, for instance, holding discussions in a room where confidentiality can be guaranteed. In addition, pseudonymisation techniques, whereby a unique reference number is assigned to participants (patients or staff) taking part in the interviews and focus groups to keep their identifiable data anonymized, could be used, including briefing the participants before the interview and group sessions.

Data Analysis

Once data collection is completed, the next stage is to analyse and interpret the data. In Westat et al. (2002), specific steps in data analysis include checking and preparing raw data for analysis, conducting an initial analysis based on the evaluation plan, conducting additional analyses based on the initial results and integrating and synthesising the findings. The team should devise appropriate quality control procedures to seek clarification where necessary, obtaining any missing data and ensuring the data collected are complete and of high quality for meaningful analysis. For instance, in questionnaires, some items which were not appropriately completed may not be analysed, and it will be essential to check whether the return rates are sufficient to provide valuable information necessary to address the evaluation questions. Recorded interviews and focus groups should be transcribed and reviewed, and where additional information or clarity is needed, another session could be scheduled. The same goes for notes recorded during observations. Statistical models and computer software deemed appropriate can be used for analysis and presentation of the results, for instance the use of tables or pie charts for descriptive statistics. Specific computer software packages for handling qualitative data can also be used to aid in organising and reorganising analysis of the data (Pope et al. 2000).

Evaluation Reporting

A report is the principal output of the evaluation process. It can be presented in various formats; however, irrespective of the format, an evaluation report should contain an introduction, evaluation questions, how information was generated and analysed to generate findings to answer each of the evaluation questions, conclusions and recommendations. A typical structure of formal evaluation reports is presented in Table 7.2.

Evaluation reports must be written in clear and easily understandable language based on the evaluation information without bias, and data should be presented in a clear manner (World Health Organization 2013). The outcome of the evaluation may be disseminated to the departments involved and the management of the healthcare organisation in the form of a report. It could also be shared in workshops in the form of a presentation for all interested parties. In the event where actions must be

Table 7.2 Evaluation report structure for SOP intervention for safety and quality improvement

Sections	Contents
Administrative	Evaluation team, evaluation participants, location, evaluation dates, evaluation type and evaluation number
Executive summary	Brief overview of intervention evaluated, methods used, main findings and conclusion
Introduction	Description of intervention evaluated, objectives and evaluation questions to be addressed and summary of evaluation plan and resources used for evaluation
Methods	Evaluation approach, techniques of data collection (questionnaire, interview, focus group, direct observation, records review), techniques used in data analysis, limitation of methods and problems encountered during evaluation
Findings	Outcomes of analysis of data collected, how each evaluation question was addressed, both positive and negative findings should be presented
Conclusions	Answers regarding objectives or overall goals of intervention, problems to be addressed, limitations and suggestions concerning intervention
Appendices	Technical terms, relevant diagrams, list of participants in evaluation
Appreciation	Thanking the staff, patients and others who contributed to evaluation

taken to address the findings, it will be the responsibility of the evaluation team to ensure all issues raised in the findings are adequately resolved and closed. An evaluation report can also be submitted using guidelines such as the Standards for Quality Improvement Reporting Excellence (SQUIRE) guidelines as the report aims at describing a system to improve the quality and safety of health care. SQUIRE provides a framework for reporting improvement work in health care. It contains various elements which can be adapted to generate a report capable of providing a better understanding of and insight into how to improve health care.

Ethics and Standards for Conducting and Reporting Evaluations

Evaluations should be designed, conducted and reported in conformity with the highest ethical and scientific standards. Ethical approval should be sought especially where it will involve patients and staff participation or looking at identifying patient records (NHS Institute for Innovation and Improvement 2005). In some African countries where there is no national ethics review body, the necessary clearances and permissions must be obtained from the management of the healthcare organisation before starting the evaluation. In carrying out the evaluation, the interests, dignity and rights of participants and other stakeholders must be recognised and respected. Consent to participate must be voluntary, and the privacy and confidentiality of the participants must be respected. If a participant is unwilling to take part in an evaluation, such a decision must be respected without having any negative impact on the relationship of the person with the evaluation team or the healthcare organisation. In general, there must be an arrangement in place to handle participants that might be affected by sensitive, embarrassing or upsetting questions.

The use of any records or data in an organisation for evaluations must follow data protection regulations, the organisation's confidentiality agreements and relevant policies and procedures. Where the evaluation team intends to record interviews and focus group discussions or use direct quotes from the participants either identifiable or anonymised in the reports, it is good practice to explain this to participants in advance and obtain consent to confirm that they are in agreement with the arrangements. Pseudonymisation could also be used where necessary. This is a process where participants' identifying information is removed or replaced with a code to ensure participants' confidentiality and enhance privacy.

It is also fundamental that the findings, limitations and conclusions of the evaluation are strictly evidence-based, that is, the reports must be distilled from the available evidence presented to the evaluation team instead of the personal bias of its members. A framework, such as SQUIRE guidelines, could provide a systematic way of reporting.

Benefits of Evaluation in Health Care in Africa

Evaluation will bring vast benefits to the healthcare environment in Africa, where insufficient funding in health care is recognised as a very acute problem. As reported by the WHO Regional Office for Africa (2013), most countries in the region are still struggling to achieve their financial goals to meet the Abuja Declaration of 2001 on increasing government funding for health and the 2008 Ouagadougou Declaration on Primary Health Care and Health Systems. Evaluation is therefore essential as it will help in ongoing data collection to monitor interventions implemented to demonstrate whether the resources, time and energy invested in those interventions represent value for the money. In healthcare organisations in the region, this information will help in reducing cost or wastage of limited resources as it will aid in the early detection and termination of any intervention which neither achieved the designed goals nor resulted in a change in work practices. In addition, evaluation can also assist in assessing whether interventions are effective and provide insight on how and why they work, their impact and sustainability and feasibility of replication (Brewster et al. 2015). This assessment will be useful in the healthcare setting in Africa as it will reduce or eliminate the chances of investing limited resources in improving local service without ensuring that the improvements being carried out are as effective as they could be and ensuring the right improvements are being made (NHS Institute for Innovation and Improvement 2005).

Barriers and Enablers to Evaluation

Evaluations, as reported by Brewster et al. (2015), pose challenges to all involved and a particular challenge typical of the African healthcare system; among those listed in the report are concerns about the impartiality and competence of the evaluation team. Indeed, the major barriers of low-resource countries of Africa in designing evaluations, collecting and analysing data and interpreting the results of the findings is finding adequate staff with the appropriate skills, experience and expertise. Collecting trustworthy data which are comprehensive and representative using both the quantitative and qualitative methods discussed in this chapter will require an evaluation team that possesses a repertoire of good skills and techniques.

In designing, conducting and reporting evaluations, as discussed in this chapter, the evaluation team will be expected to have some degree of skills, knowledge and experience necessary to manage the threat to validity, that is, the extent to which an evaluation measures what it is claiming to measure (Clarke et al. 2019). Moreover, although this design is useful in the evaluation of an intervention in many areas of health care, it is subject to a range of biases, including confounding bias, bias in study participant selection, bias due to missing data, bias in measurement of outcome and bias in the selection of reported results (Sterne et al. 2016). In Westat et al.'s (2002) report, sample bias due to the loss of sample units and response bias where responses or observations do not reflect true behaviours, characteristics or attitudes have the greatest ability to compromise the credibility of findings.

It will be important to seek expert advice on statistical rules about sampling as this will help to determine the appropriate sample size and how the sample should be selected before data collection commences (NHS Institute for Innovation and Improvement 2005). Once the issues with the sample and pitfalls associated with the data collection tools and techniques are addressed, there will be a strong probability that valid conclusions will be drawn from the ensuing analysis, resulting in credible findings.

Questionnaires also require some level of experience and expertise in their design, implementation and interpretation to reduce or eliminate pitfalls such as sampling bias, non-response bias, interviewer bias and sensitivity of respondents to the questionnaire, which might threaten the reliability and validity of the data collected. In observations, the reliability and validity of observations also depend on the skills and experience of the evaluation team and on their awareness of any bias they might introduce when conducting the observations. The evaluation must be sensitive to the fact that participants could act differently if they know they are being observed and they might devise a means to prevent this problem from occurring or to account for its effect (Minister of Public Works and Government Services 1998).

In a focus group, a member of an evaluation team who will facilitate the focus group should have the requisite experience and skill to effectively manage the group, with or without a topic guide. The facilitator should make certain that one person does not dominate the discussion but that all are given the opportunity to air their views. The facilitator should also be impartial in managing the group discussion, that is, have no personal interest that could interfere with the group opinion or the findings. Interviews as a method of data collection are no exception; they require trained and experienced evaluation teams that possess advanced skills. Gill et al. (2008) provided a set of skills deemed necessary for successful interviews, which may in turn generate reliable and valid information. These include the *"ability to listen attentively to what is being said, so that participants are able to recount their experiences as fully as possible, without unnecessary interruptions; adopting open and emotionally neutral body language, nodding, smiling, looking interested and making encouraging noises during the interview; and the strategic use of silence, if used appropriately, can also be highly effective at getting respondents to contemplate their responses, talk more, elaborate or clarify a particular issue"*.

On the other hand, some of the enablers will include creating a dedicated department to lead the project, for instance the SQD proposed in this book, trained in-house staff with expertise and experience in evaluation techniques and availability of adequate resources. In a nutshell, senior management support in combination with staff members with relevant technical, research, measurement, system leadership and engagement and implementation skills are proposed as prerequisites for successful implementation of the essential components of a healthcare system, discussed in Chap. 1 of this book, and will greatly promote evaluation projects in healthcare organisations in Africa.

Conclusion

The report from Jabot et al. (2014) titled "Evaluation: an avenue to improvement of health promotion in Africa?" confirms that evaluation, which is an essential part of quality improvement in healthcare, is not an entirely new concept in African healthcare settings. However, according to this report, there are obstacles to overcome to ensure that evaluation is effectively planned and conducted to fully meet the expectations of the stakeholders in the region. It is therefore hoped that evaluation as presented in this chapter will shed more light on the concept of evaluation in health care in the region and provide ideas on how best to resolve some of its challenges and hindrances. Specifically, it should encourage reflection on the design, conduct and use of evaluation among healthcare staff, management and other stakeholders in the region to seek solutions to practical problems and develop a deeper understanding of how best to design and implement a successful improvement programme, especially because evaluation can generate evidence-based information that is vital for decision-making, sound judgement and persuasion and knowledge that is crucial to improving patient care and quality outcomes (Health Foundation 2015).

Furthermore, evaluation could help in the early detection of problems in improvement interventions if it is carried out at the right phase of interventions. This could lead to fine-tuning or termination of interventions, thereby avoiding further waste of already scarce resources in the region on interventions which could undermine efforts to improve care. Finally, like all essential components of improving quality and safety of healthcare system discussed in the book, this chapter is not intended to make healthcare staff experts in evaluation; however, we hope it will give them the right foundation to start the journey. It will also encourage them to carry out more scientific research to further explore and increase their understanding of the topic in the local context, with the goal of promoting quality evaluation within healthcare settings by advancing the culture of and commitment to carrying out evaluations in compliance with the best standards and practices.

References

Andrew S, Halcomb EJ (2009) Mixed methods research for nursing and the health sciences. Blackwell Publishing Ltd, West Sussex

Baker LM (2006) Observation: a complex research method. Libr Trends 55:171–189

Bälter KA, Bälter O, Fondell E et al (2005) Web-based and mailed questionnaires: a comparison of response rates and compliance. Epidemiology 16:577–579

Belisario JSM, Jamsek J, Huckvale K et al (2015) Comparison of self-administered survey questionnaire responses collected using mobile apps versus other methods. Cochrane Database Syst Rev 7:MR000042. https://doi.org/10.1002/14651858.MR000042.pub2. PMID: 26212714; PMCID: PMC8152947

Black TR (1999) Doing quantitative research in the social sciences: an integrated approach to research design, measurement and statistics. Sage, London

Brewster L, Aveling E, Martin G et al (2015) What to expect when you're evaluating healthcare improvement: a concordat approach to managing collaboration and uncomfortable realities. BMJ Qual Saf 24:318–324

Bryman A, Cramer D (1997) Quantitative data analysis with SPSS for windows a guide for social scientists. Routledge, London

Centres of Disease Control and Prevention (2018) Evaluation guide: developing and using a logical model. https://www.cdc.gov/tb/programs/evaluation/Logic_Model.html. Accessed 27 Aug 2021

Chua H, Ke Q (2017) Research methods: What's in the name? Libr Inf Sci Res 39:284–294

Clarke GM, Conti S, Wolters AT et al (2019) Evaluating the impact of healthcare interventions using routine data. Br Med J 365(l2239):1–7

Coly A, Parry G (2017) Evaluating complex health interventions: a guide to rigorous research designs. Academy Health, Washington, DC

Deakin H, Wakefield K (2014) Skype interviewing: reflections of two PhD researchers. Qual Res 14(5):603–616

Deeks JJ, Dinnes J, D'Amico R et al (2003) Evaluating non-randomised intervention studies. Health Technol Assess 7(27):1–201

Dell-Kuster S, Sanjuan E, Todorov A et al (2004) Designing questionnaires: healthcare survey to compare two different response scales. BMC Med Res Methodol 14(96):1–13

Duffy B, Smith K, Terhanian G et al (2005) Comparing data from online and face-to-face surveys. Int J Mark Res 47(6):615–639

Edwards PJ, Roberts I, Clarke MJ et al (2002) Increasing response rates to postal questionnaires: systematic review. Br Med J 324:1183–1195

Gill P, Stewart K, Treasure E et al (2008) Methods of data collection in qualitative research: interviews and focus groups. Br Dent J 204(6):291–295

Groves RM (1990) Theories and methods of telephone surveys. Annu Rev Sociol 16(1):221–240

Hammersley M, Atkinson P (2007) *Ethnography. Principles in practice* (3 edn), Routledge London

Hardré PL, Crowson HM, Xie K (2012) Examining contexts-of-use for web-based and paper-based questionnaires. J Index Met 72(6):1015–1038

Heath J, Williamson H, Williams L et al (2018) "It's just more personal": using multiple methods of qualitative data collection to facilitate participation in research focusing on sensitive subjects. Appl Nurs Res 43:30–35

Hershberger PE, Kavanaugh K (2017) Comparing appropriateness and equivalence of email interviews to phone interviews in qualitative research on reproductive decisions. Appl Nurs Res 37:50–54

Iversen HH, Bjertnæs ØA, Skudal KE (2014) Patient evaluation of hospital outcomes: an analysis of open-ended comments from extreme clusters in a national survey. BMJ Open 4:1–9

Jabot F, Ridde V, Wone I et al (2014) Evaluation: an avenue to improvement of health promotion in Africa? Sante Publique 26(1):21–34

James J (2014) Patterns of Mobile phone use in developing countries: evidence from Africa. Soc Indic Res 119:687–704

James N, Busher H (2009) Online interviewing. Sage, London

Janca A, Isaac M, Bennett L et al (1995) somatoform disorders in different cultures - a mail questionnaire survey. Soc Psychiatry Psychiatr Epidemiol 30:44–48

Joseph CL, Ownby DR, Havstad SL et al (2013) Evaluation of a web-based asthma management intervention program for urban teenagers: reaching the hard to reach. J Adolesc Health 52(4):419–426

Kitzinger J (1994) The methodology of focus groups: the importance of interaction between research participants. Sociol Health Illn 16(1):103–121

Leviton LC, Khan LK, Rog D et al (2010) Evaluability assessment to improve public health policies, programs, and practices. Annu Rev Public Health 31:213–233

Marsh P, Glendenning R (2005) The primary care service evaluation toolkit: version 1.5. National Co-ordinating Centre for Research Capacity Development, London

Maxwell E (2020) Patient feedback: how effectively is it collected and used? Nurs Times 116(12):27–29

Menon S, Karl J, Wignaraja K (2009) Handbook on planning, monitoring and evaluating for development results. United Nations Development Programme (UNDP), New York

Minister of Public Works and Government Services (1998) Programme evaluation methods: measurement and attribution of Programme results, 3rd edn. Public Affairs Branch of Treasury Board of Canada Secretariat, Ottawa. https://www.tbs-sct.gc.ca/cee/pubs/meth/pem-mep-eng.pdf. Accessed 20 Jan 2021

Morgan DL (1998) The focus group guide book. Sage, London

NHS Institute for Innovation and Improvement (2005) Improvement Leaders' Guide Evaluating Improvement General improvement skills. NHS Institute for Innovation and Improvement University of Warwick Campus, Coventry

Novick G (2008) Is there a bias against telephone interviews in qualitative research? Res Nurs Health 31(4):391–398

Odendaal W, Watkins JA, Leon N et al (2020) Health workers' perceptions and experiences of using mHealth technologies to deliver primary healthcare services: a qualitative evidence synthesis. Cochrane Database Syst Rev 3(3):CD011942. https://doi.org/10.1002/14651858.CD011942.pub2. PMID: 32216074; PMCID: PMC7098082

Pedersen B, Delmar C, Falkmer U et al (2016) Bridging the gap between interviewer and interviewee: developing an interview guide for individual interviews by means of a focus group. Scand J Caring Sci 30:631–638

Pettersen KI, Veenstra M, Guldvog B et al (2004) The patient experiences questionnaire: development, validity and reliability. Int J Qual Health Care 16(6):453–463

Pope C, Ziebland S, Mays N (2000) Qualitative research in health care: Analysing qualitative data. BMJ 320:114–116

Public Health England (2018) Evaluation methods. https://www.gov.uk//government/publications/evaluation-in-health-and-well-being-overview/evaluation-methods. Accessed 8 Jan 2021

Raine R, Fitzpatrick R, Barratt H et al (2016) Challenges, solutions and future directions in the evaluation of service innovations in health care and public health. Heal Serv Del Res 16:2050–4349

Rattray J, Jones C (2007) Essential elements of questionnaire design and development. J Clin Nurs 16:234–243

Scriven M (1991) Evaluation thesaurus, 4th edn. Sage, London

Shadish W, Cook T, Leviton L (1990) Foundations of program evaluation. Sage Publications, London

Shah SK, Corley KG (2006) Building better theory by bridging the quantitative – qualitative divide. J Manag Stud 43:0022–2380

Siriwardena AN (2009) Using quality improvement methods for evaluating health care. Qual Prim Care 17:155–159

Sterne JAC, Hernán MA, Reeves BC et al (2016) ROBINS-I: a tool for assessing risk of bias in non-randomised studies of interventions. BMJ 355(i4919):1–7

The Health Foundation (2015) Evaluation: what to consider commonly asked questions about how to approach evaluation of qprovement in health care. The Health Foundation, London

Walshe C, Ewing G, Griffiths J (2011) Using observation as a data collection method to help understand patient and professional roles and actions in palliative care settings. Palliat Med 26(8):1048–1054

Watkins JOTA, Goudge J, Gómez-Olivé FX et al (2018) Mobile phone use among patients and health workers to enhance primary healthcare: a qualitative study in rural South Africa. Soc Sci Med 198:139–147

Westat JF, Frierson H, Hood S et al (2002) The 2002 user friendly handbook for project evaluation. The National Science Foundation, Arlington

WHO Regional Office for Africa (2013) State of health financing in the African region. World Health Organization, Geneva. Report number: ISBN: 978-929023213-1 (NLM Classification: W 74 HA1)

Willig C (2008) Introducing qualitative research in psychology: adventures in theory and method. Open University Press, Maidenhead

World Health Organisation (2013) WHO evaluation practice handbook. World Health Organization, Geneva

Index

Printed in the United States
by Baker & Taylor Publisher Services